The Interloper

By

Violet Jacob

(Mrs. Arthur Jacob)

Author of 'The Sheep-Stealers'

NEW YORK
DOUBLEDAY, PAGE & COMPANY
1904

AUTHOR'S NOTE

Before proceeding with this story I must apologise for a striking inaccuracy which it contains. I have represented the educated characters as speaking, but for certain turns of phrase, the ordinary English which is now universal. But, in Scotland, in the very early nineteenth century, gentle and simple alike kept a national distinction of language, and remnants of it lingered in the conversation, as I remember it, of the two venerable and unique old ladies from whom the characters of Miss Hersey Robertson and her sister are taken. They called it "Court Scots."

For the assistance of that tender person, the General Reader, I have ignored it.

V. J.

1904.

CONTENTS

BOOK I

[ix]

CONTENTS

BOOK II

THE INTERLOPER

BOOK I

CHAPTER I

THE HEIR

HALF-WAY up the east coast of Scotland the estuary of the North Lour cuts a wide cleft in an edge of the Lowlands and flows into the North Sea among the sands and salmon-nets.

The river winds in large curves through the shingles and green patches where cattle graze, overhung by woods of beech and birch, and pursuing its course through a country in full cultivation—a country of large fields where rolling woods, purple in the shadow, stretch north toward the blue Grampians.

A bridge of eight arches spans the water before it runs out to sea, the bank on its further side rising into a line of plow-fields crowning the cliffs, where flights of gulls follow the plowman and hover in his track over the upturned earth. As the turnpike runs down to the bridge, it curls round the policies of a harled white house which has stood for some two hundred years a little way in from the road, a tall house with dead-looking windows and slates on which the lichen has fastened. A clump of beech-trees presses round it on two sides, and, in their bare branches, rooks' nests make patches against the late autumn skies.

Inside the mansion of Whanland—for such is its name—on a December afternoon in the first year of the nine-

3

teenth century, two men were talking in the fading light.
The room which they occupied was panelled with wood,
polished and somewhat light-coloured, and had two
arched alcoves, one on either side of the chimney-piece.
These were filled with books whose goodly backs gave a
proper solemnity to the place. The windows were narrow and high, and looked out to the beeches. A faint
sound of the sea came droning in from the sand-hills
which flanked the shore, and were distant but the space
of a few fields.

The elder of the two men was a person who had reached
that convenient time of life when a gentleman may
attend to his creature comforts without the risk of being
blamed for it. He was well dressed and his face was free
from any obvious fault. He produced, indeed, a worse
effect than his merits warranted, for his hair, which had
the misfortune to look as though it were dyed, was, in
reality, of a natural colour. Nothing in his appearance
hinted at the fact that he was the family lawyer—or
"man of business," as it is called in Scotland—of the
young man who stood on the hearth-rug, nor did his
manner suggest that they had met that day for the
first time.

He sat looking up at Gilbert Speid* with considerable
interest. Though he was not one to whom the finer
details of another's personality were apparent, he was
yet observant in the commoner way. It did not escape
him that his companion was shy, but he did not suspect
that it was with the shyness of one who, though well
accustomed to the company of his kind, had no inti-
macies. A few hours ago, when starting to meet him at
Whanland, he had told himself that his task would be
easy, and he meant to be friendly, both from inclination
and policy, with the strange laird, who was a stranger to
his inheritance. But though he had been received with
politeness a little different from the amenity of any one

*Pronounced Speed

he had known before, he felt that he was still far from the defenses of the young man's mind. As to Gilbert's outward appearance, though it could hardly be called handsome, the lawyer was inclined to admire it. He was rather tall, and had a manner of carrying himself which was noticeable, not from affectation, but because he was a very finished swordsman, and had a precision of gesture and movement not entirely common. He did not speak with the same intonation as the gentry with whom it was Alexander Barclay's happiness to be acquainted, professionally or otherwise, for, though a Scot on both sides of his family, he had spent most of his youth abroad, and principally in Spain. His head was extremely well set and his face gave an impression of bone—well-balanced bone; it was a face rather heavy and singularly impassive, though the eyes looked out with an extraordinary curiosity on life. It seemed, to judge from them, as though he were always on the verge of speaking, and Barclay caught himself pausing once or twice for the expected words. But they seldom came and Gilbert's mouth remained closed, less from determination to silence than from settled habit.

It was in the forenoon that Gilbert Speid had arrived at Whanland to find Barclay awaiting him on the doorstep; and the two men had walked round the house and garden and under the beech-trees, stopping at points from which there was any view to be had over the surrounding country. They had strolled up a field parallel with the road which ran from the nearest town of Kaims to join the highway at the bridge. There Gilbert had taken in every detail, standing at an angle of a fence and looking down on the river as it wound from the hazy distance of bare woods.

"And my property ends here?" he asked, turning from the fascinating scene to his companion.

"At the bend of the Lour, Mr. Speid; just where you see the white cottage."

"I am glad that some of that river is mine," said Gilbert, after a long pause.

Barclay laughed with great heartiness, and rubbed his hands one over the other.

"Very satisfactory," he said, as they went on—"an excellent state of things."

When they returned to the house they found a stack of papers which the lawyer had brought to be examined, and Speid, though a little oppressed by the load of dormant responsibility it represented, sat gravely down, determined to do all that was expected of him. It was past three o'clock when Barclay pulled out his watch and inquired when he had breakfasted, for his own sensations were reminding him that he himself had done so at a very early hour.

Gilbert went to the bell, but as he stood with the rope in his hand, he remembered that he had no idea of the resources of the house, and did not even know whether there were any available servant whose duty it was to answer it. His companion sat looking at him with a half-smile, and he coloured as he saw it.

When the door opened a person peered in whom he dimly recollected seeing on his arrival in the group which had gathered to unload his post-chaise. He was a small, elderly man, whose large head shone with polished baldness. He was pale, and had the pose and expression we are accustomed to connect—perhaps unjustly—with field-preachers, and his rounded brow hung like the eaves of a house over a mild but impudent eye. He was the type of face to be seen bawling over a psalm-book at some sensational religious meeting, a face not to be regarded too long nor too earnestly, lest its owner should be spurred by the look into some insolent familiarity. He stood on the threshold looking from Speid to Barclay, as though uncertain which of the two he should address.

It took Gilbert a minute to think of what he had

wanted; for he was accustomed to the well-trained service of his father's house, and the newcomer matched
nothing that had a place in his experience.

"What is it?" inquired the man at the door.

"Is there any dinner—anything that we can have to
eat? You must forgive me, sir; but you see how it is.
I am strange here, and I foolishly sent no orders."

"I engaged a cook for you, and it is hardly possible
that she has made no preparation. Surely there is something in the kitchen, Macquean?"

"I'll away down an' see," said the man, disappearing.

"Who is that?" asked Gilbert, to whom the loss of a
dinner seemed less extraordinary than the possession of
such a servant.

"His name is Mungo Macquean. He has had charge
of the house for a great part of the time that it has stood
empty. He is a good creature, Mr. Speid, though uncouth—very uncouth."

In a few minutes the door opened again to admit Macquean's head.

"There's a chicken she'll roast to ye, an' there's brose.
An' a'm to tell her, are ye for pancakes?"

"Oh, certainly," said Gilbert. "Mr. Barclay, when
shall it be?"

"The sooner the better, I think," said the other hope-
fully.

"Then we will dine at once," said Gilbert.

Macquean's mouth widened and he stared at his master.

"You'll get it at five," he said, as he withdrew his
head.

The lawyer's face fell.

"I suppose it cannot be ready before then," he said
with a sigh.

The two drew up rather disconsolately to the fireside.
The younger man's eyes wandered round the room and
lit upon one of those oil-paintings typical of the time,

representing a coach-horse, dock-tailed, round-barrelled, and with a wonderfully long rein.

"That is the only picture I have noticed in the house," he observed. "Are there no more—no portraits, I mean?"

"To be sure there are," replied Barclay, "but they have been put in the garret, which we forgot to visit in our walk round. We will go up and see them if you wish. They are handsomely framed and will make a suitable show when we get them up on the walls."

The garret was approached by a steep wooden stair, and, as they stood among the strange collection it contained in the way of furniture and cobwebs, Speid saw that the one vacant space of wall supported a row of pictures, which stood on the floor like culprits, their faces to the wainscot. Barclay began to turn them round. It irked the young man to see his fat hands twisting the canvases about and flicking the dust from the row of faces which he regarded with a curious stirring of feeling. Nothing passed lightly over Gilbert.

He was relieved when his companion, whose heart was in the kitchen, and who was looking with some petulance at the dust which had fallen on his coat from the beams above, proposed to go down and push forward the preparations for dinner.

Speid stood absorbed before the line of vanished personalities which had helped to determine his existence, and they returned his look with all the intelligent and self-conscious gravity of eighteenth-century portraiture. Only one in the row differed in character from the others, and he took up the picture and carried it to the light. It represented a lady whose figure was cut by the oval frame just below the waist. Her hands were crossed in front of her, and her elbows brought into line with her sides, as were those of the other Speid ancestresses; there was something straight and virginal in her pose. Never had Gilbert seen such conventionality of attitude

joined to so much levity of expression. She wore a
mountain of chestnut hair piled high on her head and
curling down one side of her neck. Her open bodice
of warm cream colour suggested a bust rather fuller than
might be expected from the youthful and upright stiff-
ness of her carriage, and over her arm hung an India
muslin spotted scarf, which had apparently slipped
down round her waist. Her eyes were soft in shade and
hard in actual glance, bold, bright, scornful, under
strongly marked brows. The mouth was very red and
the upper lip fine; the lower lip protruded and drooped
a little in the middle. Her head was half turned to meet
the spectator.

Her appearance interested him, and he searched the
canvas for an inscription. Turning it round, he saw a
paper stuck upon the back and covered with writing:
"*Clementina Speid, daughter of John Lauder, Esq., of
Netherkails, and Marie La Vallance, his wife.* 1767."

The lady was his mother; and the portrait had been
painted just after her marriage, three years before his
own birth.

Never in his life had he seen any likeness of her. His
father had not once mentioned her name in his hearing,
and, as a little boy, he had been given by his nurses to
understand that she existed somewhere in that mysterious and enormous category of things about which
well-brought-up children were not supposed to inquire.
There was a certain fitness in thus meeting her unknown
face as he entered Whanland for the first time since he
left it in the early months of his infancy. She had been
here all the time, waiting for him in the dust and darkness. As he set the picture against the wall her eyes
looked at him with a secret intelligence. That he had
nothing to thank her for was a fact which he had gathered
as soon as he grew old enough to draw deductions for
himself; but all the same he now felt an unaccountable
sympathy with her, not as his mother—for such a rela-

tionship had never existed for him—but as a human being. He went to the little window under the slope of the roof and looked out over the fields. On the shore the sea lay, far and sad, as if seen through the wrong end of a telescope. The even, dreary sound came through a crack in the two little panes of glass. He turned back to the picture, though he could hardly see it in the strengthening dusk; her personality seemed to pervade the place with a brave, unavailing brightness. It struck him that, in that game of life which had ended in her death, there had been her stake, too. But it was a point of view which he felt sure no other being he had known had ever considered.

Mr. Barclay's voice calling to him on the staircase brought him back from the labyrinth of thought. He hurried out of the garret to find him on the landing, rather short of breath after his ascent.

"The Misses Robertson are below, Mr. Speid; they have driven out from Kaims to bid you welcome. I have left them in the library."

"The Misses Robertson?"

"Miss Hersey and Miss Caroline Robertson; your cousins. The ladies will not be long before they find you out, you see. They might have allowed you a little more law, all the same. But women are made inquisitive—especially the old ones."

"I think it vastly kind," said Speid shortly. "I remember now that my father spoke of them."

As they entered the library, two small figures rose from their chairs and came forward, one a little in front of the other.

The sisters were both much under middle height, and dressed exactly alike; it was only on their faces that the very great difference in them was visible. There was an appealing dignity in the full acknowledgment of her seventy years which Miss Hersey carried in her person. She had never had the smallest pretension to either intel-

lect or attraction, but her plain, thin face, with its one
beauty of gray hair rolled high above her forehead, was
full of a dignity innocent, remote, and entirely natural,
that has gone out of the modern world. Miss Caroline,
who was slightly her senior, was frankly ugly and foolish-
looking; and something fine, delicate, and persuasive
that lay in her sister's countenance had, in hers, been
omitted. Their only likeness was in the benignity that
pervaded them and in the inevitable family resemblance
that is developed with age. The fashion of their dresses,
though in no way grotesque, had been obsolete for several years.

"Welcome, Mr. Speid," said Miss Hersey, holding out
a gentle, bony hand. "Caroline, here is Mr. Speid."

It was no slight effort which the two feeble old ladies
had made in coming to do him honour, for they had
about them the strangeness which hangs round very
aged people when some unaccustomed act takes them
out of their own surroundings, and he longed to thank
them, or to say something which should express his sense
of it. But Barclay's proximity held him down. Their
greeting made him disagreeably aware of the lawyer's
presence; and his incongruity as he stood behind him
was like a cold draught blowing on his back. He made
a hurried murmur of civility, then, as he glanced again
at Miss Hersey's face, he suddenly set his heels together,
and, bending over her hand, held it to his lips.

She was old enough to look as if she had never been
young, but seventy years do not rob a woman, who has
ever been a woman, of everything; she felt like a queen
as she touched her kinsman's bent head lightly with her
withered fingers.

"Welcome, Gilbert," she said again. "God bless you,
my dear!"

"We knew your father," said the old lady, when chairs
had been brought, and she and her sister installed, one
on either side of the fireplace.

"We knew your father," echoed Miss Caroline, smiling vaguely.

"I do not remember that he was like you," said Miss Hersey, "but he was a very handsome man. He brought your mother to see us immediately after he was married."

"You'll have to keep up the custom," observed Mr. Barclay jocosely. "How soon are we to look for the happy event, Mr. Speid? There will be no difficulty among the young ladies here, I'm thinking."

"My cousin will do any lady honour that he asks, Mr. Barclay, and it is likely he will be particular," said Miss Hersey, drawing herself up.

"He should be particular," said Miss Caroline, catching gently at the last word.

"Your mother was a sweet creature," continued the younger sister. "He brought her to our house. It was on a Sunday after the church was out. I mind her sitting by me on the sofy at the window. You'll mind it, too, Caroline."

"A sweet creature indeed; a sweet creature," murmured Miss Caroline.

"She was so pleased with the lilies-of-the-valley in the garden, and I asked Robert Fullarton to go out and pull some for her. Poor thing! it is a sad-like place she is buried in, Gilbert."

"I have never seen it, ma'am," said Speid.

"It's at Garviekirk. The kirkyard is on the shore, away along the sands from the mouth of the river. Your father wished it that way, but I could never understand it."

"I shall be very pleased to show you the road there," broke in Barclay.

"It was a bitter day," continued Miss Robertson. "I wondered your father did not get his death o' cold standing there without his hat. He spoke to no one, not even to Robert Fullarton, who was so well acquainted with him. And when the gentlemen who had come to the burying arrived at the gate of Whanland, he just bade them a good-day and went in.   There was not one that was brought in to take a glass of wine.   I never saw him after; he went to England."

While her sister was speaking Miss Caroline held her peace   Her chin shook as she turned her eyes with dim benevolence from one to the other.   At seventy-two she seemed ten years older than Miss Hersey.

Gilbert could not but ask his cousins to stay and dine with him, and they assented very readily.   When at last dinner was brought he and Mr. Barclay handed them to the table.   There was enough and to spare upon it, in spite of Macquean's doubts,   and Miss Hersey, seated beside him, was gently exultant in the sense of kinship. It was a strange party.

Gilbert, who had never sat at the head of his own table before, looked round with a feeling of detachment.   It seemed to him that he was acting in a play and that his three guests, whom, a few hours before, he had never seen, were as unreal as everything else.   The environment of this coming life was closing in on him and he could not meet its forces as easily as a more elastic nature would have met them.   He accepted change with as little equanimity as a woman, in spite of the many changes of his past, because he knew that both duty and temperament would compel him to take up life, and live it with every nerve alongside the lives running parallel with his own.   He could see that he had pleased Miss Hersey and he was glad, as he had a respect for ties of blood imbibed from the atmosphere of ceremonious Spain.   He was glad to find something that had definite connection with himself and the silent house he had entered; with its wind-blown beech-trees and the face upstairs in the dust of the garret.

When dinner was over the Misses Robertson sent out for the hired coach and pair which they had considered indispensable to the occasion.   When they had taken

their leave Gilbert stood and watched the lights of the
vehicle disappearing down the road to Kaims. Their
departure relieved him, for their presence made him dislike Barclay. Their extreme simplicity might border
on the absurd, but it made the lawyer's exaggerated
politeness and well-to-do complacency look more offensive than they actually were.

It was quite dark as he turned back, and Barclay,
who was a man much in request in his own circle,
was anxious to get home to the town, where he
proposed to enjoy a bottle with some friends. He
looked forward keenly to discussing the newcomer
over it.

Before he went to bed Speid strolled out into the
damp night. He set his face toward the sea, and the
small stir of air there was blew chill upon his cheek.
Beyond a couple of fields a great light was flaring, throwing up the blunt end of some farm buildings through
which he had passed that morning in his walk with Barclay. Figures were flitting across the shine; and the
hum of human voices rose above a faint roar that was
coming in from the waste of sea beyond the sand-hills.
He strode across the paling, and made toward the light.
When he reached the place he found that a bonfire was
shooting bravely upward, and the glow which it threw
on the walls of the whitewashed dwelling-house was
turning it into a rosy pink. The black forms of twenty
or thirty persons, men and women—the former much
in the majority—were crowding and gyrating round the
blaze. Some were feeding it with logs and stacks of
brushwood; a few of the younger ones were dancing and
posturing solemnly; and one, who had made a discreet
retirement from the burning mass, was sitting in an
open doorway with an empty bottle on the threshold
beside him. Some children looked down on the throng
from an upper window of the house. The revel was
apparently in an advanced stage.

The noise was tremendous. Under cover of it, and of the deep shadows thrown by the bonfire, Gilbert slipped into a dark angle and stood to watch the scene. The men were the principal dancers, and a knot of heavy carter-lads were shuffling opposite to each other in a kind of sentimental abandonment. Each had one hand on his hip and one held conscientiously aloft. Now and then they turned round with the slow motion of joints on the spit. One was singing gutturally in time to his feet; but his words were unintelligible to Speid.

He soon discovered that the rejoicings were in honour of his own arrival, and the knowledge made him the more inclined to keep his hiding-place. He could see Macquean raking at the pile, the flame playing over his round forehead and unrefined face. He looked greatly unsuited to the occasion, as he did to any outdoor event.

All at once a little wizened woman looked in his own direction.

"Yonder's him!" she cried, as she extended a direct forefinger on his shelter.

A shout rose from the revellers. Even the man in the doorway turned his head, a thing he had not been able to do for some time.

"Heh! the laird! the laird!"

"Yon's him. Come awa', laird, an' let's get a sicht o' ye!"

"Here's to ye, laird!"

"Laird! laird! What'll I get if I run through the fire?"

"Ye'll get a pair o' burned boots!" roared the man in the doorway with sudden warmth.

Speid came out from the shadow. He had not bargained for this. Silence fell at once upon the assembly, and it occurred to him that he would do well to say a few words to these, his new dependents. He paused, not knowing how to address them.

"Friends," he began at last, "I see that you mean this—this display as a kind welcome to me."

"Just that," observed a voice in the crowd.

"I know very little about Whanland, and I do not even know your names. But I shall hope to be friendly with you all. I mean to live here and to try my best to do well by everybody. I hope I have your good wishes."

"Ye'll hae that!" cried the voice; and a man, far gone in intoxication, who had absently filled the tin mug he had drained with small stones, rattled it in accompaniment to the approving noise which followed these words.

"I thank you all," said the young man, as it subsided.

Then he turned and went up the fields to the house.

And that was how Gilbert Speid came back to Whanland.

CHAPTER II

THE woman who lay in her grave by the sands had rested there for nearly thirty years when her son stood in the grass to read her name and the date of her death. The place had been disused as a burial-ground, and it cost Gilbert some trouble to find the corner in which Clementina Speid's passionate heart had mixed with the dust from which, we are told, we emanate. The moss and damp had done their best to help on the oblivion lying in wait for us all, and it was only after half an hour of careful scraping that he had spelt out the letters on the stone. There was little to read: her name and the day she died—October 5, 1770—and her age. It was twenty-nine; just a year short of his own. Underneath was cut: "Thus have they rewarded me evil for good, and hatred for my good-will (Ps. cix. 4)."

He stood at her feet, his chin in his hand, and the salt wind blowing in his hair. The smell of tar came up from the nets spread on the shore to windward of him, and a gull flitted shrieking from the line of cliff above.

He looked up.

He had not heard the tread of nearing hoofs, for the sea sound swallowed everything in its enveloping murmur, and he was surprised to find that a person, from the outer side of the graveyard wall, was regarding him earnestly. He could not imagine how she had arrived at the place; for the strip of flat land which contained this burying-ground at the foot of the cliffs

17

appeared to him to end in the promontory standing out into the ocean a half-mile further east. The many little tracks and ravines which cut downward to the coast, and by one of which the rider had descended to ride along the bents, were unknown to him. He had not expected to see any one, and he was rather embarrassed at meeting the eyes of the middle-aged gentlewoman who sat on horseback before him. She was remarkable enough to inspire any one with a feeling of interest, though not from beauty, for her round, plain face was lined and toughened by the weather, and her shrewd and comprehensive glance seemed more suited to a man's than to a woman's countenance. A short red wig of indifferent fit protruded from under a low-crowned beaver; and the cord and tassels, with which existing taste encircled riding-hats, nodded over one side of the brim at each movement of the head below. A buff waistcoat, short even in those days of short waists, covered a figure which in youth could never have been graceful, and the lady's high-collared coat and riding-skirt of plum colour were shabby with the varied weather of many years. The only superfine things about her were her gloves, which were of the most expensive make, the mare she rode, and an intangible air which pervaded her, drowning her homeliness in its distinction.

Seeing that Gilbert was aware of her proximity, she moved on; not as though she felt concern for the open manner of her regard, but as if she had seen all she wished to see. As she went forward he was struck with admiration of the mare, for she was a picture of breeding; and whoever groomed her was a man to be respected, her contrast to the shabbiness of her rider was marked, the faded folds of the plum-coloured skirt showing against her loins like the garment of a scarecrow laid over satin.

She was a dark bay with black points, short-legged, deep-girthed; her little ears were cocked as she picked

her way through the grass into the sandy track which
led back in the direction of the Lour's mouth and the
bridge.   The lady, despite her dumpish figure, was a
horsewoman, a fact that he noticed with interest as he
turned from the mound, and, stepping through a breach
in the wall, took his way homeward in the wake of the
stranger.

It was a full fortnight since he had come to Whanland.   With the exception of Barclay and the Misses
Robertson, he had heard little and seen nothing of his
neighbours, for his time had been filled by business matters.   He knew his own servants by sight, and that was
all, but, with regard to their functions, he was completely in the dark, and glad enough to have Macquean
to interpret domestic life to him.   He had made some
progress in the understanding of his speech, which he
found an easier matter to be even with than his character;   and he was getting over the inclination either to
laugh or to be angry which he had felt on first seeing
him;   also, it was dawning on him that, in the astound-
ing country he was to inhabit, it was possible to com-
bine decent intentions with a mode of bearing and
address bordering on grossness.

As he went along and watched the rider in front, he
could not guess at her identity, having nothing to give
him the smallest clue to it;   he was a good deal attracted
by her original appearance, and was thinking that he
would ask Miss Robertson, when he next waited on her,
to enlighten him, when she put the mare to a trot and
soon disappeared round an angle of the cliff.

The clouds were low;   and the gleam of sunshine
which had enlivened the day was merging itself into a
general expectation of coming wet.   Gilbert buttoned
up his coat and put his best foot forward, with the
exhilaration of a man who feels the youth in his veins
warring pleasantly with outward circumstances.   He
was young and strong, the fascination of the place he

had just left, and the curious readiness of his rather complicated mind to dwell on it, and on the past of which it spoke, ran up, so to speak, against the active perfection of his body. He took off his hat and carried it, swinging along with his small head bare, and taking deep breaths of the healthy salt which blew to him over miles of open water from Jutland opposite. The horse he had seen had excited him. So far, he had been kept busy with the things pertaining to his new position, but, interesting as they were, it occurred to him that he was tired of them. Now he could give himself the pleasure of filling his stable. He had never lacked money, for his father had made him a respectable allowance, but, now that he was his own master, with complete control of his finance, he would be content with nothing but the best.

He thought of his two parents, one lying behind him in that God-forgotten spot by the North Sea and the other under the cypresses in Granada, where he had seen him laid barely three months ago. It would have seemed less incongruous had the woman been left with the sun and orange-trees and blue skies, and the man at the foot of the impenetrable cliffs. But it was the initial trouble: they had been mismated, misplaced, each with the other, and one with her surroundings.

For two centuries the Speids of Whanland had been settled in this corner of the Eastern Lowlands, and, though the property had diminished and was now scarcely more than half its original size, the name carried to initiated ears a suggestion of sound breeding, good physique, and unchangeable custom, with a smack of the polite arts brought into the family by a collateral who had been distinguished as a man of letters in the reign of George I. The brides of the direct line had generally possessed high looks, and been selected from those families which once formed the strength of provincial Scotland, the ancient and untitled county gentry.

From its ranks came the succession of wits, lawyers, divines, and men of the King's service, which, though known only in a limited circle, formed a society in the Scottish capital that for brilliancy of talent and richness of personality has never been surpassed.

The late laird, James Speid, had run contrary to the family custom of mating early, and was nearing forty when he set out, with no slight stir, for Netherkails, in the county of Perth, to ask Mr. Lauder, a gentleman with whom he had an acquaintance, for the hand of his daughter, Clementina. He had met this lady at the house of a neighbour and decided to pay his addresses to her; for, besides having a small fortune—not enough to allure a penniless man, but enough to be useful to the wife of one of his circumstance—she was so attractive as to disturb him very seriously. He found only one obstacle to the despatch of his business, which was that Clementina herself was not inclined toward him, and told him so with a civility that did not allay his vexation; and he returned to Whanland more silent than ever—for he was a stern man—to find the putting of Miss Lauder from his mind a harder matter than he had supposed.

But, in a few weeks, a letter came from Netherkails, not from the lady, but from her father, assuring him that his daughter had altered her mind, and that, if he were still constant to the devotion he had described, there was no impediment in his way. Mr. Speid, whose inclination pointed like a finger-post to Netherkails, was now confronted by his pride, which stood, an armed giant, straddling the road to bar his progress. But, after a stout tussle between man and monster, the wheels of the family chariot rolled over the enemy's fallen body; and the victor, taking with him in a shagreen case a pearl necklace which had belonged to his mother, brought back Clementina, who was wearing it upon her lovely neck.

Whatever may have been the history of her change of

mind, Mrs. Speid accepted her responsibilities with a
suitable face and an apparent pleasure in the interest
she aroused as a bride of more than common good looks.
Her coach was well appointed, her dresses of the best;
her husband, both publicly and in private, was precise in
his courtesy and esteem, and there was nothing left to
be desired but some sympathy of nature. At thirty-
eight he was, at heart, an elderly man, while his wife, at
twenty-seven, was a very young woman. The fact
that he never became aware of the incongruity was the
rock on which their ship went to pieces.

After three years of marriage Gilbert was born.
Clementina's health had been precarious for months, and
she all but paid for the child's life with her own. On
the day that she left her bed, a couch was placed at the
window facing seaward, and she lay looking down the
fields to the shore. No one knew what occurred, but,
that evening, there was a great cry in the house and the
servants, rushing up, met Mr. Speid coming down the
stairs and looking as if he did not see them. They
found their mistress in a terrible state of excitement and
distress and carried her back to her bed, where she
became so ill that the doctor was fetched. By the time
he arrived she was in a delirium; and, two days after,
she died without having recognised anyone.

When the funeral was over James Speid discharged
his servants, gave orders for the sale of his horses, shut
up his house, and departed for England, taking the child
with him under the charge of a young Scotchwoman
In a short time he crossed over to Belgium, dismissed
the nurse, and handed over little Gilbert to be brought
up by a peasant woman near the vigilant eye of a pasteur
with whom he had been friendly in former days. Being
an only son, Mr. Speid had none but distant relations,
and, as he was not a man of sociable character, there was
no person who might naturally come forward to take
the child. He spent a year in travel, and settled finally

in Spain, where the boy, when he had reached his fifth
birthday, joined him

Thus Gilbert was cut off from all intercourse with his
native country, growing up with the sons of a neighbouring Spanish nobleman as his companions. When, at
last, he went to school in England, he met no one who
knew anything about him, and, all mention of his
mother's name having been strictly forbidden at his
home, he reached manhood in complete ignorance of
everything connected with his father's married life.
The servants, being foreign, and possessing no channel
through which they could hear anything to explain the
prohibition, made many guesses, and, from scraps of
their talk overheard by the boy, he discovered that there
was some mystery connected with him. It was a great
deal in his mind, but, as he grew older, a certain delicacy
of feeling forbade his risking the discovery of anything
to the detriment of the mother whose very likeness he
had never seen. His father, though indifferent to him,
endeavoured to be just, and was careful in giving him
the obvious advantages of life. He grew up active and
manly, plunging with zest into the interests and amuse-
ments of his boyhood's companions. He was a good
horseman, a superb swordsman, and, his natural gravity
assimilating with something in the Spanish character, he
was popular. Mr. Speid made no demands upon his
affection, the two men respecting each other without any
approach to intimacy, and, when the day came on which
Gilbert stood and looked down at the stern, dead face,
though his grief was almost impersonal, he felt in every
fibre that he owed him a debt he could only repay by the
immediate putting into effect of his wishes. Mr. Speid
had, during his illness, informed him that he was heir to
the property of Whanland, and that he desired him to
return to Scotland and devote himself conscientiously
to it.

And so he had come home, and was now making his

way up to the bridge, wondering why he had not seen the figure of the strange lady crossing it between him and the sky. She must have turned and gone up the road leading from it to the cliffs and the little village of Garviekirk, which sat in the fields above the churchyard.

He looked at the shoe-marks in the mud as he went up the hill, following them mechanically, and, at the top, they diverged, as he had expected, from his homeward direction. As he stopped half-way and glanced over the bridge parapet into the swirling water of the Lour slipping past the masonry, the smart beat of hoofs broke on his ear. The mare was coming down toward him at a canter, the saddle empty, the stirrup-leather flying outwards, the water splashing up as she went through the puddles. Something inconsequent and half-hearted in her pace showed that whatever fright had started her had given way to a capricious pleasure in the unusual; and the hollow sound of her own tread on the bridge made her buck light-heartedly.

Gilbert stepped out into the middle of the way and held up his walking-stick. She swerved, stopped suddenly with her fore-feet well in front of her, and was going to turn when he sprang at the reins. As he grasped them she reared up, but only as a protest against interference, for she came down as quietly as if she had done nothing at which any one could take offense. She had evidently fallen, for the bit was bent and all her side plastered with mud. He plucked a handful of grass and cleaned down the saddle before starting with her towards Garviekirk. There was no one to be seen, but there stood, in the distance, a roadside cottage whose inmates might, he thought, know something of the accident. He hurried forward.

The cottage-door opened on the side-path, and, as he drew near, he saw the mare's owner standing on the threshold, watching his approach. She had been original-looking on horseback and she was now a hundred times more so; for the traces of her fall were evident, and, on one side, she was coated with mud from head to heel. Her wig was askew, her arms akimbo, and her hat, which she held in her hand, was battered out of shape. She stood framed by the lintel, her feet set wide apart; as she contemplated Gilbert and the mare, she kept up a loud conversation with an unseen person inside the cottage.

"Nonsense, woman!" she was exclaiming as he stopped a few paces from her. "Come out and hold her while this gentleman helps me to mount. Sir, I am much obliged to you."

As she spoke she walked round the animal in a critical search for damage.

"She is quite sound, madam," said Gilbert. "I trotted her as I came to make sure of it. I hope you are not hurt yourself."

"Thanky, no," she replied, rather absently.

He laid the reins on the mare's neck. The lady threw an impatient look at the house.

"Am I to be kept waiting all day, Granny Stirk?" she cried.

There was a sound of pushing and scuffling, and an old woman carrying a clumsy wooden chair filled the doorway. She was short and thin, and had the remains of the most marked good looks.

The lady broke into a torrent of speech.

"What do I want with that? Do you suppose I have come to such a pass that I cannot mount my horse without four wooden legs to help me up? Put it down, you old fool, and come here as I bid you—do you hear?"

Granny Stirk advanced steadily with the chair in front of her. She might have looked as though protecting herself with it had her expression been less decided.

"Put it down, I tell you. God bless me, am I a cripple? Leave her head, sir—she will stand—and do me the favour to mount me."

Gilbert complied, and, putting his hand under the stranger's splashed boot, tossed her easily into the saddle. She sat a moment gathering up the reins and settling her skirt; then, with a hurried word of thanks, she trotted off, standing up in her stirrup as she went to look over at the mare's feet. Granny had put down her burden and was staring at Gilbert with great interest.

"Who is that lady?" he inquired, when horse and rider had disappeared.

"Yon's Leddy Eliza Lamont," she replied, still examining him.

"Does she live near here?"

"Ay; she bides at Morphie, away west by the river."

"And how did she meet with her accident?"

"She was coming in by the field ahint the house, an' the horse just coupet itsel'. She came in-by an' tell't me. She kens me fine."

It struck Gilbert as strange that, in spite of Lady Eliza's interest as she watched him over the burying-ground wall, she had not had the curiosity to ask his name, though they had spoken and he had done her a service. He looked down at the mud which her boot had transferred to his fingers.

"Ye've filed your hands," observed Granny. "Come ben an' I'll gie ye a drappie water to them."

He followed her and found himself in a small, dark kitchen. It was clean, and a great three-legged caldron which hung by a chain over the fire was making an aggressive bubbling. A white cat, marked with black and brown, slunk deceitfully out of its place by the hearth as they entered. The old woman took an earthenware bowl and filled it. When he had washed his hands, she held out a corner of her apron to him, and he dried them.

"Sit down a whilie to the fire," she said, pushing forward the wooden chair that Lady Eliza had despised.

"Thank you, I cannot," he replied. "I must be

going for it will soon be dark; but I should like to pay you another visit one day."

"Haste ye back, then," she said, as he went out of the door.

Gilbert turned as he stood on the side-path, and looked at the old woman. A question was in her face.

"You'll be the laird of Whanland?" she inquired, rather loudly.

He assented.

"You're a fine lad," said Granny Stirk, as she went back into the cottage.

CHAPTER III

LADY ELIZA LAMONT splashed along the road and over the bridge; her heart was beating under the outlandish waistcoat, and behind her red face, so unsuggestive of emotion of any sort, a turmoil was going on in her brain. She had seen him at last.

She breathed hard, and her mouth drew into a thin line as she passed Whanland, and saw the white walls glimmering through the beech-trees. There was a light in one of the upper windows, the first she had seen there for thirty years in the many times she had ridden past.

He was so little like the picture her mind had imagined that she would scarcely have recognised him, she told herself. Yet still there was that in his look which forbade her to hate him unrestrainedly, though he represented all that had set her life awry. He was now her neighbour and it was likely they would often meet; indeed, sooner or later, civility would compel her to invite him to wait upon her. She gave the mare a smart blow with her riding-cane as they turned into the approach to Morphie House.

Up to the horse-block in the stable-yard she rode, for her fall had made her stiff, and, though she usually objected to dismounting upon it, she was glad of its help this evening. The groom who came out exclaimed as he saw her plight, but she cut him short, merely sending him for a lantern, by the light of which they examined the mare together in the growing dusk;

28

she then gathered up her skirt and went into the house by the back entrance. Her gloves were coated with mud, and she peeled them off and threw them on a table in the hall before going into the long, low room in which she generally sat. The lights had not been brought and it was very dark as she opened the door; the two windows at the end facing her were mere gray patches of twilight through which the dim, white shapes of a few sheep were visible; for, at Morphie, the grass grew up to the walls at the sides of the house. A figure was sitting by the hearth between the windows and a very tall man rose from his chair as she entered.

Lady Eliza started.

"Fullarton !" she exclaimed.

"It is I. I have been waiting here expecting you might return earlier. You are out late to-night."

"'The mare put her foot in a hole, stupid brute! A fine roll she gave me, too."

He made an exclamation, and, catching sight of some mud on her sleeve, led her to the light. She went quietly and stood while he looked at her.

"Gad, my lady! you have been down indeed! You are none the worse, I trust?"

"No, no; but I will send for a dish of tea, and drink it by the fire. It is cold outside."

"But you are wet, my dear lady."

"What does that matter? I shall take no harm. Ring the bell, Fullarton—the rope is at your hand."

Robert Fullarton did as he was desired, and stood looking at the ragged grass and the boles of the trees. His figure and the rather blunt outline of his features showed dark against the pane. At sixty he was as upright as when he and Lady Eliza had been young together, and he the first of the county gentlemen in polite pursuits. At a time when it was hardly possible to be anything else, he had never been provincial, for though he was, before anything, a sportsman, he had been one of the very few of his day capable of combining sport with wider interests.

The friendship between his own family and that of Morphie House had gone far back into the preceding century, long before Mr. Lamont, second son of an impoverished earl, had inherited the property through his mother, and settled down upon it with Lady Eliza, his unmarried sister. At his death she had stepped into his place, still unmarried, a blunt, prejudiced woman, understood by few, and, oddly enough, liked by many. Morphie was hers for life and was to pass, at her death, to a distant relation of her mother's family. She was well off, and, being the only occupant of a large house, with few personal wants and but one expensive taste, she had become as autocratic as a full purse and a life outside the struggles and knocks of the world will make anyone who is in possession of both.

The expensive taste was her stable; for, from the hour that she had been lifted as a little child upon the back of her father's horse, she had wavered only once in her decision that horses and all pertaining to them presented by far the most attractive possibilities in life. Her hour of wavering had come later.

The fire threw bright flickerings into the darkness of the room as Lady Eliza sat and drank her tea. The servant who had brought it would have brought in lights, too, but she refused to have them, saying that she was tired and that the dusk soothed her head, and she withdrew into the furthest corner of a high-backed settee, with the little dish beside her on a spindle-legged table.

Fullarton sat at the other end of the hearth, his elbows on his knees and his hands spread to the blaze. They were large hands, nervous and well-formed. His face, on which the firelight played, had a look of preoccupation, and the horizontal lines of his forehead seemed deeper than usual—at least, so his companion

thought. It was easily seen that they were very intimate, from the silence in which they sat.

"Surely you must be rather wet," said he again, after
a few minutes. "I think it would be wise if you were to
change your habit for dry clothes."

"No; I will sit here."

"You have always been a self-willed woman, my
lady."

She made no reply, merely turning her cane round and
round in her hand. A loud crash came from the fire, and
a large piece of wood fell into the fender with a sputter of
blue fireworks. He picked it up with the tongs and set
it back in its place. She watched him silently. It was
too dark to read the expression in her eyes.

"I have seen young Whanland," she said suddenly.

"Indeed," said Fullarton.

"He caught the mare and brought her to me at
Granny Stirk's house."

"What is he like?" he asked, after a pause.

"A proper young fellow. He obliged me very greatly.
Have you not met him? He has been at Whanland
this fortnight past, I am told."

"No," said Fullarton, with his eyes on the flame,
"never. I have never seen him."

"As I came by just now I saw the lights in Whanland
House. It is a long time that it has been in darkness
now. I suppose that sawney-faced Macquean is still
minding it?"

"I believe so," said the man, drawing his chair out of
the circle of the light.

"How long is it now since—since Mrs. Speid's death?
Twenty-eight or twenty-nine years, I suppose?"

"It is thirty," said Robert.

"It was a little earlier in the year than this," continued Lady Eliza. "I remember seeing Mr. Speid's
travelling-carriage on the road, with the nurse and the
baby inside it."

"You build your fires very high," said Fullarton. "I must move away, or the cold will be all the worse when I get out of doors.

"But I hope you will stay and sup, Fullarton. You have not been here since Cecilia came back."

"Not to-night," said he, rising; "another time. Present my respects to Cecilia, for I must go."

Lady Eliza sat still. He stood by the settee holding out his hand. His lips were shaking, but there was a steadiness in his voice and a measured tone that told of great control.

"Good-night," he said. "I left my horse in the stable. I will walk out myself and fetch him."

He turned to go to the door. She watched him till he had almost reached it.

"Fullarton!" she cried suddenly; "come back!"

He looked round, but stood still in his place.

"Come back; I must speak—I must tell you!"

He did not move, so she rose and stood between him and the fire, a grotesque enough figure in the dancing light.

"I know everything; I have always known it. Do you think I did not understand what had come to you in those days? Ah! I know—yes, more than ever, now I have seen him. He has a look that I would have known anywhere, Robert."

He made an inarticulate sound as though he were about to speak.

She held up her hand.

"There is no use in denying it—you cannot! How can you, with that man standing there to give you the lie? But I have understood always—God knows I have understood!"

"It is untrue from beginning to end," said Fullarton very quietly.

"You are obliged to say that," she said through her teeth. "It is a lie!"

But for this one friendship, he had lived half his life solely among men. He had not fathomed the unsparing brutality of women. His hand was on the door. She sprang towards him and clasped both hers round his arm.

"Robert! Robert!" she cried.

"Let me go," he said, trying to part the hands; "I cannot bear this. Have you *no* pity, Eliza?"

"But you will come back? Oh, Robert, listen to me! Listen to me! You think because I have spoken now that I will speak again. Never! I never will!"

"You have broken everything," said he.

"What have I done?" she asked fiercely. "Have I once made a sign of what I knew all those years? Have I, Robert?"

"No," he said thickly; "I suppose not. How can I tell?"

The blood flew up into her face, dyeing it crimson.

"What? what? Do you disbelieve me?" she cried. "How dare you, I say?"

She shook his arm. Her voice was so loud that he feared it might be overheard by some other inmate of the house. He felt almost distracted. He disengaged himself and turned to the wall, his hand over his face. The pain of the moment was so intolerable. Lady Eliza's wrath dropped suddenly and fell from her, leaving her standing dumb, for there was something in the look of Fullarton's bowed shoulders that struck her in the very centre of her heart. When she should have been silent she had spoken, and now, when she would have given worlds to speak, she could not.

He turned slowly and they looked at each other. The fire had spurted up and each could see the other's face. His expression was one of physical suffering. He opened the door and went out.

He knew his way in every corner of Morphie, and he went, as he had often done, through the passage by which she had entered and passed by the servants' offices into the stable-yard. He was so much pre-occupied that he did not hear her footsteps behind him, and he walked out, unconscious that she followed. In the middle of the yard stood a weeping-ash on a plot of grass, and she hurried round the tree and into an out-building connected with the stable. She entered and saw his horse standing on the pillar-rein, the white blaze on his face distinct in the dark. The stablemen were indoors. She slipped the rings and led him out of the place on to the cobble-stones.

Robert was standing bareheaded in the yard. He took up the rein mechanically without looking at her, and put his foot in the stirrup iron. As he was about to turn, she laid hold of the animal's mane.

"Lady Eliza!" he exclaimed, staring down through the dusk.

"You have left your hat, Fullarton," she said. "I will go in and fetch it."

Before he could prevent her, she had vanished into the house. He sat for a moment in his saddle, for there was no one to take the horse; but he followed her to the door, and dismounted there. In a couple of minutes she returned with the hat.

"Thank you—thank you," he said; "you should not have done such a thing."

"What would I not do?"

"Eliza," he said, "can I trust you?"

"You never have," she replied bitterly, "but you will need to now."

He rode out of the yard.

She reached her room without meeting anyone, and sank down in an armchair. She longed to weep; but Fate, that had denied her the human joys which she desired, but for which she had not, apparently, been created, withheld that natural relief too. The repressed womanhood in her life seemed to confront her at every

step. She lifted her head, and caught sight of herself
in a long cheval glass, her wig, her weather-beaten face,
her clumsy attitude. She had studied her reflection in
the thing many and many a time in the years gone by,
and it had become to her almost as an enemy—a candid
enemy. As a girl going to county balls with her brother,
she had stood before it trying to cheat herself into the
belief that she was less plain in her evening dress than
she had been in her morning one. Now she had lost
even the freshness which had then made her passable.
She told herself that, but for that, youth had given her
nothing which age could take away, and she laughed
against her will at the truth. She looked down at the
pair of hands shining white in the mirror. They were
her one ornament and she had taken care of them.
How small they were! how the fingers tapered! how the
pink of the filbert-shaped nails showed against the
cream of the skin! They were beautiful. Yet they
had never felt the touch of a man's lips, never clung
round a lover's neck, never held a child. Everything
that made a woman's life worth living had passed her
by. The remembrance of a short time when she had
thought she held the Golden Rose forever made her
heart ache. It was Gilbert's mother who had snatched
it from her.

And friendship had been a poor substitute for what
she had never possessed. The touch of love in the
friendship of a man and a woman which makes it so
charming, and may make it so dangerous, had been
left out between herself and Robert. She lived before
these days of profound study of sensation, but she
knew that by instinct. The passion for inflicting pain
which assails some people when they are unhappy had
carried her tongue out of all bounds, and she realised
that she was to pay for its short indulgence with a
lasting regret. She did not suppose that Fullarton
would not return, but she knew he would never forget,

and she feared that she also would not cease to remember. She could not rid her mind of the image printed on it— his figure, as he stood in the long-room below with his face turned from her. She had suffered at that moment as cruelly as himself, and she had revelled in her own pain.

When she had put off her riding-habit, she threw on a wrapper and lay down on the bed, for she was wearied, body and soul, and her limbs were beginning to remind her of her fall. It was chilly and she shivered, drawing up the quilt over her feet. The voices of two servants, a groom and a maid, babbled on by the ash-tree in the yard below; she could not distinguish anything they said, but the man's tone predominated. They were making love, no doubt. Lady Eliza pressed her head into the pillow and tried to shut out the sound.

She was half asleep when someone tapped at the door, and, getting no answer, opened it softly.

"Is it Cecilia?" said she, sitting up.

"My dearest aunt, are you asleep? Oh, I fear I have awakened you."

The girl stood holding back the curtains. As she looked at the bed her lips trembled a little.

"I have only this moment heard of your accident," she said.

"I am not hurt, my dear, so don't distress yourself."

"Thank Heaven!" exclaimed the other.

"My patience, Cecilia, you are quite upset! What a little blockhead you are!"

For answer, Cecilia took Lady Eliza's hand in both her own, and laid her cheek against it. She said nothing.

"It must be almost supper-time," said the elder woman. "I will rise, for you will be waiting."

"May I not bring something up to your room, ma'am? I think you should lie still in bed. I am very well alone."

"Nonsense, child! Go downstairs, and let me get up.

I suppose you think I am too old to take care of myself."

Cecilia went out as she was bid, and took her way to the dining-room. Her face was a little troubled, for she saw that Lady Eliza was more shaken than she had been willing to admit, and she suspected the presence of some influence which she did not understand; for the two women, so widely removed in character and age, had so strong a bond of affection, that, while their minds could never meet on common ground, there was a sympathy between them apart from all individual bias.

Cecilia was one of those unusual people whose outward personalities never look unsuitable to the life encompassing them, though their inward beings may be completely aloof from everything surrounding them physically. She sat down by the table, her gray gown melting into the background of the walls, and the whiteness of her long neck rising distinct from it. Her dress was cut open in front and bordered by a narrow line of brown fur which crossed on her bosom. Though she was so slim, the little emerald brooch which held the fastening of it together sank into the hollow made by her figure; her hair was drawn up on the top of her head, and piled in many rolls round a high, tortoiseshell comb. Her long eyes, under straight brows, seemed, in expression, to be holding something hidden behind the eyelashes—something intangible, elusive. To see her was to be reminded, consciously or unconsciously, of mists, of shadows, of moonlit things—things half seen, things remembered. Her lips closed evenly, though in beautiful lines, and the upper, not short enough for real beauty, had an outward curve, as it rested on its fellow, which held a curious attraction. She was very pale with a pallor that did not suggest ill-health.

Though she was the only young inhabitant of Morphie, she existed among the dusty passages—dusty with the powdering of ages—and the sober unconventionality of the place as naturally as one of those white plants which haunt remote waterways exists among the hidden hollows and shadows of pools. She was very distantly related to Lady Eliza Lamont, but, when the death of both parents had thrown her on the world, a half-grown, penniless girl, she had come to Morphie for a month to gain strength after an illness, and remained there twelve years. Lady Eliza, ostentatiously grumbling at the responsibility she had imposed upon herself, found, at the end of the time, that she could not face the notion of parting with Cecilia. It was the anxiety of her life that, though she had practically adopted the girl, she had nothing she could legally leave her at her death but her own personal possessions.

A few minutes later she came down in the ancient pelisse which she found comfortable after the exertions of the day. She had taught Cecilia something of the activity which, though now a part of most well-bred women's lives, was then almost an eccentricity. The female part of the little society which filled Kaims in the winter months nodded its "dressed" head over its cards and teacups in polished dismay at the effect such ways would surely have on the young women; at other times one might hardly have guessed at the lurking solicitude in so many womanly bosoms; for, though unwilling, for many reasons, to disagree with Lady Eliza, their owners were apt, with the curious reasoning of their sex, to take her adopted daughter as a kind of insult to themselves. It was their opinion that Miss Cecilia Raeburn, though a sweet young lady, would, of course, find the world a *very* different place when her ladyship's time should come, and they only hoped she was sensible of the debt she owed her; these quiet-looking girls were often very sly. With prudent eyes the matrons congratulated themselves and each other that their own Carolines and Amelias were "less unlike other people," and had defined, if modest, prospects; and such of the

Carolines and Amelias who chanced to be privily listening would smirk in secure and conscious unison. Even
Miss Hersey Robertson, who mixed a little in these
circles, was inclined to be critical.

The advent of a possible husband, though he would
present in himself the solution of all difficulties, had only
vaguely entered Lady Eliza's mind. Like many parents,
she supposed that the girl would "marry some day,"
and, had anyone questioned the probability in her
presence, it is likely that she would have been very
angry. Fullarton, who was consulted on every subject,
had realised that the life at Morphie was an unnatural
one for Cecilia and spoken his mind to some purpose.
He suggested that she should pass a winter in Edinburgh,
and, though Lady Eliza refused stubbornly to plunge
into a society to whose customs she felt herself unable
to conform, it was arranged by him that a favourite
cousin, widow of the late Lord Advocate of Scotland,
should receive the girl. This lady, who was childless,
and longed for someone to accompany her to those routs
and parties dear to her soul, found in her kinsman's
suggestion something wellnigh providential. So kind
a welcome did she extend, that her charge, whose
pleasure in the arrangement had been but a mixed
business, set out with an almost cheerful spirit.

A nature inclined to study and reflection, and nine
years of life with a person of quick tongue, had bred in
Cecilia a different calibre of mind to that of the provincial
young lady of her time; and Lady Eliza had procured
her excellent tuition. The widow had expected to find
in her guest a far less uncommon personality, and it was
with real satisfaction that she proceeded to introduce
her to the very critical and rather literary society which
she frequented. There were some belonging to it who
were to see in Miss Raeburn, poor as she was, an ideal
future for themselves. Cecilia, when she returned to
Morphie, left more than one very sore heart behind her.

To many it seemed wonderful that her experiences had not spoiled her, and that she could take up life again in the draughty, ill-lit house, whose only outward signs of animation were the sheep grazing under its windows and the pigeons pluming in rows under the weathercock swinging crazily on the stable roof.

What people underrated was her devoted attachment to Lady Eliza, and what they could not understand was the fact that, while she was charmed, interested, and apparently engrossed by many things, her inner life might hold so completely aloof as never to have been within range of them.

CHAPTER IV

Jimmy

INLAND from the river's mouth the dark plough-fields stretched sombre, restful, wide, uncut by detail. The smaller roads intersecting the country were treeless in the main, and did not draw the eye from the majesty of the defined woods. There was everything to suggest breadth and full air; and the sky, as Gilbert rode up toward a farm cresting the swell of the high horizon, was as suggestive of it as the earth. The clear gray meeting the sweep of the world was an immensity on which cloud-masses, too high for rain, but full of it, looked as though cut adrift by some Titanic hand and left to sail derelict on the cold heavens.

The road he was travelling was enlivened by a stream of people, all going in the same direction as himself, and mostly on foot, though a couple of gigs, whose occupants looked as much too large for them as the occupants of country gigs generally do, were ascending to the farm at that jog which none but agriculturally-interested persons can suffer.

A displenishing sale, or "roup," as it is called, had been advertised there, which was drawing both thrifty and extravagant to its neighbourhood. Curiosity was drawing Gilbert. A compact little roan, bought for hacking about the country, was stepping briskly under him, showing its own excellent manners and the ease and finish of its rider's seat. Beside the farm a small crowd was gathered round the pursy figure of a water-butt on high legs, which stood out against the sky.

As he went, he observed, coming down a cart-road, two other mounted people, a man and a woman. He judged that he and they would meet where their respective ways converged, and he was not wrong, for in another minute he was face to face with Robert Fullarton and Lady Eliza Lamont. He drew aside to let them pass on. Lady Eliza bowed and her mare began to sidle excitedly to the edge of the road, upset by the sudden meeting with a strange horse.

"Good-day to you, sir," she said, as she recognised him. "I am fortunate to have met you. It was most obliging of you to come and inquire for me as you did."

"Indeed, I could do no less," replied Gilbert, hat in hand, "and I am very glad to see your ladyship on horseback again."

"Lord, sir, I was out the next day. Fullarton, let me make you acquaint with Mr. Speid, of Whanland. Sir, Mr. Robert Fullarton, of Fullarton."

The two gentlemen bowed gravely.

Lady Eliza was so anxious to assure the man beside her of her perfect good faith and good feeling after the painful meeting of a few weeks ago that she would willingly have gone arm-in-arm to the "roup" with Gilbert, had circumstances and decorum allowed it. She brought her animal abreast of the roan and proceeded with the two men, one on either side of her. Robert, understanding her impulse, would have fallen in with it had not the sharp twinge of memory which the young man's presence evoked almost choked him. It was a minute before he could speak.

"You are newly come, sir," he said at last. "I am to blame for not having presented myself at Whanland before."

Gilbert made a civil reply.

"I hear this is likely to be a large sale," observed Fullarton, as they rode along. "There is a great deal of

live stock, and some horses. Have you any interest
in it?"

"The simple wish to see my neighbours has brought
me," replied Gilbert. "I have so much to learn that I
lose no chance of adding anything to my experience."

While they were yet some way from their destination
the crowd parted for a moment, and Lady Eliza caught
sight of the object in its midst. She pointed towards it.

"Ride, Fullarton! ride, for God's sake, and bid for the
water-butt!" she cried

"Tut, tut, my lady. What use have you for it?"

"It will come very useful for drowning the stable terrier's puppies. She has them continually. Ride, I tell
you, man! Am I to be overrun with whelps because
you will not bestir yourself?"

Gilbert could scarce conceal his amusement, and was
divided between his desire to laugh aloud and an uneasy
feeling that the lady would appeal to him.

The auctioneer was seen at this juncture to leap down
from the wood-pile on which he stood, and a couple of
men hurried forward and began to remove the water-
butt. It was being hustled away like some corpulent
drunkard, its legs trailing the ground stiffly and raising a
dust that threatened to choke the bystanders.

The yard was full of people, and, as the auctioneer had
paused between two lots, and was being refreshed at the
expense of the farm's owner, tongues were loose, and the
air was filled with discussion, jests, and the searching
smell of tobacco and kicked-up straw. Among the few
women present Gilbert perceived Granny Stirk, seated
precariously on the corner of the wood-pile from which
the auctioneer had just descended. Beside her was a
tall, shock-headed lad of nineteen or so, whom only the
most unobservant could suspect of belonging to the
same category as the farm-boys, though his clothes were
of the same fashion as their own, and his face wore the
same healthy tanned red. He was spare and angular,

and had that particular focus of eye which one sees in men who steer boats, drive horses, pay out ropes, and whose hands can act independently while they are looking distant possibilities in the face. A halter dangled from his arm. He was very grave, and his thoughts were evidently fixed on the door of the farm stable. In spite of his sharp-cut personality, he stood by Granny Stirk in a way that suggested servitude.

Gilbert left his companions and went toward the couple. Granny's face was lengthened to suit the demands of a public occasion, and her little three-cornered woollen shawl was pinned with a pebble brooch.

"What ails ye that ye canna see the,laird of Whanland?" she said, turning to the boy as Speid stopped beside them.

He shuffled awkwardly with his cap.

"He's ma grandson, an' it's a shelt* he's after."

Gilbert was getting a little more familiar with local speech.

"Do you intend to buy?" he said to the lad.

Jimmy Stirk brought his eyes back to his immediate surroundings, and looked at the speaker. They were so much lighter than the brown face in which they were set, and their gaze was so direct, that Gilbert was almost startled. It was as though someone had gripped him.

"Ay, that's it. He's to buy," broke in Granny. "He's aye wanted this, an' we'd be the better of twa, for the auld ane's getting fairly done."

"I doubt I'll no get it yet," said the boy.

"He's sold near a' the things he's got," continued Granny, looking at her grandson's feet, which Gilbert suddenly noticed were bare. "A'm fair ashamed to be seen wi' him."

"How much have you got together?" inquired the young man.

* Pony.

Jimmy opened his hand. There were ten pounds in the palm.

"He got half that, July month last, from a gentleman that was like to be drowned down by the river's mouth; he just gaed awa an' ca'ed him in by the lugs,"* explained his grandmother.

"Did you swim out?" asked Speid, interested.

"Ay," replied Jimmy, whose eyes had returned to the door.

"That was well done."

"I kenned I'd get somethin'," observed the boy.

The auctioneer now emerged from the farm-house and the crowd began to draw together like a piece of elastic. He came straight to the wood-pile.

"Are you needing all that to yoursel'?" he enquired, looking jocosely at the bystanders as he paused before Granny Stirk.

"Na, na; up ye go, my lad. The biggest leer in the armchair," said the old woman as she rose.

"It's ill work meddling wi' the Queen o' the Cadgers," remarked a man who stood near.

Gilbert determined to stay in his place by the Stirks, for the commotion and trampling going on proclaimed that the live stock were on the eve of being brought to the hammer. The cart-horses were the first to be disposed of, so, having found someone who offered to put the roan into a spare stall, he abandoned himself to the interest with which the scene inspired him.

Jimmy Stirk's face, when the last team had been led away, told him the all-important moment had come. The boy moistened his lips with his tongue and looked at him. His hand was shut tightly upon the money it held.

It was difficult to imagine what use the owner of the farm might have found for the animal being walked

* Ears.

about before the possible buyers, for he was just fifteen hands and seemed far too light to carry a heavy man, or to be put between the shafts of one of those clumsy gigs which rolled unevenly into Kaims on market-days. In spite of the evident strain of good blood, he was no beauty, being somewhat ewe-necked and too long in the back. But his shoulder sloped properly to the withers, and his length of stride behind, as he was walked round, gave promise of speed; his full eye took a nervous survey of the mass of humanity surrounding him. The man who led him turned him abruptly round and held him facing the wood-pile. Gilbert could hear Jimmy Stirk breathing hard at his shoulder.

The auctioneer looked round upon the crowd with the noisome familiarity of his class, a shepherd's crook which he held ready to strike on the planks at his feet substituting the traditional hammer.

"You'll no' hae seen the like o' lot fifty-seven hereabout," he began. "Yon's a gentleman's naig—no ane o' they coorse deevils that trayvels the road at the term wi' an auld wife that's shifting hoose cocked up i' the cart—he wouldna suit you, Granny."

He looked down at the old woman, the grudge he bore her lurking in his eye.

"Hoots!" she exclaimed; "tak him yoursel', gin ye see ony chance o' bidin' on his back!"

The auctioneer was an indifferent horseman.

"A gentleman's naig, I'm telling ye! Fit for the laird o' Fullarton, or maybe her ladyship hersel'," he roared, eager to cover his unsuccessful sally and glancing toward Robert and Lady Eliza, who sat on horseback watching the proceedings. "Aicht pounds! Aicht pounds! Ye'll na get sic a chance this side o' the New Year!"

There was a dead silence, but a man with a brush of black whisker, unusual to his epoch, cast a furtive glance at the horse.

"Speak up, Davie MacLunder! speak up!"

Another dead silence followed.

"Fiech!" said David MacLunder suddenly, without moving a muscle of his face.

"Seven pound! Seven pounds! Will nane o' you speak? Will I hae to bide here a' the day crying on ye? Seven pound, I tell ye! Seven pound!"

"Seven pound five," said a slow voice from behind a haystack.

"I canna see ye, but you're a grand man for a' that," cried the auctioneer, "an' I wish there was mair like ye!"

"Seven ten," said Jimmy Stirk.

"Aicht," continued the man behind the haystack.

Though Gilbert knew lot fifty-seven to be worth more than all the money in Jimmy's palm, he hoped that the beast's extreme unsuitability to the requirements of those present might tell in the lad's favour. The price rose to eight pound ten.

"Nine," said Jimmy.

"And ten to that," came from the haystack.

"Ten pound," said the boy, taking a step forward.

There was a pause, and the auctioneer held up his crook.

"Ten pounds!" he cried. "He's awa at ten pounds! Ane, twa——"

"Ten pound ten!" shouted Davie MacLunder.

Jimmy Stirk turned away, bitter disappointment in his face. In spite of his nineteen years and strong hands, his eyes were filling. No one knew how earnestly he had longed for the little horse.

"Eleven," said Gilbert.

"Eleven ten!"

"Twelve."

The auctioneer raised his crook again, and threw a searching glance round.

"Twelve pound! Twelve pound! Twelve pound for the last time! Ane, twa, three——"

The crook came down with a bang.

"Twelve pound. The laird of Whanland."

"He is yours," said Speid, taking the bewildered Jimmy by the elbow. "Your grandmother was very civil to me the first time I saw her, and I am glad to be able to oblige her."

The boy looked at him in amazement.

Gilbert had slipped some money into his pocket before starting for the sale; he held the two gold pieces out to him.

"You can take him home with you now," he said, smiling.

Jimmy Stirk left the "roup" in an internal exultation which had no outward nor visible sign but an additional intensity of aspect, the halter which had hung over his arm adorning the head of the little brown horse, on whose back he jogged recklessly through the returning crowd His interest in the sale had waned the moment he had become owner of his prize; but his grandmother, who had set out to enjoy herself and meant to do so thoroughly, had insisted on his staying to the end She kept her seat at the foot of the wood-pile till the last lot had changed hands, using her tongue effectively on all who interfered with her, and treating her grandson with a severity which was her way of marking her sense of his good fortune.

Granny Stirk, or "the Queen of the Cadgers," as local familiarity had christened her, was one of those vigorous old people, who, having lived every hour of their own lives, are always attracted by the possibilities of youth, and whose sympathy goes with the swashbuckling half of the world. For the tamer portion of it, however respectable, they have little feeling, and are often rewarded by being looked upon askance during life and very much missed after death. They exist, for the most part, either in primitive communities or in very old-fashioned ones, and rarely in that portion of society which lies between the two. Gilbert, with his appear-

ance of a man to whom anything in the way of adventure
might happen, had roused her interest the moment she
saw him holding Lady Eliza's mare outside her own
cottage door. His expression, his figure, his walk, the
masculine impression his every movement conveyed,
had evoked her keenest sympathy, and, besides being
grateful for his kindness to Jimmy, she was pleased to
the core of her heart by the high-handed liberality he had
shown. It was profitable to herself and it had become·
him well, she considered.

The cadgers, or itinerant fish-sellers, who formed a
distinct element in the population of that part of the
coast, were a race not always leniently looked upon by
quiet folk, though there was, in reality, little evil that
could be laid to their charge but the noise they made.
While they had a bad name, they were neither more nor
less dishonest and drunken than other people, and had,
at least, the merit of doing their business efficiently.
It was they who carried the fish inland after the boats
came in, and those who stood on their own feet and were
not in the pay of the Kaims fishmongers, kept, like the
Stirks, their own carts and horses. When the haul came
to be spread and the nets emptied, the crowding cadgers
would buy up their loads, either for themselves or for
their employers, and start inland, keeping a smart but
decent pace till they were clear of the town, and, once
on the road, putting the light-heeled screws they affected
to their utmost speed. Those whose goal was the town
of Blackport, seven or eight miles from the coast, knowing that the freshest fish commanded the highest price,
used the highroad as a racecourse, on which they might
be met either singly or in a string of some half-dozen
carts, pursuing their tempestuous course.

The light carts which they drove were, in construction,
practically flat boxes upon two wheels, on the front of
which sat the driver, his legs dangling between the
shafts. As they had no springs and ran behind horses

to which ten miles an hour was the business of life, the rattle they made, as they came bowling along, left no one an excuse for being driven over who had not been born deaf. Those in the employ of the Kaims fish-mongers would generally run in company, contending each mile hotly with men who, like Jimmy Stirk, traded for themselves and took the road in their own interests.

More than forty years before the time of which I speak, Granny Stirk, then a strikingly handsome young woman, lived with her husband in the cottage which was still her home. Stirk, a cadger well known on the road for his blasphemous tongue and the joyfulness of his Saturday nights, was reported to be afraid of his wife, and it is certain that, but for her strong hand and good sense, he would have been a much less successful member of society. As it was, he managed to lead an almost decent life, and was killed, while still a young man, in an accident.

Mrs. Stirk thus found herself a widow, with two little boys under ten, a cart, a couple of angular horses, and no male relations; in spite of the trouble she had had with him, she missed her man, and, after his funeral, prepared herself to contend with two things—poverty and the dulness of life. She cared little for the company of her own sex, and the way in which her widowhood cut her off from the world of men and movement galled and wearied her. So it was from inclination as well as necessity that she one day mounted the cart in her husband's vacant place, and appeared at Kaims after the boats came in, to be greeted with the inevitable jeers. But the jeers could not stop her shrewd purchasing, nor alter the fact that she had iron nerves and a natural judgment of pace, and in the market she was soon let alone as one with whom it was unprofitable to bandy words. For curses she cared little, having heard too many; to her they were light things to encounter in the fight for her bread, her children, and the joy of life.

Her position became assured one day, when, after a time of scarcity in the fish-market, a good haul held out the prospect of an unusual sale inland. A string of cadgers who had started before Mrs. Stirk were well out on the road when she appeared from a short-cut considered unfit for wheels, and having hung shrewdly to their skirts, passed them just outside Blackport, her heels on the shaft, her whip ostentatiously idle, and her gold earrings swinging in her ears.

When her eldest son was of an age to help her, he ran away to sea; and when she gave up the reins to the second, she retired to the ordinary feminine life of her class with the nickname of the "Queen of the Cadgers" and a heavier purse. Behind her were a dozen years of hard work. When her successor died, as his father had done, in the prime of life, the sailor son, as a sort of rough payment for his own desertion, sent his boy Jimmy to take his place; the arrangement suited Mrs. Stirk, and her grandson took kindly to his trade. They had spent a couple of years together when Gilbert Speid came into their lives as owner of the land on which their cottage stood.

Lady Eliza remained in her saddle for the whole of the sale, though Fullarton put his horse in the stable. She beckoned to Gilbert to join them, and the two men stood by her until the business was over and the crowd began to disperse. They rode homeward together, their roads being identical for a few miles, threading their way through the led horses, driven cattle, and humanity which the end of the "roup" had let loose. Jimmy Stirk passed them on his new acquisition, for he had flung himself on its back to try its paces, leaving his grandmother to follow at her leisure.

"Did you buy that horse for the saddle or for harness?" inquired Fullarton, as the boy passed them.

"He is not mine," replied Gilbert. "It was young Stirk who bought him."

"But surely I heard the auctioneer knock him down to you."

"I outbid him by two pounds. He had not enough, so I added that on for him. I never saw anyone so much in earnest as he was," explained Gilbert.

Fullarton was silent, and Lady Eliza looked curiously at the young man.

"I don't know anything about the boy," he added, feeling rather foolish under her scrutiny. "I fear you think me very soft-hearted."

"That is to your credit," said Fullarton, with the least touch of artificiality.

"Perhaps you have the quality yourself, sir, and are the more leniently inclined toward me in consequence," replied Gilbert, a little chafed by the other's tone.

"We shall have all our people leaving us and taking service at Whanland," said Lady Eliza. "You have obliged me also, for my fish will arrive the fresher."

"Do you deal with the Stirks?" inquired Gilbert.

"I have done so ever since I came to this part of the country, out of respect for that old besom, Granny. I like the boy, too; there is stout stuff in that family."

"Then I have committed no folly in helping him?" said Speid.

"Lord, no, sir! Fullarton, this is surely not your turning home?"

"It is," said he, "and I will bid you good evening, for Mr. Speid will escort you. Sir, I shall wait upon you shortly, and hope to see you later at my house."

Gilbert and Lady Eliza rode on together, and parted at the principal gate of Morphie; for, as he declined her invitation to enter on the plea of the lateness of the hour, she would not suffer him to take her to the door.

From over the wall he got a good view of the house as he jogged down the road, holding back the little roan, who, robbed of company, was eager for his stable. With its steep roofs and square turrets at either end of the

façade, it stood in weather-beaten dignity among the
elms and ashes, guiltless of ornament or of that outburst
of shrubs and gravel which cuts most houses from their
surroundings, and is designed to prepare the eye for the
transition from nature to art. But Morphie seemed an
accident, not a design; an adjunct, in spite of its considerable size, to the pasture and the trees. The road
lay near enough to it for Speid to see the carved coat-of-
arms over the lintel, and the flagged space before the
door stretching between turret and turret. He hurried
on when he had passed it, for splashes of rain were beginning to blow in his face, and the wind was stirring in the
tree-tops.

Where a field sloped away from the fringe of wood, he
paused a moment to look at one of those solid stone dove-
cotes which are found in the neighbourhood of so many
gentlemen's houses in the northern lowlands of Scotland.
Its discoloured whitewash had taken all the mellow tones
that exposure and damp can give, and it stood, looking
like a small, but ancient fort, in a hollow among the
ragged thorn-trees. At either end of its sloping roof a
flight of crowsteps terminated in a stone ball cutting the
sky. Just above the string-course which ran round the
masonry a few feet below the eaves was a row of pigeon-
holes; some birds circling above made black spots against
the gray cloud.

Gilbert buttoned up his coat, and let the roan have
his way.

CHAPTER V

MR. BARCLAY held the happy position of chief bachelor in the polite circles of Kaims. Although he had viewed with displeasure the advent of a young and sporting banker and the pretensions of the doctor's eldest son, who had an agreeable tenor voice, his position remained unshaken. Very young ladies might transfer their interest to those upstarts and their like, but, with the matrons who ruled society, he was still the backbone of every assembly, and its first male ornament. He was an authority on all local questions, and there clung about him that subdued but conscious gallantry acceptable to certain female minds.

It was a cold night when he gave his overcoat and muffler to the maid in the hall of a house which stood a little back from the High Street. A buzz of talk came to him through an open door, and, as he ascended the stairs, the last notes of a flute had just died away. The wife of the coastguard inspector was giving a party, at which tea, conversation, and music were the attractions. The expression which had been arranging itself on his face culminated as he entered the drawing-room.

Mrs. Somerville, the inspector's wife, formed the link in the chain between town and county, and numbered both elements in her acquaintance; her husband, who, disabled by a wound, had retired from the active branch of his profession, being the only representative of His Majesty's service in the neighbourhood. Her parties, therefore, were seen by Kaims through a certain halo

54

caused by the presence, outside the house, of a string of family chariots, and the absence, inside it, of one of Captain Somerville's legs.

The room was half full. A group of young ladies and two or three young men were at the piano, and near the drawn curtains of the window a whist-table was set, at which four elderly people were seated in the throes of their game.

The two Miss Robertsons occupied a sofa a little apart from the rest of the company and Miss Hersey was talking to Captain Somerville, whose infirmity forbade him to rise and welcome individual guests, while it enabled him to consistently entertain the principal ones.

"You are late, Mr. Barclay," said the hostess, as she held out her hand. "We had been hoping for you to join the rubber which is going on, but some of our friends were impatient, and so they have settled down to it."

"I was detained, ma'am," said the lawyer. "I have been out to Whanland, and nothing would content Speid but that I should stay and dine with him."

"See what it is to be such a popular man!" exclaimed the coastguard's lady, looking archly over her fan.

She was not above the acceptance of the little compliments with which Barclay, who was socially ambitious, plied her.

"You flatter me sadly, I fear, Mrs. Somerville; but that is your kindness and not merit."

"I have not yet seen Mr. Speid," said Mrs. Somerville, "but I hear he is a very well-looking young man. Quite the dandy, with his foreign bringing up."

"Yes, that is exactly what I tell him," replied Barclay. "A very affable fellow, too. He and I are great friends. Indeed, he is always plaguing me to go out to Whanland."

That he had never gone there on any errand but business was a fact which he did not reveal to his hostess.

"So many stories are afloat respecting his—his antecedents," said the lady, dropping her eyes, "one hardly knows what to believe. However, there he is, master of his—of the Speid property. I think bygones should be bygones, don't you, Mr. Barclay?"

As she said this, she glanced toward a corner of the room in which Lucilla Somerville, a homely virgin in' white muslin and red arms, was whispering with a girl friend.

Barclay knew as much as his hostess of Gilbert's history and very little more, whatever his conjectures might be, but he relapsed instantly from the man of the world into the omniscient family lawyer

"Ah!" he exclaimed, raising two fingers; "forbidden ground with me, madam—forbidden ground, I fear!"

"Well, I will not be naughty, and want to know what I should not hear," said the lady. "I fear it is a sad world we live in, Mr. Barclay."

"It would be a much sadder one if there were no fair members of your sex ready to make it pleasant for us," he replied, with a bow.

"You are incorrigible!" she exclaimed, as she turned away.

At this moment a voice rose from the neighbourhood of the piano, whence the doctor's son, who had discovered an accompanist among the young ladies, sent forth the first note of one of a new selection of songs. It was known to be a new one, and the company was silent.

> " Give me a glance, a witching glance,
>   This poor heart to illume,
> Or else the rose that through the dance
>   Thy tresses did perfume.
>
> " Keep, cruel one, the ribbon blue
>   From thy light hand that flows;
> Keep it—it binds my fond heart true;
>   But oh, give me the rose!"

"How well it suits Mr. Turner's voice," said Lucilla, as the singer paused in the interval between the verses.

"The words are lovely," said her friend—"so full of feeling!"

"The sighs that, drawn from mem'ry's fount,
My aching bosom tear—
O bid them cease ! nor, heartless, count
My gestures of despair.

"Take all I have—the plaints, the tears
That hinder my repose,
The heart that's faithful through the years;
But oh, give me the rose !"

A polite murmur ran through the room as Mr. Turner laid down his music.

"I notice that our musical genius keeps his eyes fixed on one particular spot as he sings," observed an old gentleman at the whist-table, as he dealt the cards. "I wonder who the young puppy is staring at."

"If you had noticed that I threw away my seven of clubs, it would have been more to the purpose, and we might not have lost the trick," remarked the spinster who was his partner, acidly.

"People have no right to ask one to play whist in a room where there is such a noise going on," said the first speaker.

"Did I hear you say *whist?*" inquired the lady sarcastically.

Mr. Barclay passed on to the little group formed by his host and the Misses Robertson.

"How are you, Barclay?" said the sailor, looking up from his chair, and reflecting that, though the lawyer was more than a dozen years his junior, and had double as many legs as himself, he would not care to change places with him. He was a man of strong prejudices.

"I have not had the pleasure of meeting you since our afternoon together at Whanland," said Barclay, pausing before the sofa with a bow which was as like Gilbert's as he could make it.

"We go out very little, sir," said Miss Hersey.

"Speid will be a great acquisition," continued Barclay; "we all feel the want of a few smart young fellows to wake us up, don't we, Miss Robertson?"

"We like our cousin particularly," said Miss Hersey; "it has been a great pleasure to welcome him back."

Miss Caroline's lips moved almost in unison with her sister's, but she said nothing and sat still, radiating an indiscriminate pleasure in her surroundings. She enjoyed a party.

"That must be another arrival even later than myself," remarked the lawyer, as a vehicle was heard to draw up in the street outside. "I understand that you expect Lady Eliza Lamont; if so, that is likely to be her carriage."

Mrs. Somerville began to grow visibly agitated as the front door shut and voices were audible on the staircase. In a few moments Lady Eliza Lamont and Miss Raeburn were announced.

It was only a sense of duty which had brought Lady Eliza to Mrs. Somerville's party, and it would hardly have done so had not Robert Fullarton represented to her that having three times refused an invitation might lay her open to the charge of incivility. As she entered, all eyes were turned in her direction; she was dressed in the uncompromising purple gown which had served her faithfully on each occasion during the last ten years that she had been obliged, with ill-concealed impatience, to struggle into it. She held her fan as though it had been a weapon of offence; on her neck was a beautifully wrought amethyst necklace. Behind her came Cecilia in green and white, with a bunch of snowdrops on her breast and her tortoiseshell comb in her hair.

"We had almost despaired of seeing your ladyship," said Mrs. Somerville; "and you, too, dear Miss Raeburn. Pray come this way, Lady Eliza. Where will you like to sit?"

"I will take that seat by Captain Somerville," said the newcomer, eyeing a small cane-bottomed chair which stood near the sofa, and longing to be rid of her hostess.

"Oh, not there!" cried the lady. "Lucilla, my dear,

roll up the velvet armchair. Pray, pray allow me, Lady Eliza! I cannot let you sit in that uncomfortable seat —indeed I cannot!"

But her victim had installed herself.

"I am not able to offer you this one," said Captain Somerville; "for I am a fixture, unfortunately."

"Lady Eliza, let me beg you——"

"Much obliged, ma'am; I am very comfortable here. Captain Somerville, I am glad to find you, for I feared you were away," said Lady Eliza. She had a liking for the sailor which had not extended itself to his wife.

"I have been up the coast these last three weeks inspecting; my wife insisted upon my getting home in time for to-night. I had not intended to, but I obeyed her, you see."

"And why did you do that?"

"God knows," said the sailor.

The sound of the piano checked their conversation, as a young lady with a roving eye was, after much persuasion, beginning to play a selection of operatic airs. To talk during music was not a habit of Lady Eliza's, so the two sat silent until the fantasia had ended in an explosion of trills and a chorus of praise from the listeners.

"Is that your daughter?" she inquired; "I move so seldom from my place that I know very few people here."

"Heaven forbid, ma'am! That's my Lucy standing by the tea-table."

"You don't admire that kind of music?"

"If anyone had presumed to make such a noise on any ship of mine, I'd have put 'em in irons," said Captain Somerville.

They both laughed, and Lady Eliza's look rested on Cecilia, who had been forced into the velvet chair, and sat listening to Barclay as he stood before her making conversation. Her eyes softened.

"What do you think of my girl?" she said.

"I have only seen one to match her," replied the old man, "and that was when I was a midshipman on board the flagship nearly half a century ago. It was at a banquet in a foreign port where the fleet was being entertained. She was the wife of some French grandee. Her handkerchief dropped on the floor, and when I picked it up she gave me a curtsey she might have given the King, though I was a boy more fit to be birched at school than to go to banquets. Another young devil, a year or two my senior, said she had done it on purpose for the flag-lieutenant to pick up instead of me; he valued himself on knowing the world."

Lady Eliza's eyes were bright with interest.

"I taught him a little more of it behind the flag-lieutenant's cabin next morning, and got my leave ashore stopped for it; but it was a rare good trouncing," added Captain Somerville, licking his lips.

"I am sorry your leave was stopped," said his companion; "I would have given you more if I had been in command."

"You can't eat your cake and have it, ma'am—and I enjoyed my cake."

"I suppose you never saw her again," said she.

"Never; but I heard of her—she was guillotined in the Revolution a dozen years later. I shall never forget my feelings when I read it. She made a brave business of it, I was told; but no one could look at her and mistake about that."

They sat silent for some time, and, Mrs. Somerville appropriating Barclay, Cecilia had leisure to turn to Miss Hersey; both she and Lady Eliza had a regard for the old ladies, though between them there was little in common save good breeding. But that can be a strong bond.

"Come, come; we cannot allow you to monopolise Miss Raeburn any more!" exclaimed Mrs. Somerville, tapping the lawyer playfully on the arm. "We need you at the tea-table; duty first and pleasure after, you know."

"If you will watch my destination, Mrs. Somerville, you will see that it is purely duty which animates me," said Barclay, starting off with a cup of tea in one hand and a plate of sweet biscuits in the other.

His hostess watched him as he offered the tea with much action to Miss Caroline Robertson.

"Fie, sir! fie!" she exclaimed, as he returned; "that is too bad!"

"For my part, I would shut up all members of your sex after forty," said he, rather recklessly.

"Indeed?" said Mrs. Somerville, struggling with her smile. She was forty-seven.

"I meant sixty, ma'am—sixty, of course," gasped Barclay, with incredible maladroitness.

"That would be very sad for some of our friends," she observed, recovering stoutly from the double blow and looking with great presence of mind at Lady Eliza. "How old would you take her ladyship to be, for instance?"

Barclay happened to know that Lady Eliza would, if she lived, keep her fifty-third birthday in a few months; it was a fact of which some previous legal business had made him aware.

"I should place her at forty-eight," he replied, "though, of course, if she understood the art of dress as you do, she might look nearly as young as yourself."

"Go away; you are too foolish, Barclay! Mr. Turner, we are talking of age: at what age do gentlemen learn wisdom?"

"Never, very often," replied Turner, who, in spite of his tenor voice, had a sour nature.

Barclay gave him a vicious glance; he did not admire him at the best of times, and the interruption annoyed him. He turned away.

"I trust you have been attended to, Miss Robertson," said the hostess.

She despaired of separating her husband and Lady Eliza, and approached Miss Hersey, whose intimate connection with the county made her presence and that of her sister desirable adjuncts to a party. The old lady made room for her on the sofa.

"Yes, many, many thanks to you; we have enjoyed our evening. Caroline, Mrs. Somerville is asking if we have all we need. We have been very much diverted."

Miss Caroline smiled; she had not quite caught the drift of her sister's words, but she felt sure that everything was very pleasant.

Mrs. Somerville did not know whether the vague rumours about Gilbert's parentage which had been always prevalent, and which had sprung up afresh with his return, had ever reached the old ladies' ears. Their age and the retirement in which they lived had isolated them for a long time, but she reflected that they had once taken part in the life surrounding them and could hardly have remained in complete ignorance. She longed to ask questions.

"Mr. Barclay seems a great favourite at Whanland," she began.

"He was there when we went to welcome my cousin," replied Miss Hersey; "he is his man of business."

"He is most agreeable—quite the society man too. I do not wonder that Mr. Speid likes to see him; it is a dull life for a young gentleman to lead alone in the house—such a sad house, too, what with his poor mother's death there and all the unfortunate talk there was. But I have never given any credit to it, Miss Robertson, and I am sure you will say I was right. I am not one of those who believe everything they hear."

The old lady made no reply, staring at the speaker; then her face began to assume an expression which Mrs. Somerville, who did not know her very well, had never seen on it, and the surprise which this caused her had the effect of scattering her wits.

"I despise gossip, as you know," she stammered; "indeed, I always said—I always say—if there's anything unkind, do not bring it to *me;* and I said—what does it matter to *me?* I said—his poor mother is dead and buried, and if there *is* anything discreditable——"

Miss Hersey rose from the sofa, and turned to her sister.

"Come, Caroline, it is time we went home. Ma'am," she said, curtseying as deeply as her age would permit to the astonished Mrs. Somerville, "we have outstayed your good manners. I have the honour to wish you a good-evening."

The Misses Robertson's house stood barely a hundred yards from that of Captain Somerville, so Miss Hersey had decided that the coach which was usually hired when they went abroad was unnecessary; the maid-servant who was to have presented herself to escort them home had not arrived when they put on their cloaks, so they went out alone into the moonlit street.

"What was that she was saying, Hersey?" inquired Miss Caroline, as she clung to her sister's arm, rather bewildered by her situation, but accepting it simply.

"Mrs. Somerville is no gentlewoman, sister. She was bold enough to bring up some ill-talk to which I have never been willing to listen."

"That was very wrong—very wrong," said Miss Caroline.

Miss Hersey was murmuring to herself.

"Discreditable?" she was saying—"discreditable? The impertinence!"

CHAPTER VI

THE DOVECOTE OF MORPHIE

THE vehicle used by Captain Somerville on his tours of inspection was standing in the Whanland coach-house; it was an uncommon-looking concern, evolved from his own brain and built by local talent. The body was hung low, with due regard to the wooden leg of its owner, and the large permanent hood which covered it faced backwards instead of forwards, so that, when driving in the teeth of bad weather, the Captain might retire to its shelter, with a stout plaid to cover his person and his snuffbox to solace it.

This carriage was made to convey four people—two underneath the hood and one in front on a seat beside the coachman. On fine days the sailor would drive himself, defended by the Providence that watches over his profession; for he was a poor whip.

It was a soft night, fresh and moist; the moon, almost at the full, was invisible, and only the dull light which pervaded everything suggested her presence behind the clouds. Captain Somerville, sitting with Gilbert over his wine at the dining-room table, was enjoying a pleasant end to his day; for Speid, knowing that his inspection work would bring him to the neighbourhood of Whanland, had delayed his own dinner till a comparatively late hour, and invited the old gentleman to step aside and share it before returning to Kaims.

A sound behind him made the younger man turn in his chair and meet the eyes of Macquean, who had entered.

64

"Stirk's wantin' you," he announced, speaking to his master, but looking sideways at Captain Somerville.

"Tell him to wait," said Gilbert; "I will see him afterwards."

Macquean slid from the room.

The two men talked on until they were again aware of his presence. He stood midway between Speid and the door, rubbing one foot against the other.

"It's Stirk," he said.

"I am not ready to see him," replied Gilbert with some impatience; "I will ring when I am."

When they had risen from the table and the sailor had settled himself in an armchair, Gilbert summoned Macquean.

"What does young Stirk want with me?" he inquired.

Macquean cast a circular look into space, as though his master's voice had come from some unexpected quarter.

"It's poachers," he said apologetically.

"*What?*" shouted Somerville.

"Just poachers."

"But where? What do you mean?" cried Gilbert.

"It's poachers," said Macquean again. "Stirk's come for you."

"Where are they?"

"They're awa west to net the doo'cot o' Morphie; but they'll likely be done by now," added Macquean.

"Is that what he wanted me for?" cried Gilbert.

"Ay."

Captain Somerville had dragged himself up from his chair.

"But, God bless my sinful soul!" he exclaimed, "why did you not tell us?"

Macquean grinned spasmodically.

"I'm sure I couldna say," he replied.

Gilbert took him by the shoulders and pushed him out of his way, as he ran into the hall shouting for Jimmy;

the boy was waiting outside for admittance, and he almost knocked him down.

"It's they deevils frae Blackport that's to net the doo-cot o' Morphie!" began Jimmy breathlessly.

"How do you know?"

"I'm newly come from Blackport mysel', an' I heard it i' the town."

Speid's eyes glittered.

"Where is your cart? We will go, Jimmy."

"It's no here, sir; I ran."

The sailor had come to the door, and was standing behind his friend.

"My carriage is in the yard," he said. "Take it, Speid, it holds four. Are you going, boy?"

Jimmy did not think reply necessary.

"Macquean, run to the farm, and get any men you can find. I will go to the stable, Captain Somerville, and order your phaëton; my own gig only holds two. Oh, if I had but known of this earlier! What it is to have a fool for a servant!"

"It is worse to have a stick for a leg," said Somerville; "but I am coming, for all that, Speid. Someone must drive, and someone must hold the horse."

"Do, sir, do!" cried Gilbert, as he disappeared into the darkness.

With Jimmy's help, he hurried one of his own horses into the shafts of the Captain's carriage and led it to the doorstep. As the sailor gathered up the reins, Macquean returned breathless.

"I didna see onybody," he explained; "they're a' bedded at the farm."

An exclamation broke from Gilbert.

"But you should have knocked them up, you numskull! What do you suppose I sent you for?"

Macquean shook his head with a pale smile of superiority.

"They wadna rise for me," he said; "I kenned that when I went."

"Then you shall come yourself!" cried Speid. "Get in, I tell you! get in behind with Jimmy!"

Macquean shot a look of dismay at his master, and his mouth opened.

"Maybe I could try them again," he began; "I'll awa and see."

"Get in!" thundered Gilbert.

At this moment Jimmy Stirk's arm came out from under the hood, and Macquean was hauled into the seat beside him; Captain Somerville took a rein in each hand, and they whirled down the short drive, and swung out into the road with a couple of inches to spare between the gatepost and the box of the wheel.

"You will hardly find that man of yours very useful," observed the sailor, as they were galloping down the Morphie road; "I cannot think why you brought him."

Gilbert sat fuming; exasperation had impelled him to terrify Macquean, and, as soon as they had started, he realised the futility of his act.

"The boy behind is worth two," he said

"There may be four or five of these rascals at the dovecote."

"We must just do our best," said Gilbert, rather curtly.

Somerville thought of his leg and sighed; how dearly he loved a fray no one knew but himself.

As they approached Morphie, they stopped to extinguish their lights, and he began, in consequence, to drive with what he considered great caution, though Gilbert was still forced to cling to the rail beside him; Macquean, under the hood, was rolled and jolted from side to side in a manner that tended to make him no happier. His companion, seldom a waster of words, gave him little comfort when he spoke.

"Ye've no gotten a stick wi' ye," he observed, as they bowled through the flying mud.

"Na," said Macquean faintly.

"Ye'll need it."

There was a pause.

"I kent a man that got a richt skelp from ane o' they Blackport laddies," continued Jimmy; "'twas i' the airm, too. It swelled, an' the doctor just wheepit it off. I mind it well, for I was passin' by the house at the time, an' I heard him skirl."

There was no reply from the corner of the hood and they pressed on; only Somerville, who had a habit of chirruping which attacked him the moment he took up the reins and only left him when he laid them down, relieved the silence. Thanks to the invisible moon, the uniform grayness which, though not light, was yet luminous, made the way plain, and the dark trees of Morphie could be seen massed in the distance.

"I wonder they wad choose sic a night as this," remarked Jimmy; "it's a peety, too, for they'll likely see us if we dinna gang cannylike under the trees. Can ye run, Mr. Macquean?"

"Ay, can I," replied the other, grinning from under the safe cover of the darkness. A project was beginning to form itself in his mind.

"There'll be maire nor three or four. I'd like fine if we'd gotten another man wi' us; we could hae ta'en them a' then. They're ill deevils to ficht wi'."

"I could believe that," said Macquean.

His expression was happily invisible to Stirk.

"If I'd time, I could cut ye a bit stick frae the hedge," said Jimmy.

"Heuch! dinna mind," replied Macquean soothingly.

They were nearing the place where the dovecote could be seen from the road and Captain Somerville pulled up. Gilbert and Jimmy got out quietly and looked over a gate into the strip of damp pasture in which the building stood. There was enough light to see its shape distinctly, standing as it did in the very centre of the clearing among the thornbushes. It was not likely that the thieves would use a lantern on such a night, and the two strained their eyes for the least sign of any moving thing that might pass by the foot of the bare walls. Macquean's head came stealthily out from under the hood, as the head of a tortoise peers from beneath its shell. No sound came from the dovecote and Gilbert and Jimmy stood like images, their bodies pressed against the gateposts. Somerville, on the driving-seat, stared into the gray expanse, his attention fixed. They had drawn up under a roadside tree, for better concealment of the carriage. Macquean slipped out into the road, and, with a comprehensive glance at the three heads all turned in one direction, disappeared like a wraith into the night.

Presently, to the straining ears of the watchers came the sound of a low whistle.

"There," said Speid under his breath, "did you hear that, Jimmy?"

The boy nodded.

"Let Macquean hold the horse," burst out Somerville, who was rolling restlessly about on the box. "I might be of use even should I arrive rather late. At least, I can sit on a man's chest."

At this moment Jimmy looked into the back of the carriage."

"Mr. Macquean's awa'!" he exclaimed as loudly as he dared.

Gilbert ground his teeth; only the necessity for silence stopped the torrent which rose to the sailor's lips.

Speid and Jimmy slid through the bars of the gate; they dared not open it nor get over it for fear it should rattle on its hinges. They kept a little way apart until they had reached the belt of thorn-trees, and, under

cover of these, they drew together again and listened.
Once they heard a boot knock against a stone; they
crept on to the very edge of their shelter, until they were
not thirty yards from the dovecote. The door by which
it was entered was on the farther side from the road, and
the pigeon-holes ran along the opposite wall a few feet
below the roof. Three men were standing by the door,
their outlines just distinguishable. Jimmy went on his
hands and knees, and began to crawl, with that motion
to which the serpent was condemned in Eden, towards
a patch of broom that made a spot like an island in the
short stretch of open ground between the thorns and
the building, Gilbert following.

Now and then they paused to listen, but the voices
which they could now hear ran on undisturbed, and,
when they had reached their goal, they were close
enough to the dovecote to see a heap lying at its foot
which they took to be a pile of netting. Evidently the
thieves had not begun their night's work.

The nearest man approached the heap and began to
shake it out.

"I'll gi'e ye a lift up, Robbie," said one of the voices;
"there's stanes stickin' out o' the wa' at the west side.
I had a richt look at it Sabbath last when the kirk was
in."

"My! but you're a sinfu' man!" exclaimed Robbie.

"We're a' that," observed a third speaker piously.

Two of the men took the net, and went round the
dovecote wall till they found the stones of which their
companion had spoken; these rough steps had been
placed there for the convenience of anyone who might
go up to mend the tiling.

"Lie still till they are both up," whispered Gilbert.
"There are two to hold the net, and one to go in and beat
out the birds."

They crouched breathless in the broom till they saw
two figures rise above the slanting roof between them

and the sky. Each had a length of rope which he secured round one of the stone balls standing at either end above the crowsteps; it was easy to see that the business had been carefully planned. Inside the dovecote, a cooing and gurgling showed that the birds were awakened.

The two men clambered down by the crowsteps, each with his rope wound round his arm and supporting him as he leaned over to draw the net over the pigeon-holes.

"Now then, in ye go," said Robbie's voice.

The key was in the door, for the third man unlocked it and entered.

Speid and Jimmy Stirk rose from the broom; they could hear the birds flapping among the rafters as the intruder entered, and the blows of his stick on the inner sides of the walls. They ran up, and Gilbert went straight to the open doorway and looked in. His nostrils were quivering; the excitement which, with him, lay strong and dormant behind his impassive face, was boiling up. It would have been simple enough to turn the key of the dovecote on its unlawful inmate, but he did not think of that.

"You scoundrel!" he exclaimed—"you damned scoundrel!"

The man turned round like an animal trapped, and saw his figure standing against the faint square of light formed by the open door; he had a stone in his hand which he was just about to throw up into the fluttering, half-awakened mass above his head. He flung it with all his might at Speid, and, recognising his only chance of escape, made a dash at the doorway. It struck Gilbert upon the cheek-bone, and its sharp edge laid a slanting gash across his face. He could not see in the blackness of the dovecote, so he leaped back, and the thief, meeting with no resistance, was carried stumbling by his own rush a few feet into the field, dropping his stick as he went. As he recovered himself, he turned upon his enemy; he was a big man, bony and heavy, and, had he known it, the want of light was all in his favour against a foe like Gilbert Speid, to whom self-defence, with foil or fist, was the most fascinating of sciences. Flight did not occur to him, for he was heavy-footed, and he saw that his antagonist was smaller than himself.

Speid cursed the darkness; he liked doing things neatly, and the situation was sweet to him; it was some time since he had stood up to any man, either in play or in earnest. He determined to dodge his opponent until he had reversed their positions and brought him round with his back to the whitewash of the dovecote; at the present moment he stood against the dark background of the trees. The two closed together, and, for some minutes, the sound of blows and heavy breathing mingled with the quiet of the night.

The blood was dripping down Gilbert's face, for the stone had cut deep; he was glad the wound was below his eye, where the falling drops could not hamper his sight. He guarded himself very carefully, drawing his enemy slowly after him, until he stood silhouetted sharply against the whitewash. He looked very large and heavy, but the sight pleased Speid; he felt as the bull feels when he shakes his head before charging; his heart sang aloud and wantonly in his breast. Now that he had got the position he desired, he turned from defence to attack, and with the greater interest as his antagonist was no mean fighter. He had received a blow just below the elbow, and one on the other side of his face, and his jaw was stiff. He grew cooler and more steady as the moments went by. He began to place his blows carefully, and his experience told him that they were taking effect. Breath and temper were failing his enemy; seeing this, he took the defensive again, letting him realise the futility of his strength against the skill he met. Suddenly, the man rushed in, hitting wildly at him. He was struck under the jaw by a blow that had the whole weight of Gilbert's body behind it, and he went over backwards, and lay with his face to the sky. He had had enough.

Meanwhile, the two men on the dovecot had been a good deal startled by hearing Gilbert's exclamation and the noise of the rush through the door. One, who had fastened the net on the eaves, clambered up the crow-steps, and, holding fast to the stone ball, looked over to see that his friend's design had been frustrated by someone who was doing his utmost to destroy his chances of escape. He came down quickly to the lower end of the roof, meaning to drop to the ground and go to his assistance; but he found himself confronted by Jimmy Stirk, who had sidled round the walls, and stood below, looking from himself to his partner with the air of a terrier who tries to watch two rat-holes at once. A few birds had come out of the pigeon-holes, and were struggling, terrified, in the meshes. The two men did the most sensible thing possible: they dropped, one from either end of the tiling, and ran off in opposite directions.

Unable to pursue both, the boy pounced upon the man on his left, and would have laid hands on him as he landed, had he not slipped upon a piece of wet mud and stumbled forward against the wall. When he recovered himself, his prey had put twenty yards between them, and was running hard towards the thorn-trees. The net had fallen to the ground, and the pigeons were escaping from it, flying in agitated spirals above the dovecote; their companions were emerging from the holes, dismayed with the outraged dismay felt by the feathered world when its habits are disturbed. The air was a whirl of birds. Jimmy gathered himself together and gave chase with all his might.

Captain Somerville's state of mind as he watched Gilbert and Jimmy Stirk disappear was indescribable;

as he sat on the box and the minutes went by, his feelings grew more poignant, for impotent wrath is a dreadful thing. Had he happened upon Macquean, he would have been congenially occupied for some time, but the darkness had swallowed Macquean, and there was nothing for him to do but sit and gaze into the grayness of the field.

At last he heard what he fancied was Speid's voice and the clattering of feet upon the dovecote roof. The night was still, and, though middle-age was some way behind him, his hearing was acute. He found his position beyond his endurance.

The horse was old, too, and stood quiet while he descended painfully to the ground. He led him to the gatepost and tied him to it securely; to squeeze between the bars as Jimmy and Gilbert had done was impossible for him, so he opened it with infinite caution, and closed it behind him. Then he set out as best he could for the thorn-trees.

His wooden leg was a great hindrance in the moist pasture, for the point sunk into the earth as he walked, and added to his exertions. He paused in the shadow of the branches, as his friends had done, and halted by a gnarled bush with an excrescence of tangled arms. While he stood, he heard steps running in his direction from the dovecote. He held his breath.

A figure was coming towards him, making for the trees. As it passed, the sailor took firm hold of a stem to steady himself, and stuck out his wooden leg. The man went forward with a crash, his heels in the air, his head in the wet moss, and before he knew what had happened, a substantial weight had subsided upon his back.

"My knife is in my hand," observed Captain Somerville, laying the thin edge of his metal snuff-box against the back of the thief's neck, "but, if you move, it will be in your gizzard."

By the time his absence was discovered, Macquean had put some little distance between himself and the carriage. For the first few minutes of his flight he crept like a shadow, crouching against the stone wall which flanked one side of the road, and terrified lest his steps should be heard. He paused now and then and stood still to listen for the sound of pursuit, taking courage as each time the silence remained unbroken. The white face of a bullock standing by a gate made his heart jump as it loomed suddenly upon him. When he felt safe, he took his way with a bolder aspect—not back towards Whanland, but forward toward Morphie House. He burned with desire to announce to someone the sensational events that were happening, and he realised very strongly that it would be well to create an excuse for his own defection.

He was panting when he pealed the bell and knocked at the front-door, feeling that the magnitude of his errand demanded an audience of Lady Eliza herself. It was opened by a maidservant with an astonished expression.

"Whaur's her ladyship?" said Macquean. "A'm to see her."

"What is't?" inquired the girl, closing the door until it stood barely a foot open.

"A'm seeking her leddyship, a' tell ye."

She looked at him critically.

"Who is there?" said a cool voice from the staircase.

The maid stood back, and Cecilia came across the hall.

"Where do you come from?" she asked, as the lamp-light struck Macquean's bald head, making it shine in the darkness.

"From Whanland," replied he. "You'll be Miss Raeburn? Eh! There's awfu' work down i' the field by the doo'cot! The laird's awa' there, an' Jimmy Stirk, an' the ane-leggit Captain-body frae Kaims. They're to net it an' tak' the birds."

"What?" exclaimed Cecilia, puzzled, and seeing visions of the inspector engaged in a robbery. "Do you mean Captain Somerville?"

"A' do, indeed," said Macquean, wagging his head, "an' a'm sure a' hope he may be spared. He's an auld man to be fechtin' wi' poachers, but we're a' in the hands o' Providence."

A light began to break on Cecilia.

"Then, are the poachers at the dovecote? Is that what you have come to say?"

Macquean assented.

The maid servant, who had been listening open-mouthed, now flew up to Lady Eliza's bedroom, and found her mistress beginning to prepare herself for the night. She had not put off her dress, but her wig stood on a little wooden stand on the toilet-table. She made a snatch at it as the girl burst in with her story.

"Cecilia, what is all this nonsense?" exclaimed Lady Eliza, seeing her adopted niece's figure appear on the threshold. "(Stop your havering, girl, till I speak to Miss Raeburn.) Come here, Cecilia. I can't hear my own voice for this screeching limmer. (Be quiet, girl.) What is it, Cecilia? Can't you answer, child?"

The maid had all the temperament of the female domestic servant, and was becoming hysterical.

"Put her out!" cried Lady Eliza. "Cecilia! put her into the passage."

"There's a man downstairs," sobbed the maid, who had talked herself into a notion that Macquean was a poacher trying to effect an entrance into the house.

"A man, is there? I wish there were more, and then we should not have a parcel of whingeing* women to serve us! I wish I could put you all away, and get a few decent lads in, instead. Take her away, Cecilia, I I tell you!"

When the door was shut behind the servant, and

* Whining.

Lady Eliza had directed her niece to have the stablemen sent with all despatch to the dovecote, she drew a heavy plaid shawl from the cupboard and went downstairs to sift the matter. Her wig was replaced and she had turned her skirt up under the plaid.

Macquean was still below. Having delivered himself of his news, he had no wish to be sent out again. He did not know where the servants' hall might be, or he would have betaken himself there, and the maid had fled to her own attic and locked herself in securely.

"Have you got a lantern?" said Lady Eliza over the banisters. "I am going out, and you can light me."

"Na," said Macquean, staring.

Without further comment she went out of the house, beckoning him to follow. She crossed the yard and opened the stable-door, to find Cecilia, a cloak over her shoulders, caressing the nose of the bay mare. Seeing the maid's distracted state of mind, she had roused the men herself. A small lantern stood on the corn-bin. The mare whinnied softly, but Lady Eliza took no notice of her.

"Here, my dear; give the lantern to Macquean," she exclaimed. "I am going to see what is ado in the field."

"It gives little light," said Cecilia. "The men have taken the others with them."

"Ye'd best bide whaur ye are," said Macquean suddenly. "It's terrible dark."

Lady Eliza did not hear him. She had gone into the harness-room, and the two women were searching every corner for another lantern. Finding the search fruitless, they went into the coach-house. There was no vestige of such a thing, but, in a corner, stood a couple of rough torches which had been used by the guizardsö * at Hogmanay.

When Macquean, compelled by Lady Eliza, had lit

* Masqueraders, who, in Scotland, go from house to house at Hogmanay, or the last day of the year.

one, she ordered him to precede her, and they left the stable, Cecilia following. The arms of the trees stood out like black rafters as they went under them, the torchlight throwing them out theatrically, as though they made a background to some weird stage scene. Occasionally, when Macquean lowered the light, their figures went by in a fantastic procession on the trunks of the limes and ashes. The darkness overhead seemed measureless. The fallen twigs cracked at their tread, and beech-nuts underfoot made dry patches on the damp moss among the roots. As they emerged from the trees and looked down the slope, they saw the stable-men's lanterns and heard the voices of men.

Lady Eliza redoubled her pace. When they had almost come to the dovecote, she told Macquean to hold up his torch. Cecilia, whose gown had caught on a briar, and who had paused to disentangle herself, hurried after her companions, and rejoined them just as he raised the light.

As she looked, the glare fell full upon the walls, and on the figure of Gilbert Speid standing with the blood running down his face.

CHAPTER VII

THE LOOKING-GLASS

GILBERT hurried forward as he saw Lady Eliza.

"The pigeons are safe," he said. "I have locked up two of these rascals in the dovecote. The third, I fear, has got away."

"Indeed, sir, I am vastly obliged to you," exclaimed she. "You seem considerably hurt."

"He has had a stiff fight, ma'am," said Captain Somerville.

"You are very good to have protected my property," she continued, looking at the two gentlemen. "All I can do now is to send for the police from Kaims, unless the dovecote is a safe place for them until morning."

"Young Stirk has gone to Kaims with my carriage, said Somerville, "for the door is not very strong, and I fancy your men have no wish to watch it all night."

"It seems," said Lady Eliza, turning to Speid, "that I have only to be in a difficulty for you to appear."

Her voice was civil, and even pleasant, but something in it rang false. Gilbert felt the undercurrent instinctively, for, though he had no idea of her real sentiments towards himself, he recognised her as a person in whose doings the unexpected was the natural.

"I think I can do nothing more," he said, with a formality which came to him at times, "so I will wish your ladyship a good-night."

"May I· ask where you are going, sir, and how you propose to get there in that condition?"

"It is nothing," replied Gilbert, "and Whanland is a

79

bare four miles from here. With your permission I will
start at once."

"Nonsense, Mr. Speid! You will do nothing of the
sort. Do you suppose I shall allow you to walk all that
way, or to leave Morphie till your face has been attended
to? Come, Captain Somerville, let us go to the house.
Sir, I insist upon your coming with us."

The men from the stable were instructed to remain at
the dovecote door until Jimmy should return with the
police, and Gilbert recognised Macquean as Lady Eliza
again drove him forward to light the party back under
the trees. He made no comment, feeling that the
moment was unsuitable, and being somewhat interested
in the fact that a young woman, of whose features he
could only occasionally catch a glimpse, was walking
beside him; as the torchlight threw fitful splashes across
her he could see the outline of a pale face below a crown
of rather elaborately dressed dark hair. Lady Eliza
had directed him to follow his servant, and was herself
delayed by the sailor's slow progress. Though he had
never seen his companion before, she was known to him
by hearsay. Her silent step, and the whiteness of her
figure and drapery against the deep shadows between
the trees, gave him a vague feeling that he was walking
with Diana. He grew aware of his bloody face, and immediately became self-conscious.

"I fear I am a most disagreeable object, Miss Raeburn," he said.

"I had not observed it, sir," she replied.

"You are very kind, but you must think me unpleasant
company in this condition, all the same."

"I can think of nothing but that you have saved my
aunt's pigeons. She says little, but I know she is
grateful. There has always been a large flock at
Morphie, and their loss would have vexed her very
much."

"I owe Stirk—Stirk, the young cadger—a debt for

bringing me word of what was going to happen. He heard of it in Blackport, and came straight to tell me."

"I wonder why he went to you instead of warning us," said she.

"We are rather friendly, he and I. I suppose he thought he would like the excitement, and that I should like it, too. He was not wrong, for I do," replied Gilbert, unconsciously using the present tense.

"Then what has brought Captain Somerville? It all happened so suddenly that there has been no time for surprise. But it is strange to find him here."

"He was dining with me when the news was brought, and he insisted on coming. He managed to trip a man up, and sit on him till Stirk and I came to his help. He did it with his wooden leg, I believe," said Gilbert, smiling in spite of his injured face.

Cecilia laughed out.

"I think that is charming," she said.

Gilbert had known many women more or less intimately, but never one of his own countrywomen. He had heard much of the refinement and delicacy of the British young lady. This one, who seemed, from the occasional view he could obtain of her, and from the sound of her voice, to possess both these qualities in the highest degree, struck him as having a different attitude towards things in general to the one he had been led to expect in the class of femininity she represented. As she had herself said, there had been no time for surprise, and he now suddenly found that he was surprised—surprised by her presence, surprised to find that she seemed to feel neither agitation nor any particular horror at what had happened. He had known women in Spain who found their most cherished entertainment in the bull-ring, but he had never met one who would have taken the scene she had broken in upon so calmly.

The changed customs of our modern life have made it hard to realise that, in the days when Gilbert and Cecilia

met by torchlight, it was still a proof of true sensibility
to swoon when confronted by anything unusual, and
that ladies met cows in the road with the same feelings
with which they would now meet man-eating tigers.
Indeed, the woman of the present moment, in the face
of such an encounter, would probably make some more
or less sensible effort towards her own safety, but, at
the time of which I speak, there was nothing for a lady
to do at the approach of physical difficulties but subside
as rapidly as possible on to the cleanest part of the path.
But Cecilia had been brought up differently. Lady
Eliza led so active a life, and was apt to require her to
do such unusual things, that she had seen too many
emergencies to be much affected by them. There was
a deal of the elemental woman in Cecilia, and she had
just come too late to see the elemental man in Speid
brush away the layer of civilisation, and return to
his natural element of fight. She was almost sorry she
had been too late.

She walked on beside him, cool, gracious, the folds of
her skirt gathered up into her hand, and he longed for
the lamp-lit house, that he might see her clearly.

"The man with the torch is your servant, is he not?"
said she. "He told me he had come from Whanland."

"He is," replied Speid; "but how long he will remain
so is another matter. I am very angry with him—dis-
gusted, in fact."

"What has he done, sir, if I may ask?"

"Everything that is most intolerable. He drove me
to the very end of my patience, in the first instance."

"How long is your patience, Mr. Speid?"

"It was short to-night," replied Gilbert.

"And then?"

"Then I brought him here to be of some use, and
while I was looking over the wall for these thieving
ruffians, he ran away."

"He does not look very brave," observed Cecilia, a

smile flickering round her lips. "He arrived at the door, and rang up the house, and I could see that he was far from comfortable."

"He will be more uncomfortable to-morrow," said Gilbert grimly.

"Poor fellow," said Cecilia softly. "It must be a terrible thing to be really afraid."

"It is inexcusable in a man."

"I suppose it is," replied she slowly, "and yet——"

"And yet—you think I should put up with him? He has enraged me often enough, but he has been past all bearing to-night."

"Do you really mean to send him away? He has been years at Whanland, has he not?"

"He has," said Gilbert; "but let us forget him, Miss Raeburn, he makes me furious."

When they reached the house, Lady Eliza led the way to the dining-room, and despatched such servants as were to be found for wine. Her hospitable zeal might even have caused a fresh dinner to be cooked, had not the two men assured her that they had only left the table at Whanland to come to Morphie.

"If I may have some water to wash the cut on my face, I will make it a little more comfortable," said Speid.

He was accordingly shown into a gloomy bedroom on the upper floor, and the maid who had opened the door to Macquean, having recovered from her hysterics, was assiduous in bringing him hot water and a sponge. As the room was unused, it had, all the deadness of a place unfrequented by humanity, and the heavy curtains of the bed and immense pattern of birds and branches which adorned the wallpaper gave everything a lugubrious look. He examined his cut at the looking-glass over the mantelshelf, an oblong mirror with a tarnished gilt frame.

The stone which had struck him was muddy, and he

found, when he had washed the wound, that it was deeper than he supposed. It ached and smarted as he applied the sponge, for the flint had severed the flesh sharply. As he dried his wet cheek in front of the glass, he saw a figure which was entering the room reflected in it.

"Lady Eliza has sent me with this. Can I help you, sir?" said Cecilia rather stiffly, showing him a little case containing plaster.

She held a pair of scissors in her hand. He turned.

"Ah!" she exclaimed, as she saw the long, red scar; "that is really bad! Do, pray, use this plaster. Look, I will cut it for you."

And she opened the case, and began to divide its contents into strips.

"You are very good," he said awkwardly, as he watched the scissors moving.

She did not reply.

"I had no intention of disturbing the house in this way," he continued; "it is all owing to Macquean's imbecility. You need never have known anything till to-morrow morning."

"You are very angry with Macquean," said Cecilia. "I cannot bear to think of his leaving a place where he has lived so long. But you will be cooler to-morrow, I am sure. Now, Mr. Speid, I have made this ready. Will you dip it in the water and put this strip across the cut?"

Gilbert did as he was bid, and, pressing the edges of the wound together, began to lay the plaster across his cheek.

"You can hardly see," said she. "Let me hold the light."

She raised the candle, and the two looked intently into the glass at his fingers, as he applied the strip. He met with scant success, for it stuck to his thumb and curled backwards like a shaving. He made another and more careful attempt to place it, but, with the callous obstinacy often displayed by inanimate things, it refused to lie flat.

The two pairs of eyes met in the looking-glass.

"I cannot make it hold," said he. "It is not wet enough, and I am too clumsy."

His arm ached where it had been hit below the elbow; it was difficult to keep it steady.

"I can do it," said Cecilia, a certain resolute neutrality in her voice. "Hold the candle, sir."

She took the strip from him, and, dipping it afresh in the water, laid it deftly across his cheekbone.

As her cool fingers touched his hot cheek he dropped his eyes from her face to the fine handkerchief which she had tucked into her bosom, and which rose and fell with her breathing. She took it out, and held it pressed against the plaster.

"You will need two pieces," she said. "Keep this upon the place while I cut another strip."

He had never been ordered in this way by a girl before. Caprice he had experience of, and he had known the exactingness of spoilt women, but Cecilia's impersonal commanding of him was new, and it did not displease him. He told himself, as he stood in front of her, that, were he to describe her, he would never call her a girl. She was essentially a woman.

"That is a much better arrangement," observed Captain Somerville, as Gilbert entered the dining-room alone. "I did not know you were such a good surgeon, Speid."

"Don't praise me. I was making such a clumsy job of it that Miss Raeburn came to my help; she has mended it so well that a few days will heal it, I expect."

"You will have a fine scar, my lad," said the sailor.

"That doesn't matter. I assure you, the thing is of no consequence. It is not really bad."

"It is quite bad enough," said Lady Eliza.

"You think far too much of it, ma'am."

"At any rate, sit down and help yourself to some wine. I have not half thanked you for your good offices."

"I fancy he is repaid," said Somerville dryly, glancing at the strips of plaster.

Lady Eliza had ordered a carriage to be got ready to take Speid and the sailor home, and Captain Somerville had sent a message to Kaims by Jimmy Stirk, telling his family to expect his return in the morning, as he had accepted Gilbert's suggestion that he should remain at Whanland for the night. He looked kindly on this arrangement, for he was over sixty, and it was a long time since he had exerted himself so much.

While they stood in the hall bidding Lady Eliza goodnight, Cecilia came downstairs. She had not followed Gilbert to the dining-room. She held out her hand to him as he went away.

"Thank you," said he, looking at her and keeping it for a moment.

He leaned back in the carriage beside Somerville, very silent, and, when they reached Whanland and he had seen his friend installed for the night, he went to his own room What had become of Macquean he did not know and did not care. He sat late by the fire, listening to the snoring of the sailor, which reached him through the wall.

A violent headache woke him in the morning, and he lay thinking of the events of the preceding night. He put his hand up to his cheek to feel if the plaster was in its place. Macquean came in, according to custom, with his shaving-water, looking neither more nor less uncouth and awkward than usual. Though he shifted from foot to foot, the man had a complacency on his face that exasperated his master.

"What did you mean by leaving the carriage last night?" said Gilbert.

"A' went awa' to Morphie," said Macquean.

"And who told you to do that?"

"Aw! a' didna' speir* about that. A' just tell't them to gang awa' down to the doo'cot. Her ladyship was vera well pleased," continued Macquean, drawing his lips back from his teeth in a chastened smile.

"Get out of the room, you damned fellow! You should get out of the house, too, if it weren't for—for—get out, I say!" cried Gilbert, sitting up suddenly.

Macquean put down the shaving-water and went swiftly to the door. When he had shut it behind him he stood a moment to compose himself on the door-mat.

"He shouldna speak that way," he said very solemnly, wagging his head.

* Ask.

CHAPTER VIII

THE HOUSE IN THE CLOSE

To say that the Miss Robertsons were much respected in Kaims was to give a poor notion of the truth. The last survivors of a family which had lived—and, for the most part, died—in the house they still occupied, they had spent the whole of their existence in the town.

It was nearly a hundred years since a cousin of the Speid family, eldest and plainest of half a dozen sisters, had, on finding herself the sole unmarried member of the band, accepted the addresses and fortune of a wealthy East India merchant whose aspiring eye was turned in her direction.

The family outcry was loud at his presumption, for his birth was as undistinguished as his person, and the married sisters raised a chorus of derision from the calm heights of their own superiority. Mr. Robertson's figure, which was homely; his character, which was ineffective; his manners, which were rather absurd, all came in for their share of ridicule. The only thing at which they did not make a mock was his money.

But Isabella was a woman of resolute nature, and, having once put her hand to the plough, she would not look back. She not only married Mr. Robertson in the face of her family, but had the good sense to demean herself as though she were conquering the earth; then she settled down into a sober but high-handed matrimony, and proceeded to rule the merchant and all belonging to him with a rod of iron. The only mistake she made was that of having thirteen children.

88

And now the tall tombstone, which rose, with its draped urn, from a forest of memorials in the church-yard of Kaims, held records of the eleven who lay under it beside their parents. The women had never left their own place; two or three of the men had gone far afield, but each one of the number had died unmarried, and each had been buried at home. The two living would look in at it, on the rare occasions on which they passed, with a certain sense of repose.

After his marriage, Mr. Robertson had met with reverses, and the increase of his family did not mend his purse. At his death, which took place before that of his wife, he was no more than comfortably off; and the ample means possessed by Miss Hersey and Miss Caroline were mainly due to their own economical habits, and the accumulated legacies of their brothers and sisters.

In the town of Kaims the houses of the bettermost classes were completely hidden from the eye, for they stood behind those fronting on the street, and were approached by "closes," or narrow, covered ways, running back between the buildings. The dark doorways opening upon the pavement gave no suggestion of the respectable haunts to which they led. The Robertson house stood at the end of one of these. Having dived into the passages, one emerged again on a paved path, flanked by deep borders of sooty turf, under the windows of the tall, dead-looking tenements frowning squalidly down on either side, and giving a strange feeling of the presence of unseen eyes, though no sign of humanity was visible behind the panes. From the upper stories the drying underwear of the poorer inhabitants waved, parti-coloured, from long poles. The house was detached. It was comfortable and spacious, with a wide staircase painted in imitation of marble, and red baize inner doors; very silent, very light, looking on its further side into a garden.

It was Sunday; the two old ladies, who were strict

Episcopalians, had returned from church, and were sitting dressed in the clothes held sacred to the day, in their drawing-room. June was well forward, and the window was open beside Miss Hersey, as she sat, hand-kerchief in hand, on the red chintz sofa. The strong scent of lilies of the valley came up from outside, and pervaded that part of the room. At her elbow stood a little round table of black lacquer inlaid with mother-of-pearl pagodas. Miss Caroline moved about rather aim-lessly among the furniture, patting a table-cover here and shifting a chair there, but making no appreciable difference in anything she touched. Near the other window was set out a tray covered with a napkin, holding some wineglasses, a decanter, and two plates of sponge-cakes.

The Miss Robertsons' garden formed a kind of oasis in the mass of mean and crowded houses which lay between the High Street and the docks; for the populous part of Kaims, where the sailors, dockmen, and fishing-people lived, stretched on every side. A wide grass-plot, which centered in a wooden seat, crept close under the drawing-room windows, and from this a few steps ran down to the walled enclosure in which flower and kitchen garden were combined. The gate at their foot was overhung by an old jessamine plant which hid the stone lintel in a shower of white stars. Round the walls were beds of simple flowering plants, made with no pretence of art or arrangement, and dug by some long-forgotten gardener who had died unsuspicious of the oppressive niceties which would, in later times, be brought into his trade. Mignonette loaded the air with its keen sweetness, pansies lifted their falsely-innocent faces, sweet-williams were as thick as a velvet-pile carpet in shades of red and white, the phlox swayed stiffly to the breeze, and con-volvulus minor, most old-fashioned of flowers, seemed to have sprung off all the Dresden bowls and plates on which it had ever been painted, and assembled itself in

a corner alongside the lilies of the valley. The whole
of the middle part of the place was filled with apple-trees,
and the earth at their feet was planted with polyanthus
and hen-and-chicken daisies. At the foot of the garden
a fringe of white and purple lilacs stood by the gravel
path, and beyond these, outside the walls, a timber-
merchant's yard made the air noisy with the whirring
of saws working ceaselessly all the week.

But to-day everything was quiet, and the Miss
Robertsons sat in their drawing-room expecting their
company.

The Edinburgh coach reached Kaims late on Saturday
nights, and those who expected mails or parcels were
obliged to wait for them until Sunday morning, when,
from half-past one to two o'clock, the mail-office was
opened, and its contents handed out to the owners.
Church and kirk were alike over at the time of distribu-
tion, and the only inconvenience to people who had
come in from the country was the long wait they had to
endure after their respective services had ended, till
the moment at which the office doors were unlocked.
From time immemorial the Miss Robertsons had opened
their house to their friends between church hour and
mail hour, and this weekly reception was attended by
such county neighbours as lived within reasonable
distance of the town, and did not attend the country
kirks. Their carriages and servants would be sent to
wait until the office should open, while they themselves
would go to spend the interval with the old ladies.

Like moss on an ancient wall, a certain etiquette had
grown over these occasions, from which no one who
visited at the house in the close would have had the
courage or the ill-manners to depart. Miss Hersey,
who had virtually assumed the position of elder sister,
would sit directly in the centre of the sofa, and, to the
vacant places on either side of her, the two ladies whose
rank or whose intimacy with herself entitled them to

the privilege, would be conducted. She was thinking
to-day of the time when Clementina Speid had sat for
the first time at her right hand and looked down upon
the lilies of the valley. Their scent was coming up now.

The drawing-room was full on a fine Sunday, and Miss
Caroline, who generally retired to a little chair at the
wall, would smile contentedly on her guests, throwing,
from time to time, some mild echo of her sister's words
into the talk around her. When all who could reasonably be expected had arrived, Miss Hersey would turn
to the husband of the lady occupying the place of honour,
and, in the silence which the well-known action invariably
created, would desire him to play the host.

"Mr. Speid, will you pour out the wine?"

Sunday upon Sunday the words had been unaltered;
then, for thirty years, a different name. But now it
was the same again, and Gilbert, like his predecessor,
would, having performed his office, place Miss Hersey's
wineglass on the table with the mother-of-pearl pagodas.

It was nearing one o'clock before the marble-painted
entrance-hall echoed to the knocker, but, as one raindrop
brings many, its first summons was the beginning of a
succession of others, and the drawing-room held a good
many people when Gilbert arrived. Two somewhat
aggressive-looking matrons were enthroned upon the
sofa, a group of men had collected in the middle of the
room, and a couple or so of young people were chattering
by themselves. Miss Caroline on her chair listened to
the halting remarks of a boy just verging on manhood,
who seemed much embarrassed by his position, and who
cast covert and hopeless glances towards his own kind
near the window.

Robert Fullarton was standing silent by the mantelpiece looking out over the garden as Miss Hersey had
done, and thinking of the same things; but whereas,
with her, the remembrance was occasional, with him it
was constant. He had hardly missed his Sunday visit

once since the Sunday of which he thought, except when he was absent from home. It was a kind of painful comfort to him to see the objects which had surrounded her and which had never changed since that day. He came back into the present at the sound of Miss Hersey's voice.

"You have not brought your nephew with you," she said, motioning him to a chair near her.

"Ah, he is well occupied, ma'am," replied Robert, sitting down, "or, at least, he thinks he is. He has gone to Morphie kirk."

"One may be well occupied there also," said Miss Hersey, from the liberality of her Episcopalian point of view. "I did not know that he was a Presbyterian."

"Neither is he," said Fullarton, raising his eyebrows oddly, "but he has lately professed to admire that form of worship."

Miss Robertson felt that there was the suspicion of something hidden in his words, and was a little uncomfortable. She did not like the idea of anything below the surface. The two women beside her, who were more accustomed to such allusions, smiled.

"I do not understand, sir," said the old lady. "You seem to have some other meaning."

"I fancy there is another meaning to his zeal, and that it is called Cecilia Raeburn," said Fullarton.

"Oh, indeed!" exclaimed one of the ladies, putting on an arch face, "that is an excellent reason for going to church."

Robert saw that Miss Hersey was annoyed by her tone.

"I dare say he profits by what he hears as much as another," he said. "One can hardly be surprised that a young fellow should like to walk some of the way home in such attractive company. There is no harm in that, is there, Miss Robertson?"

"No, no," said Miss Hersey, reassured.

"Mr. Crauford Fordyce has a fine property in Lanarkshire, I am told," said one of the ladies, who seldom took the trouble to conceal her train of thought.

"His father has," replied Fullarton.

Gilbert had entered quietly, and, in the babble of voices, Miss Hersey had not heard him announced. Having paid his respects to her sister, he did not disturb her, seeing she was occupied; but, for the last few minutes, he had been standing behind Fullarton in the angle of a tall screen. His face was dark.

"Ah, Gilbert," exclaimed the old lady; "I was wondering where you could be."

"Take my chair, Speid," said Fullarton. "I am sure Miss Robertson is longing to talk to you."

"You are like a breath of youth," said Miss Hersey, as he sat down. "Tell me, what have you been doing since I saw you?"

Gilbert made a great effort to collect himself. The lady who had been speaking possessed an insatiable curiosity, and was bombarding Fullarton with a volley of questions about his nephew and the extent of his nephew's intimacy at Morphie, for she was a person who considered herself privileged.

"For one thing, I have bought a new cabriolet," said the young man.

"And what is it like?" asked Miss Hersey.

Carriages and horses were things that had never entered the range of her interest, but, to her, any belonging of Gilbert's was important.

"It is a high one, very well hung, and painted yellow. I drive my iron-gray mare in it."

"That will have a fine appearance, Gilbert."

"It would please me very much to take you out, ma'am," said he, "but the step is so high that I am afraid you would find it inconvenient."

"I am too old, my dear," said Miss Hersey, looking

delighted; "but some day I will come to the head of the close and see you drive away."

Gilbert's ears were straining towards Fullarton and his companion, who, regardless of the reticence of his answers, was cross-examining him minutely.

"I suppose that Lady Eliza would be well satisfied," she was saying, "and I am sure she should, too. *Of course*, it would be a grand chance for Miss Raeburn if Mr. Fordyce were to think seriously of her; she has no fortune. I happen to know that. For my part, I never can admire those pale girls."

The speaker, who had the kind of face that makes one think of domestic economy, looked haughtily from under her plumed Leghorn bonnet.

Fullarton grew rather uncomfortable, for he suspected the state of Gilbert's mind, and the lady, whom social importance rather than friendship with Miss Robertson had placed on the red chintz sofa, was a person whose tongue knew no bridle. He rose to escape. Gilbert rose also, in response to a nameless impulse, and a newcomer appropriating his chair, he went and stood at the window.

Though close to the lady who had spoken, he turned from her, unable to look in her direction, and feeling out of joint with the world. His brows were drawn together and the scar on his cheek, now a white seam, showed strong as he faced the light. It was more than three months since Cecilia had doctored it and he had watched her fingers in the looking-glass. He had met her many times after that night, for Lady Eliza had felt it behoved her to show him some attention, and had, at last, almost begun to like him. Had her feelings been unbiassed by the past, there is little doubt that she would have become heartily fond of him, for, like Granny Stirk, she loved youth; and her stormy explanation with Fullarton constantly in the back of her mind, she strove with herself to accept the young man's presence naturally.

To Fullarton, Gilbert was scarcely sympathetic, even
laying aside the initial fact that he was the living cause
of the loss whose bitterness he would carry to the grave.
A cynicism which had grown with the years was almost
as high as his heart, like the rising shroud supposed to
have been seen by witches round the bodies of doomed
persons.   In spite of his wideness of outlook in most
matters, there was a certain insularity in him, which
made him resent, as a consequence of foreign up-bringing,
the very sensitive poise of Gilbert's temperament.   And,
in the young man's face, there was little likeness to his
mother to rouse any feeling in Robert's breast.

Speid's thoughts were full of Cecilia and Crauford
Fordyce.   He had seen the latter a couple of times—for
it was some weeks since he had arrived to visit his uncle
—and he had not cared for him.   Once he had overtaken
him on the road, and they had walked a few miles
together.   He had struck him as stupid, and possibly,
coarse-fibred.   He only realised, as he stood twirling
the tassel of the blind, how important his occasional
meetings with Cecilia had become to him, how much she
was in his thoughts, how her words, her ways, her
movements, her voice, were interwoven with every fancy
he had.   He had been a dullard, he told himself, stupid
and coarse-fibred as Fordyce.   He had been obliged to
wait until jealousy, like a flash of lightning, should
show him that which lay round his feet.   Fool, idiot,
and thrice idiot that he was to have been near to such a
transcendent creature, and yet ignorant of the truth!
Though her charm had thrilled him through and through,
it was only here and now that the chance words of a
vulgar woman had revealed that she was indispensable
to him.

Though self-conscious, he was not conceited, and he
sighed as he reflected that he could give her nothing
which Fordyce could not also offer.   From the little he
had heard, he fancied him to be a richer man than him-

self. Cecilia did not strike him as a person who, if her heart were engaged, would take count of the difference. But what chance had he more than another of engaging her heart? Fordyce was not handsome, certainly, but then, neither was he ill-looking. Gilbert glanced across at a mirror which hung in the alcove of the window, and saw in it a rather sinister young man with a scarred face. He was not attractive, either, he thought. Well, he had learned something.

"Mr. Speid, will you pour out the wine?"

Miss Hersey's voice was all ceremony. Not for the world would she have called him Gilbert at such a moment.

He went forward to the little tray and did as she bid him.

CHAPTER IX

ON FOOT AND ON WHEELS

THE yellow cabriolet stood at the entrance to the close. The iron-gray mare, though no longer in her first youth, abhorred delay, and was tossing her head and moving restlessly, to the great annoyance of the very small English groom who stood a yard in front of her nose, and whose remonstrances were completely lost on her. Now and then she would fidget with her forefeet, spoiling the "Assyrian stride" which had added pounds to her price and made her an object of open-mouthed amasement to the youth of the Kaims gutter.

A crowd of little boys were collected on the pavement; for the company which emerged from the Miss Robertsons' house on Sundays was as good as a peep-show to them, and the laird of Whanland was, to their minds, the most choice flower of fashion and chivalry which this weekly entertainment could offer. Not that that fact exempted him from their criticism—no fact yet in existence could protect any person from the tongue of the Scotch street-boy—and the groom, who had been exposed to their comment for nearly twenty minutes, was beginning, between the mare and the audience, to come to the end of his temper.

"Did ever ye see sic a wee, wee mannie?" exclaimed one of the older boys, pointing at him.

"He's terrible like a monkey."

"An' a'm fell feared he'll no grow. What auld are ye, mun?" continued the other, raising his voice to a shout.

There was no reply.

"Hech! he winna speak!"

"He'll no be bigger nor Jockie Thompson. Come awa here, Jockie, an' let's see!"

A small boy was hauled out from the crowd and pushed forward.

"Just stand you aside him an' put your heedie up the same prood way he does."

The urchin stepped down off the pavement, and standing as near the victim as he dared, began to inflate himself and to pull such faces as he conceived suitable. As mimicry they had no merit, but as insult they were simply beyond belief.

A yell of approval arose.

The groom was beginning to meditate a dive at the whipsocket when the solid shape of Jockie Thompson's father appeared in the distance. His son, who had eluded him before kirk and who still wore his Sunday clothes, sprang back to the pavement, and was instantly swallowed up by the group.

By the time that the groom had recovered his equanimity the mare began to paw the stones, for she also had had enough of her present position.

"Whoa, then!" cried he sharply, raising his hand.

"Gie her the wheep," suggested one of the boys.

Though there was an interested pause, the advice had no effect.

"He's feared," said a boy with an unnaturally deep voice. "He's no muckle use. The laird doesna let him drive; ye'll see when he comes oot o' the close an' wins into the machine, he'll put the mannie up ahint him an' just drive himsel'."

"Ay, will he."

The man threw a vindictive glance into the group, and the mare, having resumed her stride, tossed her head up and down, sending a snow-shower of foam into the air. A spot lit upon his smart livery coat, and he pulled out his handkerchief to flick it off.

A baleful idea suggested itself to the crowd.

"Eh, look—see!" cried a tow-headed boy, "gie's a handfu' o' yon black durt an' we'll put a piece on his breeks that'll match the t'other ane!"

Two or three precipitated themselves upon the mud, and it is impossible to say what might have happened had not Gilbert, at this moment, come up the close.

"Whisht! whisht! here's Whanland! Michty, but he's fine! See now, he'll no let the mannie drive."

"Gosh! but he's a braw-lookin' deevil!"

"Haud yer tongue. He doesna look vera canny the day. I'd be sweer* to fash him."

Gilbert got into the cabriolet gathering up the reins, his thoughts intent upon what he had heard in the house. The mare, rejoiced to be moving, took the first few steps forward in a fashion of her own, making, as he turned the carriage, as though she would back on to the curbstone. He gave her her head, and drew the whip like a caress softly across her back. She plunged forward, taking hold of the bit, and trotted down the High Street, stepping up like the great lady she was, and despising the ground underneath her.

However preoccupied, Speid was not the man to be indifferent to his circumstances when he sat behind such an animal. As they left the town and came out upon the flat stretch of road leading towards Whanland, he let her go to the top of her pace, humouring her mouth till she had ceased to pull, and was carrying her head so that the bit was in line with the point of the shaft. A lark was singing high above the field at one side of him, and, at the other, the scent of gorse came in puffs on the wind from the border of the sandhills. Beyond was the sea, with the line of cliff above Garviekirk graveyard cutting out into the immeasurable water. The sky lay pale above the sea-line. They turned into the road by the Lour bridge from where the river could

* Loth.

be seen losing itself in an eternity of distance. In the extraordinary Sunday stillness, the humming of insects was audible as it only is on the first day of the week, when nature itself seems to suggest a suspension of all but holiday energy. The natural world, which recognises no cessation of work, presents almost the appearance of doing so at such times, so great is the effect of the settled habit of thousands of people upon its aspect.

The monotony of the motion and the balm of the day began to intoxicate Gilbert. It is not easy to feel that fate is against one when the sun shines, the sky smiles, and the air is quivering with light and dancing shadow; harder still in the face of the blue, endless sea-spaces of the horizon; hard indeed when the horse before you conveys subtly to your hand that he is prepared to transport you, behind the beating pulse of his trot, to Eldorado— to the Isles of the Blessed—anywhere.

His heart rose in spite of himself as he got out of the cabriolet at the door of Whanland, and ran his hand down the mare's shoulder and forelegs. He had brought her in hotter than he liked, and he felt that he should go and see her groomed, for he was a careful horse-master. But somehow he could not. He dismissed her with a couple of approving slaps, and watched her as she was led away. Then, tossing his hat and gloves to Macquean, who had come out at the sound of wheels, he strolled up to the place at which he had once paused with Barclay, and stood looking up the river to the heavy woods of Morphie.

"If she were here!" he said to himself, "if she were here!"

.   *   *   *   *   '   *   *

As Speid's eyes rested upon the dark woods, the little kirk which stood at their outskirts was on the point of emptying, for public worship began in it later than in the kirks and churches of Kaims.

The final blessing had been pronounced, the last paraphrase sung, and Lady Eliza, with Cecilia, sat in the Morphie pew in the first row of the gallery. Beside them was Fullarton's nephew, Crauford Fordyce, busily engaged in locking the Bibles and psalm-books into their box under the seat with a key which Lady Eliza had passed to him for the purpose. His manipulation of the peculiarly constructed thing showed that this was by no means the first time he had handled it.

The beadle and an elder were going their rounds with the long-handled wooden collecting-shovels, which they thrust into the pews as they passed; the sound of dropping pennies pervaded the place, and the party in the Morphie seat having made their contributions, that hush set in which reigned in the kirk before the shovel was handed into the pulpit, and the ring of the minister's money gave the signal for a general departure not unlike a stampede. Lady Eliza leaned, unabashed, over the gallery to see who was present.

When the expected sound had sent the male half of the congregation like a loosed torrent to the door, and the female remainder had departed more peacefully, the two women went out followed by Fordyce.

Lady Eliza was in high good temper. Though content to let all theological questions rest fundamentally, she had scented controversy in some detail of the sermon, and was minded to attack the minister upon them when next he came in her way. Fordyce, who was apt to take things literally, was rash enough to be decoyed into argument on the way home, and not adroit enough to come out of it successfully.

Robert Fullarton's nephew—to give him the character in which he seemed the most important to Lady Eliza—belonged to the fresh-faced, thickset type of which a loss of figure in later life may be predicted. Heavily built, mentally and physically, he had been too well brought up to possess anything of the bumpkin, or, rather, he had been too much brought up in complicated surroundings

to indulge in low tastes, even if he had them. He took
considerable interest in his own appearance, though he
was not, perhaps, invariably right in his estimate of it,
and his clothes were always good and frequently unsuitable. He was the eldest son of an indulgent father, who
had so multiplied his possessions as to become their
adjunct more than their owner; to his mother and his
two thick-ankled, elementary sisters he suggested Adonis,
and he looked to politics as a future career. Owing to
some slight natural defect, he was inclined to hang his
under-lip and breathe heavily through his nose. Though
he was of middle height, his width made him look short
of it, and the impression he produced on a stranger was
one of phenomenal cleanliness and immobility.

The way from the kirk to Morphie house lay through
the fields, past the home farm, and Lady Eliza stopped
as she went by to inquire for the health of a young cart-
horse which had lamed itself. Cecilia and Crauford
waited for her at the gate of the farmyard. A string of
ducks was waddling toward a ditch with that mixture
of caution and buffoonery in their appearance which
makes them irresistible to look at, and a hen's discor-
dant Magnificat informed the surrounding world that
she had done her best for it; otherwise everything was
still.

"We shall have to wait some time, I expect, if it is
question of a horse," observed Cecilia, sitting down upon
a log just outside the gate.

"*I* shall not be impatient," responded Fordyce, showing two very large, very white front teeth as he smiled.

"I was thinking that Mr. Fullarton might get tired of
waiting for you and drive home. The mails will have
been given out long ago, and he is probably at Morphie
by this time."

"Come now, Miss Raeburn; I am afraid you think me
incapable of walking to Fullarton, when, in reality, I
should find it a small thing to do for the pleasure of sit-

ting here with you. Confess it: you imagine me a poor
sort of fellow—one who, through the custom of being
well served, can do little for himself. I have seen it in
your expression."

Cecilia laughed a little. "Why should you fear that?"
she asked.

"Because I am extremely anxious for your good
opinion," he replied—"and, of course, for Lady Eliza's
also."

"I have no doubt you have got it," she said lightly.

"You are not speaking for yourself, Miss Raeburn. I
hope that you think well of me."

"Your humility does you credit."

"I wish you would be serious. It is hard to be set
aside by those whom one wishes to please."

"But I do not set you aside. You are speaking most
absurdly, Mr. Fordyce," said Cecilia, who was growing
impatient.

"But you seem to find everyone else preferable to
me—Speid, for instance."

"It has never occurred to me to compare you, sir."

Her voice was freezing.

"I hope I have not annoyed you by mentioning his
name," said he clumsily.

"You will annoy me if you go on with this conversation," she replied. "I am not fond of expressing
my opinion about anyone."

Fordyce looked crestfallen, and Cecilia, who was not
inclined to be harsh to anybody, was rather sorry; she
felt as remorseful as though she had offended a child; he
was so solid, so humourless, so vulnerable. She wondered what his uncle thought of him; she had wondered
often enough what Fullarton thought about most things,
and, like many others, she had never found out. It
often struck her that he was a slight peg for such friendship as Lady Eliza's to hang on. "Il y'a un qui baise et
un qui tend la joue." She knew that very well, and she

had sometimes resented the fact for her adopted aunt, being a person who understood resentment mainly by proxy.

As she glanced at the man beside her she thought of the strange difference in people's estimates of the same thing; no doubt he represented everything to someone, but she had spoken with absolute truth when she said that it had not occurred to her to compare him to Speid. She saw the same difference between the two men that she saw between fire and clay, between the husk and the grain, between the seen and the unseen. In her twenty-four years she had contrived to pierce the veils and shadows that hide the eyes of life, and, having looked upon them, to care for no light but theirs. The impression produced on her when she first saw Gilbert Speid by the dovecote was very vivid, and it was wonderful how little it had been obliterated or altered in their subsequent acquaintance. His quietness and the forces below it had more meaning for her than the obvious speeches and actions of other people. She had seen him in a flash, understood him in a flash, and, in a flash, her nature had risen up and paused, quivering and waiting, unconscious of its own attitude. Simple-minded people were inclined to call Cecilia cold.

"I am expecting letters from home to-day," said Fordyce at last. "I have written very fully to my father on a particular subject, and I am hoping for an answer."

"Indeed?" said she, assuming a look of interest; she felt none, but she was anxious to be pleasant.

"I should like you to see Fordyce Castle," said he. "I must try to persuade Lady Eliza to pay us a visit with you."

"I am afraid you will hardly be able to do that," she answered, smiling. "I have lived with her for nearly twelve years, and I have never once known her to leave Morphie."

"But I feel sure she would enjoy seeing Fordyce," he

continued; "it is considered one of the finest places in Lanarkshire, and my mother would make her very welcome; my sisters, too, they will be delighted to make your acquaintance. You would suit each other perfectly; I have often thought that."

"You are very good," she said, "and the visit would be interesting, I am sure. The invitation would please her, even if she did not accept it. You can but ask her."

"Then I have your permission to write to my mother?" said Crauford earnestly.

It struck Cecilia all at once that she was standing on the brink of a chasm. Her colour changed a little.

"It is for my aunt to give that," she said. "I am always ready to go anywhere with her that she pleases.

The more Fordyce saw of his companion the more convinced was he, that, apart from any inclination of his own, he had found the woman most fitted to take the place he had made up his mind to offer her. The occasional repulses which he suffered only suggested to him such maidenly reserve as should develop, with marriage, into a dignity quite admirable at every point. Her actual fascination was less plain to him than to many others, and, though he came of good stock, his admiration for the look of breeding strong in her was not so much grounded in his own enjoyment of it as in the effect he foresaw it producing on the rest of the world, in connection with himself. Her want of fortune seemed to him almost an advantage. Was he not one of the favoured few to whom it was unnecessary? And where would the resounding fame of King Cophetua be without his beggar-maid?

The letter he had written to his father contained an epitome of his feelings—at least, so far as he was acquainted with them; and, when he saw Lady Eliza emerge from a stable-door into the yard, and knew that there was no more chance of being alone with Cecilia, he was all eagerness to step out for Morphie, where his uncle had promised to call for him on his way home from Kaims.   Fullarton might even now be carrying the all-important reply in his pocket.

He wondered, as they took their way through the fragrant grass, how he should act when he received it, for he had hardly settled whether to address Miss Raeburn in person or to lay his hopes before Lady Eliza, with a due statement of the prospects he represented. He leaned toward the latter course, feeling certain that the elder woman must welcome so excellent a fate for her charge, and would surely influence her were she blind enough to her own happiness to refuse him.   But she would never refuse him.   Why should she?   He could name twenty or thirty who would be glad to be in her place.   He had accused her of preferring Speid's company to his own, but he had only half believed the words he spoke.   For what was Whanland?   and what were the couple of thousand a year Speid possessed?

Yet poor Crauford knew, though he would scarce admit the knowledge to himself, that the only situation in which he felt at a disadvantage was in Speid's society.

CHAPTER X

> "FORDYCE CASTLE,
> "LANARK.
> "*June* 26, 1801.

"MY DEAR SON,

"Your letter, with the very important matter it contains, took me somewhat by surprise, for although you had mentioned the name of the young lady and that of Lady Eliza Lamont, I was hardly prepared to hear that you intended to do her the honour you contemplate. A father's approval is not to be lightly asked or rashly bestowed, and I have taken time to consider my reply. You tell me that Miss Raeburn is peculiarly fitted, both in mind and person, to fill the position she will, as your wife, be called upon to occupy. With regard to her birth I am satisfied. She is, we know, connected with families whose names are familiar to all whose approval is of any value. I may say, without undue pride, that my son's exceptional prospects might have led him to form a more brilliant alliance, and I have no doubt that Miss Cecilia Raeburn, possessing such qualities of mind as you describe, will understand how high a compliment you pay to her charms in overlooking the fact. Your statement that she is dowerless is one upon which we need not dwell; it would be hard indeed were the family you represent dependent upon the purses of those who have the distinction of entering it. I am happy to say that my eldest son need be hampered by no such considerations, and that Mrs. Crauford Fordyce will lack

nothing suitable to her station, and to the interest that
she must inevitably create in the society of this county.
It now only remains for me to add that, having expressed
my feelings upon your choice, I am prepared to consent.

"Your mother is, I understand, writing to you, though
I have only your sister's authority for saying so, for I
have been so much occupied during the last day or two as
to be obliged to lock the door of my study. I am afraid,
my dear Crauford (between ourselves), that, though she
knows my decision, your mother is a little disappointed
—upset, I should say. I think that she had allowed herself to believe, from the pleasure you one day expressed
in the society of Lady Maria Milwright when she was
with us, that you were interested in that direction.
Personally, though Lord Milborough is an old friend of
the family, and his daughter's connection with it would
have been eminently suitable, her appearance would
lead me to hesitate, were I in your place and contem-
plating marriage. But that is an objection, perhaps,
that your mother hardly understands.

"I am, my dear Crauford,
"Your affectionate father,
"THOMAS FORDYCE."

"P.S.—Agneta and Mary desire their fond love to
their brother."

Fordyce was sitting in his room at Fullarton with his
correspondence in front of him; he had received two
letters and undergone a purgatory of suspense, for, by
the time he reached Morphie, his uncle had been kept
waiting for him some time. Finding nothing for himself
in his private mail-bag, Fullarton had it put under the
driving-seat, and the suggestion hazarded by his nephew
that it should be brought out only resulted in a curt
refusal. The elder man hated to be kept waiting, and the
culprit had been forced to get through the homeward
drive with what patience he might summon.

Lady Fordyce's letter lay unopened by that of Sir Thomas, and Crauford, in spite of his satisfaction with the one he had just read, eyed it rather apprehensively. But, after all, the main point was gained, or what he looked upon as the main point, for to the rest of the affair there could be but one issue. He broke the seal of his mother's envelope, and found a second communication inside it from one of his sisters.

"MY DEAR CRAUFORD (began Lady Fordyce),

"As your father is writing to you I will add a few words to convey my good wishes to my son upon the *decided step* he is about to take. Had I been consulted I should have advised a little more reflection, but as you are *bent on pleasing yourself*, and your father (*whether rightly or wrongly* I cannot pretend to say) is upholding you, I have no choice left but to express my *cordial good wishes*, and to hope that you *may never live to regret it.* Miss Cecilia Raeburn may be all you say, *or she may not*, and I should fail in my duty if I did not remind you that a young lady brought up in a provincial neighbourhood is not likely to step into *such a position as that of the wife of Sir Thomas Fordyce's eldest son* without the risk of having her head turned, or, *worse still*, of being incapable of maintaining her dignity. As I have not had the privilege of speaking to your father alone for two days, and as he has *found it convenient* to sit up till all hours, I do not know whether the consent he has (apparently) given is an unwilling one, but I should be acting *against my conscience* were I to hide from you that I suspect it most strongly. With *heartfelt wishes* for your truest welfare,

"I remain, my dear Crauford,

"Your affectionate mother,

"LOUISA CHARLOTTE FORDYCE."

"P.S.—Would it not be *wise* to delay your plans until you have been once more at home, and had every oppor-

tunity of thinking it over? You might return here in a
few days, and conclude your visit to your uncle *later on—*
say, at the end of September."

Crauford laid down the sheet of paper; he was not apt
to seize on hidden things, but the little touch of nature
which cropped up, like a daisy from a rubbish-heap, in
the end of his father's letter gave him sympathy to imagine what the atmosphere of Fordyce Castle must have
been when it was written. He respected his mother, not
by nature, but from habit, and the experiences he had
sometimes undergone had never shaken his feelings, but
only produced a sort of distressed bewilderment. He
was almost bewildered now. He turned again to Sir
Thomas's letter, and re-read it for comfort.

The enclosure he had found from his sister was much
shorter.

"MY DEAR BROTHER,
"Mary and I wish to send you our very kind love, and
we hope that you will be happy. Is Miss Raeburn
dark or fair? We hope she is fond of tambour-work.
We have some new patterns from Edinburgh which are
very pretty. We shall be very glad when you return.
Our mother is not very well. There is no interesting
news. Mrs. Fitz-Allen is to give a fête-champêtre with
illuminations next week, but we do not know whether
we shall be allowed to go, as she behaved *most unbe-
comingly* to our mother, trying to take precedence of
her at the prize-giving in the Lanark flower show.
Lady Maria Milwright is coming to visit us in September.
We shall be very pleased.
                         "Your affectionate sister,
                              "AGNETA FORDYCE."

Fullarton's good-humour was quite restored as uncle
and nephew paced up and down the twilit avenue that

evening. A long silence followed the announcement which the young man had just made.

"Do you think I am doing wisely, sir?" he said at last.

Fullarton smiled faintly before he replied; Crauford sometimes amused him.

"In proposing to Cecilia? One can hardly tell," he replied; "that is a thing that remains to·be seen." Perplexity was written in Crauford's face.

"But surely—surely—" he began, "have you not a very high opinion of Miss Raeburn?"

"The highest," said the·other dryly.

"But then——"

"What I mean is, do you care enough to court a possible rebuff? You are not doing wisely if you don't consider that. I say, a *possible* rebuff," continued his uncle.

"Then you think she will refuse me?"

"Heaven knows," responded Robert. "I can only tell you that to-day, when Miss Robertson enquired where you were, and I said that you were walking home from Morphie kirk with Cecilia, Speid was standing by looking as black as thunder."

To those whose ill-fortune it is never to have been crossed in anything, a rival is another name for a rogue. Fordyce felt vindictive; he breathed heavily.

"Do you think that Miss Raeburn is likely to—notice Speid?"

Robert's mouth twitched. "It is difficult not to notice Gilbert Speid," he replied.

"I really fail to see why everyone seems so much attracted by him."

"I am not sure that he attracts me," said the elder man.

"He looks extremely ill-tempered—most unlikely to please a young lady."

"There I do not altogether agree with you. We are always being told that women are strange things," said Fullarton.

"I am astonished at the view you take, uncle. After all, I am unable to see why my proposal should be less welcome than his—that is, if he intends to make one."

"You certainly have solid advantages. After all, that is the main point with the women," said the man for whose sake one woman, at least, had lost all. The habit of bitterness had grown strong.

"I shall go to Morphie to-morrow, and ride one of your horses, sir, if you have no objection."

"Take one, by all means; you will make all the more favourable impression. It is a very wise way of approaching your goddess—if you have a good seat, of course. Speid looks mighty well in the saddle."

He could not resist tormenting his nephew.

The very sound of Gilbert's name was beginning to annoy Fordyce, and he changed the subject. It was not until the two men parted for the night that it was mentioned again.

"I am going out early to-morrow," said Robert, "so I may not see you before you start. Good luck, Crauford."

Fordyce rode well, and looked his best on horseback, but Cecilia having gone into the garden, the only eye which witnessed his approach to Morphie next day was that of a housemaid, for Lady Eliza sat writing in the long room.

She received him immediately.

"I am interrupting your ladyship," he remarked apologetically.

"Not at all, sir, not at all," said she, pushing her chair back from the table with a gesture which had in it something masculine; "you are always welcome, as you know very well."

"That is a pleasant hearing," replied he, "but to-day it is doubly so I have come on business of a—I may say—peculiar nature. Lady Eliza, I trust you are my friend?"

"I shall be happy to serve you in any way I can, Mr. Fordyce."

"Then I may count on your good offices? My uncle is so old a friend of your ladyship's that I am encouraged to——"

"You are not in any difficulty with him, I hope," said Lady Eliza, interrupting him rather shortly.

"Far from it; indeed, I have his expressed good wishes for the success of my errand."

"Well, sir?" she said, setting her face and holding her beautiful hands together. She was beginning to see light.

"You may have rightly interpreted the frequency of my visits here. In fact, I feel sure that you have attributed them—and truly—to my admiration for Miss Raeburn."

"I have hardly attributed them to admiration for myself," she remarked, with a certain grim humour.

Crauford looked rather shocked.

"Have you said anything to my niece?" she inquired, after a moment.

"I have waited for your approval."

"That is proper enough."

Her eyes fixed themselves, seeing beyond Crauford's clean, solemn face, beyond the panelled walls, into the dull future when Cecilia should have gone out from her daily life. How often her spirits had flagged during the months she had been absent in Edinburgh!

"Cecilia shall do as she likes. I will not influence her in any way," she said at last.

"But you are willing, Lady Eliza?"

"—— Yes."

There was not the enthusiasm he expected in her voice, and this ruffled him; a certain amount was due to him, he felt.

"You are aware that I can offer Miss Raeburn a very suitable establishment," he said. "I should not have taken this step otherwise."

"Have you private means, sir?" asked Lady Eliza, drumming her fingers upon the table, and looking over his head.

"No; but that is of little importance, for I wrote to my father a short time ago, and yesterday, after leaving you, I received his reply. He has consented, and he assures me of his intention to be liberal—especially liberal, I may say."

She was growing a little weary of his long words and his unvaried air of being official. She was disposed to like him personally, mainly from the fact that he was the nephew of his uncle, but the prospect of losing Cecilia hung heavily over any satisfaction she felt at seeing her settled. Many and many a time had she lain awake, distressed and wondering, how to solve the problem of the girl's future, were she herself to die leaving her unmarried; it had been her waking nightmare. Now there might be an end to all that. She knew that she ought to be glad and grateful to fate—perhaps even grateful to Crauford Fordyce. Tears were near her eyes, and her hot heart ached in advance to think of the days to come. The little share of companionship and affection, the wreckage she had gathered laboriously on the sands of life, would soon slip from her. Her companion could not understand the pain in her look; he was smoothing out a letter on the table before her.

She gathered herself together, sharp words coming to her tongue, as they generally did when she was moved.

"I suppose my niece and I ought to be greatly flattered," she said, "I had forgotten that part of it."

"Pray do not imagine such a thing. If you will read this letter you will understand the view my father takes. The second sheet contains private matters; this is the first one."

"Sit down, Mr. Fordyce; the writing is so close that I must carry it to the light."

She took the letter to one of the windows at the end of the room, and stood by the curtain, her back turned.

A smothered exclamation came to him from the embrasure, and he was wondering what part of the epistle could have caused it when she faced him suddenly, looking at him with shining eyes, and with a flush of red blood mounting to her forehead.

"In all my life I have never met with such an outrageous piece of impertinence!" she exclaimed, tossing the paper to him. "How you have had the effrontery to show me such a thing passes my understanding! Take it, sir! Take it, and be obliging enough to leave me. You are never likely to 'live to regret' your marriage with Miss Raeburn, for, while I have any influence with her, you will never have the chance of making it. You may tell Lady Fordyce, from me, that the fact that she is a member of your family is sufficient reason for my forbidding my niece to enter it!"

Crauford stood aghast, almost ready to clutch at his coat like a man in a gale of wind, and with scarcely wits left to tell him that he had given Lady Eliza the wrong letter. The oblique attacks he had occasionally suffered from his mother when vexed were quite unlike this direct onslaught. He went towards her, opening his mouth to speak. She waved him back.

"Not a word, sir! not a word! I will ring the bell and order your horse to be brought."

"Lady Eliza, I beg of you, I implore you, to hear what I have got to say!"

He was almost breathless.

"I have heard enough. Do me the favour to go, Mr. Fordyce."

"It is not my fault! I do assure you it is not my fault! I gave you the wrong letter, ma'am. I had never dreamed of your seeing that."

"What do I care which letter it is? That such impertinence should have been written is enough for me. Cecilia 'unable to support the dignity of being your wife'! Faugh!"

"If you would only read my father's letter," exclaimed Crauford, drawing it out of his pocket, "you would see how very different it is. He is prepared to do everything—anything."

"Then he may be prepared to find you a wife elsewhere," said Lady Eliza.

At this moment Cecilia's voice was heard in the passage. He took up his hat.

"I will go," he said, foreseeing further disaster. "I entreat you, Lady Eliza, do not say anything to Miss Raeburn. I really do not know what I should do if she were to hear of this horrible mistake!"

He looked such a picture of dismay that, for a moment, she pitied him.

"I should scarcely do such a thing," she replied.

"You have not allowed me to express my deep regret —Lady Eliza, I hardly know what to say."

"Say nothing, Mr. Fordyce. That, at least, is a safe course."

"But what can I do? How can I induce you or Miss Raeburn to receive me? If she were to know of what has happened, I should have no hope of her ever listening to me! Oh, Lady Eliza—pray, pray tell me that this need not destroy everything!"

The storm of her anger was abating a little, and she began to realise that the unfortunate Crauford was deserving of some pity. And he was Robert's nephew.

"I know nothing of my niece's feelings," she said, "but you may be assured that I shall not mention your name to her. And you may be assured of this also: until Lady Fordyce writes such a letter as I shall approve when you show it to me, you will never approach her with my consent."

CHAPTER XI

THE MOUSE AND THE LION

HE who is restrained by a paternal law from attacking the person of his enemy need not chafe under this restriction; for he has only to attack him in the vanity, and the result, though far less entertaining, will be twice as effective. Gilbert Speid, in spite of his dislike to Mr. Barclay, did not bear him the slightest ill-will; nevertheless, he had dealt his "man of business" as shrewd a blow as one foe may deal another. Quite unwittingly, he had exposed him to some ridicule.

The lawyer had "hallooed before he was out of the wood," with the usual consequences.

Kaims had grown a little weary of the way in which he thrust his alleged intimacy at Whanland in its face, and when Speid, having come to an end of his business interviews, had given him no encouragement to present himself on a social footing, it did not conceal its amusement.

As Fordyce dismounted, on his return from Morphie, Barclay was on his way to Fullarton, for he was a busy man, and had the law business of most of the adjoining estates on his hands. Robert, who had arranged to meet him in the early afternoon, had been away all day, and he was told by the servant who admitted him that Mr. Fullarton was still out, but that Mr. Fordyce was on the lawn. The lawyer was well pleased, for he had met Crauford on a previous visit, and had not forgotten that he was an heir-apparent of some importance. He smoothed his hair, where the hat had disarranged it,

with a fleshy white hand, and, telling the servant that
he would find his own way, went through the house and
stepped out of a French window on to the grass.

Fordyce was sitting on a stone seat partly concealed
by a yew hedge, and did not see Barclay nor hear his
approaching footfall on the soft turf. He had come out
and sat down, feeling unable to occupy himself or to get
rid of his mortification. He had been too much horrified
and surprised at the time to resent anything Lady Eliza
had said, but, on thinking over her words again, he felt
that he had been hardly treated. He could only hope
she would keep her word and say nothing to Cecilia, and
that the letter he had undertaken to produce from Lady
Fordyce would make matters straight. A ghastly fear
entered his mind as he sat. What if Lady Eliza in her
rage should write to his mother? The thought was so
dreadful that his brow grew damp. He had no reason
for supposing that she would do such a thing, except
that, when he left her, she had looked capable of anything.

"Good heavens! good heavens!" he ejaculated.

He sprang up, unable to sit quiet, and found himself
face to face with Barclay.

"My dear sir," exclaimed the lawyer, "what is the
matter?"

"Oh, nothing—nothing," said Crauford, rather startled
by the sudden apparition. "Good-morning, Mr. Barclay; pray sit down."

The lawyer was as inquisitive as a woman, and he
complied immediately.

"Pardon me," he said, "but I can hardly believe that.
I sincerely hope it is nothing very serious."

"It is nothing that can be helped," said Fordyce
hurriedly; "only a difficulty that I am in."

"Then I may have arrived in the nick of time," said
Barclay. "Please remember it is my function to help
people out of difficulties. Come, come—courage."

He spoke with a familiarity of manner which Crauford might have resented had he been less absorbed in his misfortunes. He had an overwhelming longing to confide in someone.

"What does the proverb say? 'Two heads are better than one,' eh, Mr. Fordyce?"

Crauford looked at him irresolutely.

"I need hardly tell you that I shall be silent," said the lawyer in his most professional voice.

Fordyce had some of the instincts of a gentleman, and he hesitated a little before he could make up his mind to mention Cecilia's name to a stranger like Barclay, but he was in such dire straits that a sympathiser was everything to him, and the fact that his companion knew so much of his uncle's affairs made confidence seem safe. Besides which, he was not a quick reader of character.

"You need not look upon me as a stranger," said the lawyer, "there is nothing that your uncle does not tell me."

This half-truth seemed so plausible to Crauford that it opened the floodgates of his heart.

"You know Miss Raeburn, of course," he began.

Barclay bowed and dropped his eye ostentatiously. The action seemed to imply that he knew her more intimately than anyone might suppose.

"She is a very exceptional young lady. I had made up my mind to propose to her."

"She has not a penny," broke in Barclay.

"That is outside the subject," replied Fordyce, with something very much like dignity. "I wrote to my father, telling him of my intention, and yesterday I got his consent. He told me to expect a most liberal allowance, Mr. Barclay."

"Naturally, naturally; in your circumstances that would be a matter of course."

"I thought it best to have Lady Eliza's permission

before doing anything further. I was right, was I not, sir?"

"You acted in a most gentlemanly manner."

"I went to Morphie. Lady Eliza was cool with me, I thought. I confess I expected she would have shown some—some——"

"Some gratification—surely," finished Barclay.

"I took my father's letter with me, and unfortunately, I had also one in my pocket from my mother. It was not quite like my father's in tone; in fact, I am afraid it was written under considerable—excitement. I think she had some other plan in her mind for me. At any rate, I took it out, mistaking it for the other, and gave it to her ladyship to read. Mr. Barclay, it was terrible."

The lawyer was too anxious to stand well with his companion to venture a smile.

"Tut, tut, tut, tut!" he said, clicking his tongue against his teeth.

"My only comfort is that she promised to say nothing to Miss Raeburn; I sincerely trust she may keep her word. I am almost afraid she may write to my mother, and I really do not know what might happen if she did. That is what I dread, and she is capable of it."

"She is an old termagant," said the other.

"But what am I to do? What can I do?"

There was a silence in which the two men sat without speaking a word. Barclay crossed his knees, and clasped his hands round them; Fordyce's eyes rested earnestly upon his complacent face.

"I suppose you know that she used to set her cap at your uncle years ago?" said the lawyer at last.

"I knew they were old friends."

"You must persuade him to go and put everything straight. He can if he likes; she will keep quiet if he tells her to do so, trust her for that. That's my advice, and you will never get better."

Fordyce's face lightened; he had so lost his sense of

THE MOUSE AND THE LION 123

the proportion of things that this most obvious solution had not occured to him.

"It seems so simple now that you have suggested it," he said. "I might have thought of that for myself."

"What did I tell you about the two heads, eh?"

"Then you really think that my uncle can make it smooth?"

"I am perfectly sure of it. Will you take another hint from a well-wisher, Mr. Fordyce?"

"Of course, I shall be grateful!"

"Well, do not let the grass grow under your feet, for Speid is looking that way too, if I am not mistaken."

Crauford made a sound of impatience.

Barclay leaned forward, his eyes keen with interest.

"Then you don't like him?" he said.

"Oh, I scarcely know him," replied Fordyce, a look that delighted the lawyer coming into his face.

"He is one of those who will know you one day and look over your head the next. It would be a shame if you were set aside for a conceited coxcomb of a fellow like that—a sulky brute, too, I believe. I hate him."

"So do I," exclaimed Crauford, suddenly and vehemently.

Barclay wondered whether his companion had any idea of the tissue of rumours hanging round Gilbert, but he did not, just then, give voice to the question. It was a subject which he thought it best to keep until another time. Fullarton might return at any minute and he would be interrupted. The friendly relations which he determined to establish between himself and Fordyce would afford plenty of opportunity. If he failed to establish them, it would be a piece of folly so great as to merit reward from a just Providence. All he could do was to blow on Crauford's jealousy—an inflammable thing, he suspected—with any bellows that came to his hand. Speid should not have Cecilia while he was there to cheer him on.

"You should get Mr. Fullarton to go to Morphie to morrow, or even this afternoon; my business with him will not take long, and I shall make a point of going home early and leaving you free."

"You are really most kind to take so much interest," said Crauford. "How glad I am that I spoke to you about it."

"The mouse helped the king of beasts in the fable, you see," said the lawyer.

The simile struck Crauford as a happy one. He began to regain his spirits. His personality had been almost unhinged by his recent experience, and it was a relief to feel it coming straight again, none the worse, apparently, for its shock.

Barclay noted this change with satisfaction, knowing that to reunite a man with his pride is to draw heavily on his gratitude, and, as Fordyce's confidence grew, he spoke unreservedly; his companion made him feel more in his right attitude toward the world than anyone he had met for some time. Their common dislike of one man was exhilarating to both, and when, on seeing Fullarton emerge from the French window some time later, they rose and strolled towards the house, they felt that there was a bond between them almost amounting to friendship. At least that was Crauford's feeling; Barclay might have omitted the qualifying word.

CHAPTER XII

GRANNY TAKES A STRONG ATTITUDE

If an Englishman's house is his castle, a Scotchman's cottage is his fortress. The custom prevailing in England by which the upper and middle classes will walk, uninvited and unabashed, into a poor man's abode has never been tolerated by the prouder dwellers north of the Tweed. Here, proximity does not imply familiarity. It is true that the Englishman, or more probably the Englishwoman, who thus invades the labouring man's family will often do so on a charitable errand; but, unless the Scot is already on friendly terms with his superior neighbour, he neither desires his charity nor his company. Once invited into the house, his visit will at all times be welcomed; but the visitor will do well to remember, as he sits in the best chair at the hearth, that he does so by privilege alone. The ethics of this difference in custom are not understood by parochial England, though its results, one would think, are plain enough. Among the working classes of European nations the Scot is the man who stands most preëminently upon his own feet, and it is likely that the Millennium, when it dawns, will find him still doing the same thing.

When Granny Stirk, months before, had stood at her door, and cried, "Haste ye back, then," to Gilbert Speid, she meant what she said, and was taken at her word, for he returned some days after the roup, and his visit was the first of many. Her racy talk, her shrewd sense, and the masterly way in which she dominated her small world pleased him, and he guessed that her friendship, once given, would be a solid thing. He had accepted it, and he returned it. She made surprising confidences and asked very direct questions, in the spring evenings when the light was growing daily, and he would stroll out to her cottage for half an hour's talk. She advised him lavishly on every subject, from underclothing to the choice of a wife and her subsequent treatment, and from these conversations he learned much of the temper and customs of those surrounding him.

In the seven months which had elapsed since his arrival he had learned to understand his poorer neighbours better than his richer ones. The atmosphere of the place was beginning to sink into him, and his tenants and labourers had decided that they liked him very well; for, though there were many things in him completely foreign to their ideas, they had taken these on trust in consideration of other merits which they recognised. But, with his equals, he still felt himself a stranger; there were few men of his own age among the neighbouring lairds, and those he had met were as local in character as the landscape. Not one had ever left his native country, or possessed much notion of anything outside its limits. He would have been glad to see more of Fullarton, but the elder man had an unaccountable reserve in his manner toward him which did not encourage any advance. Crauford Fordyce he found both ridiculous and irritating. The women to whom he had been introduced did not impress him in any way, and four only had entered his life— the Miss Robertsons, who were his relations; Lady Eliza, who by turns amused, interested, and repelled him; and Cecilia Raeburn, with whom he was in love. The two people most congenial to him were Granny Stirk and Captain Somerville.

Between himself and the sailor a cordial feeling had

grown, as it will often grow between men whose horizon is wider than that of the society in which they live, and, though Somerville was almost old enough to be Speid's grandfather, the imperishable youth that bubbled up in his heart kept it in touch with that wide world in which he had worked and fought, and which he still loved like a boy. The episode at the dovecote of Morphie had served to cement the friendship.

Jimmy Stirk also reckoned himself among Gilbert's allies. Silent, sullen, fervid, his mind and energies concentrated upon the business of his day, he mentally contrasted every gentleman he met with the laird of Whanland, weighed him, and found him wanting. The brown horse, whose purchase had been such an event in his life, did his work well, and the boy expended a good deal more time upon his grooming than upon that of the mealy chestnut which shared the shed behind the cottage with the newcomer, and had once been its sole occupant. On finding himself owner of a more respectable-looking piece of horseflesh than he had ever thought to possess, he searched his mind for a name with which to ornament his property; it took him several days to decide that Rob Roy being, to his imagination, the most glorious hero ever created, he would christen the horse in his honour. His grandmother, systematically averse to new notions, cast scorn on what she called his "havers"; but as time went by, and she saw that no impression was made upon Jimmy, she ended in using the name as freely as if she had bestowed it herself.

It occurred to Mr. Barclay, after leaving Fullarton, that, as Granny Stirk knew more about other people's business than anyone he could think of, he would do sensibly in paying her a visit. That Gilbert often sat talking with her was perfectly well known to him, and if she had any ideas about the state of his affections and intentions, and could be induced to reveal her knowledge, it would be valuable matter to retail to Fordyce. Her roof had been mended a couple of months since, and he had made the arrangements for it, so he was no stranger to the old woman. It behoved him in his character of "man of business" to examine the work that had been done, for he had not seen it since its completion. He directed his man to drive to the cottage, and sat smiling, as he rolled along, at the remembrance of Fordyce's dilemma and his own simple solution of it.

Jimmy's cart, with Rob Roy in the shafts, was standing at the door, and had to be moved away to enable him to draw up; it had been freshly painted, and the three divisions of the tailboard contained each a coloured device. In the centre panel was the figure of a fish; those at the sides bore each a mermaid holding a looking-glass; the latter were the arms of the town of Kaims. Barclay alighted, heavily and leisurely, from his phaëton.

"How is the business, my laddie?" he enquired affably, and in a voice which he thought suitable to the hearty habits of the lower orders.

"It's fine," said Jimmy.

"The horse is doing well——eh?"

"He's fine," said Jimmy again. .   .

"And your grandmother? I hope she is keeping well this good weather."

"She's fine."

True to his friendly pose, the lawyer walked round the cart, running his eye over it and the animal in its shafts with as knowing an expression as he could assume. As he paused beside Rob Roy he laid his hand suddenly on his quarter, after the manner of people unaccustomed to horses; the nervous little beast made a plunge forward which nearly knocked Jimmy down, and sent Barclay flying to the sanctuary of the doorstep. His good-humour took flight also.

"Nasty, restive brute!" he exclaimed.

The boy gave him an expressive look; he was not apt to pay much attention to anyone, whether gentle or simple, beyond the pale of his own affairs, and Barclay had hitherto been outside his world. He now entered it as an object of contempt.

The sudden rattle of the cart brought Granny to the door.

"That is a very dangerous horse of yours," said the lawyer, turning round.

"Whisht! whisht!" exclaimed she, "it was the laird got yon shelt to him; he'll no thole * to hear ye speak that way."

"May I come in?" asked Barclay, recalled to his object.

She ushered him into the cottage.

"Yes, yes, I have heard about that," he remarked, as he sat down. "No doubt Jimmy is proud of the episode; it is not often a gentleman concerns himself so much about his tenant's interests. I dare say, Mrs. Stirk, that you have no wish to change your landlord, eh?"

"No for onybody hereabout," said the old woman.

"Then I gather that you are no admirer of our gentry?"

"A' wasna saying that."

"But perhaps you meant it. We do not always say what we mean, do we?" said Barclay, raising his eyebrows facetiously.

"Whiles a' do," replied the Queen of the Cadgers, with some truth.

"You speak your mind plainly enough to Mr. Speid, I believe," said Barclay.

"Wha tell't ye that?"

"Aha! everything comes round, to me in time, I assure you, my good soul; my business is confidential—very confidential. You see, as a lawyer, I am concerned with all the estates in this part of the country."

"Where the money is, there will the blayguards be gathered together," said Granny, resenting the patronage in his tone.

* Endure.

"Come, come! that is surely rather severe," said Barclay, forcing a smile. "You don't treat the laird in that way when he comes to see you, I am sure, he would not come so often if you did."

"He canna come ower muckle for me."

"What will you do when he gets a wife? He will not have so much idle time then."

"Maybe she'll come wi' him."

"That'll depend on what kind of lady she is," observed Barclay; "she may be too proud."

"Then Whanland 'll no tak' her," replied Granny decisively.

It did not escape Mrs. Stirk that Barclay, who had never before paid her a visit unconnected with business, had now some special motive for doing so. It was in her mind to state the fact baldly and gratify herself with the sight of the result, but she decided to keep this pleasure until she had discovered something more of his object. She sat silent, waiting for his next observation. She had known human nature intimately all her life, and much of it had been spent in driving bargains. She was not going to speak first.

"Well, every man ought to marry," said Barclay at last; "don't you think so, Mrs. Stirk?"

"Whiles it's so easy done," said she; "ye havna managed it yersel', Mr. Barclay."

"Nobody would have me, you see," said the lawyer, chuckling in the manner of one who makes so preposterous a joke that he must needs laugh at it himself.

"Ye'll just hae to bide as ye are," observed Granny consolingly; "maybe it would be ill to change at your time of life."

Barclay's laugh died away; he seemed to be no nearer his goal than when he sat down, and Granny's generalities were not congenial to him. He plunged into his subject.

"I think Mr. Speid should marry, at any rate," he

said; "and if report says true, it will not be long before he does so."

A gleam came into the old woman's eye; she could not imagine her visitor's motives, but she saw what he wanted, and determined instantly that he should not get it. Like many others, she had heard the report that Gilbert Speid was paying his addresses to Lady Eliza Lamont's adopted niece, and in her secret soul had made up her mind that Cecilia was not good enough for him. All femininity, in her eyes, shared that short-coming.

"He'll please himsel', na doubt," she observed.

"But do you think there is any truth in what we hear?" continued Barclay.

"A'll tell ye that when a' ken what ye're speirin' about."

"Do you believe that he is courting Miss Raeburn?" he asked, compelled to directness.

"There's jus' twa that can answer that," said Granny, leaning forward and looking mysterious; "ane's Whanland, and ane's the lassie."

"Everybody says it is true, Mrs. Stirk."

"A'body's naebody," said the old woman, "an' you an' me's less."

"It would be a very suitable match, in my opinion," said the lawyer, trying another tack.

"Aweel, a'll just tell Whanland ye was speirin' about it," replied Granny. "A' can easy ask him. He doesna mind what a' say to him."

"No, no, my good woman; don't trouble yourself to do that! Good Lord! it does not concern me."

"A' ken that, but there's no mony folk waits to be concairned when they're seeking news. A' can easy do it, sir. A' tell ye, he'll no tak' it ill o' me."

"Pray do not dream of doing such a thing!" exclaimed Barclay. "Really, it is of no possible interest to me. Mrs. Stirk, I must forbid you to say anything to Mr. Speid."

"Dod! ye needna fash yersel'; a'll do it canny-like.
'Laird,' a'll say, 'Mr. Barclay would no have ye think
it concairns him, but he'd like fine to ken if ye're courtin'
Miss Raeburn. He came here sperin' at me,' a'll
say——"

"You will say nothing of the sort," cried he "Why
I should even have mentioned it to you I cannot think."

"A' dinna understand that mysel'," replied Granny.

All Barclay's desire for discovery had flown before his
keen anxiety to obliterate the matter from his companion's mind. He cleared his throat noisily.

"Let us get to business," he said. "What I came
here for was not to talk; I have come to ask whether the
repairs in the roof are satisfactory, and to see what has
been done. I have had no time to do so before. My
time is precious."

"It'll do weel eneuch. A' let Whanland see it when
he was in-by," replied she casually.

"It's my duty to give personal inspection to all
repairs in tenants' houses," said he, getting up.

She rose also, and preceded him into the little scullery
which opened off the back of the kitchen; it smelt
violently of fish, for Jimmy's working clothes hung on a
peg by the door. Barclay's nose wrinkled.

She was pointing out the place he wished to see when
a step sounded outside, and a figure passed the window.
Someone knocked with the head of a stick upon the
door.

"Yon's the laird!" exclaimed Granny, hurrying back
into the kitchen.

Barclay's heart was turned to water, for he knew that
the old woman was quite likely to confront him with
Speid, and demand in his name an answer to the questions he had been asking. He turned quickly from the
door leading from scullery to yard, and lifted the latch
softly. As he slipped out he passed Jimmy, who, with
loud hissings, was grooming Rob Roy.

"Tell your grandmother that I am in a hurry," he cried. "Tell her I am quite satisfied with the roof."

"Sit down, Whanland," said Granny, dusting the wooden armchair as though the contact of the lawyer's body had made it unfit for Gilbert's use; "yon man rinnin' awa's Mr. Barclay. Dinna tak' tent o' him, but bide ye here till a' tell ye this."

The sun was getting low and its slanting rays streamed into the room. As Gilbert sat down his outline was black against the window. The light was burning gold behind him, and Granny could not see his face, or she would have noticed that he looked harassed and tired.

It was pure loyalty which had made her repress Barclay, for curiosity was strong in her, and it had cost her something to forego the pleasure of extracting what knowledge she could. But though she had denied herself this, she meant to speak freely to Gilbert. The lawyer had escaped through her fingers and robbed her of further sport, but she was determined that Speid should know of his questions. She resented them as a great impertinence to him, and as an even greater one to herself. She was inclined to be suspicious of people in general, and everything connected with her landlord made her smell the battle afar off, like Job's war-horse, and prepare to range herself on his side.

"Laird, are ye to get married?" said she, seating herself opposite to the young man.

"Not that I am aware of," said Gilbert. "Why do you ask, Granny? Do you think I ought to?"

"A' couldna say as to that, but Mr. Barclay says ye should."

"What has he to do with it?" exclaimed Gilbert, his brows lowering.

"Fegs! A' would hae liked terrible to ask him that mysel'. He came ben an' he began, an' says he, 'A've heard tell he's to get married,' says he; an' 'What do ye think about it?' says he. A' was that angered, ye ken,

laird, an' a' just says till him, 'Just wait,' says I, 'an'
a'll speir at him,' says I, 'an' then ye'll ken. A'll tell
him ye're terrible taken up about it—impident deevil
that ye are.' A' didna say 'deevil' to him, ye ken,
laird, but a' warrant ye a' thocht it. What has the
likes of him to do wi' you? Dod! a' could see by the
face o' him he wasna pleased when a' said a'd tell ye.
'My good woman,' says he "—here Granny stuck out her
lips in imitation of Barclay's rather protrusive mouth,
"'dinna fash yersel' to do that;' an' syne when ye came
in-by, he was roond about an' up the road like an auld
dog that's got a skelp wi' a stick."

"Did he say anything more?" inquired Gilbert
gravely.

"Ay, did he—but maybe a'll anger ye, Whanland."

"No, no, Granny, you know that. I have a reason for
asking. Tell me everything he said."

"Ye'll see an' no be angered, laird?"

"Not with you, Granny, in any case."

"Well, he was sayin' a'body says ye're courtin' Miss
Raeburn. 'Let me get a sicht o' the roof,' says he,
'that's what a' come here for.' By Jarvit! he didna
care very muckle about that, for a' the lang words he
was spittin' out about it!"

Gilbert got up, and stood on the hearth with his head
turned from the old woman.

"A've vexed ye," she said, when she saw his face
again.

"Listen to me, Granny," he began slowly; "I am very
much annoyed that he—or anyone—should have joined
that lady's name and mine together. Granny, if you
have any friendship for me, if you would do me a kindness, you will never let a word of what you have heard
come from your lips."

As he stood looking down on the Queen of the Cadgers
the light from the evening sun was full upon her marked
features and the gold ear-rings in her ears.

"Ye needna fear, Whanland," she said simply.

"I will tell you why," burst out Gilbert, a sudden impulse to confidence rushing to his heart like a wave; "it is true, Granny—that is the reason. If I cannot marry her I shall never be happy again."

Sitting alone that night, he asked himself why he should have spoken.

What power, good or evil, is answerable for the sudden gusts of change that shake us? Why do we sometimes turn traitor to our own character? How is it that forces, foreign to everything in our nature, will, at some undreamed-of instant, sweep us from the attitude we have maintained all our lives? The answer is that our souls are more sensitive than our brains.

But Gilbert, as he thought of his act, did not blame himself. Neither did eternal wisdom, which watched from afar and saw everything.

CHAPTER XIII

PLAIN SPEAKING

THE outward signs of Lady Eliza's wrath endured for
a few days after Crauford's untimely mistake, and then
began to die a lingering death; but her determination
that the enemy should make amends was unabated.
In her heart, she did not believe that Cecilia cared for
her suitor, and that being the case, she knew her well
enough to be sure that nothing would make her marry
him. For this she was both glad and sorry. It would
have been easy, as Crauford had applied to her, to discover the state of the girl's feelings; and should she find
her unwilling to accept him, convey the fact to Fullarton
and so end the matter.

But that course was not at all to her mind; Lady
Fordyce should, if Cecilia were so inclined, pay for her
words. She should write the letter her son had undertaken to procure, and he should present it and be refused.
She was thinking of that as she sat on a bench in the
garden at Morphie, and she smiled rather fiercely.

The development she promised herself was, perhaps, a
little hard on Crauford, but, as we all know, the sins of
the fathers are visited upon the children, and that did
not concern her; written words had the powerful effect
upon her that they have upon most impulsive people.
She was no schemer, and was the last being on earth to
sit down deliberately to invent trouble for anyone; but
all the abortive maternity in her had expended itself upon
Cecilia, and to slight her was the unforgivable sin.

She sat in the sun looking down the garden to the

fruit-covered wall, her shady hat, which, owing, perhaps, to the wig beneath it, was seldom at the right angle, pulled over her eyes. No other lady of those days would have worn such headgear, but Lady Eliza made her own terms with fashion All the hot part of the afternoon she had been working, for her garden produce interested her, and she was apt to do a great deal with her own hands which could more safely have been left to the gardeners. Cecilia, who was picking fruit, had forced her to rest while she finished the work, and her figure could be seen a little way off in a lattice of raspberry bushes; the elder woman's eyes followed her every movement. Whether she married Fordyce or whether she did not, the bare possibility seemed to bring the eventual separation nearer, and make it more inevitable Lady Eliza had longed for such an event, prayed for it; but now that it had come she dreaded it too much. It was scarcely ever out of her mind.

When her basket was full Cecilia came up the path and set it down before the bench "There is not room for one more," she said lightly.

"Sit down, child," said her companion; "you look quite tired. We have got plenty now. That will be— let me see—five baskets. I shall send two to Miss Robertson—she has only a small raspberry-bed—and the rest are for jam."

"Then perhaps I had better go in and tell the cook, or she will put on all five to boil."

"No, my dear, never mind; stay here. Cecilia, has it occurred to you that we may not be together very long?"

The idea was so unexpected that Cecilia was startled, and the blood left her face. For one moment she thought that Lady Eliza must have some terrible news to break, some suddenly acquired knowledge of a mortal disease.

"Why?" she exclaimed. "Oh, aunt, what do you mean?"

"I suppose you will marry, Cecilia. In fact, you must some day."

The blood came back rather violently.

"Don't let us think of that, ma'am," she said, turning away her head.

"You do not want to leave me, Cecilia?"

The two women looked into each other's eyes, and the younger laid her hand on that of her companion. The other seized it convulsively, a spasm of pain crossing her features.

"My little girl," she said; "my darling!"

In those days, endearments, now made ineffective by use and misuse, had some meaning. Young people addressed their elders as "ma'am" and "sir," and equals, who were also intimates, employed much formality of speech. While this custom was an unquestionable bar to confidence between parents and children, it emphasised any approach made by such as had decided to depart from it; also, it bred strange mixtures. To address those of your acquaintance who had titles as "your lordship" or "your ladyship" was then no solecism. Women, in speaking to their husbands or their men friends, would either use their full formal names or dispense with prefix altogether; and Lady Eliza, whose years of friendship with Fullarton more than justified his Christian name on her tongue, called him "Fullarton," "Robert," or "Mr. Fullarton," with the same ease, while to him she was equally "your ladyship" or "Eliza." Miss Hersey Robertson spoke to "Gilbert" in the same breath in which she addressed "Mr. Speid."

Though Cecilia called her adopted aunt "ma'am," there existed between them an intimacy due, not only to love, but to the quality of their respective natures. The expectancy of youth which had died so hard in Lady Eliza had been more nearly realised in the loyal and tender devotion of her adopted niece than in any other circumstance in life. There was so fine a sympathy in

Cecilia, so great a faculty for seizing the innermost soul of things, that the pathos of her aunt's character, its nobility, its foibles, its prejudices, its very absurdities, were seen by her through the clear light of an understanding love!

"I suppose you have guessed why Mr. Crauford Fordyce has been here so much?" said Lady Eliza in a few minutes. "You know his feelings, I am sure."

"He has said nothing to me."

"But he has spoken to me. We shall have to decide it, Cecilia. You know it would be a very proper marriage for you, if—if—— He annoyed me very much the other day, but there is no use in talking about it. Marry him if you like, my dear—God knows, I ought not to prevent you. I can't bear his family, Cecilia, though he is Fullarton's nephew—insolent fellow! I have no doubt he is a very worthy young man. You ought to consider it."

"What did you say to him, ma'am?"

"Oh—well, I cannot exactly tell you, my dear. I would not bias you for the world."

"But you promised him nothing, aunt? You do not mean that you wish me to accept him?" exclaimed Cecilia, growing pale again.

"You are to do what you please. I have no doubt he will have the face to come again. I wish you were settled."

"If he were the only man in the world, I would not marry him," said the girl firmly.

"Thank Heaven, Cecilia! What enormous front teeth he has—they are like family, tombstones. Take the raspberries to the cook, my dear; I am so happy."

As Cecilia went into the house a man who had ridden up to the stable and left his horse there entered the garden. Fullarton's shadow lay across the path, and Lady Eliza looked up to find him standing by her. Her thoughts had been far away, but she came back to the present with a thrill. He took a letter from his pocket, and handed it to her, smiling.

"This is from my sister," he said. "If you knew her as well as I do you would understand that it has taken us some trouble to get it. But here it is. Be lenient, Eliza."

Robert, if he had given himself the gratification of teasing his nephew, had yet expressed himself willing to take the part of Noah's dove, and go out across the troubled waters to look for a piece of dry land and an olive-branch. His task had not been an easy one at first, and he had been obliged to make a personal matter of it before he could smooth the path of the unlucky lover. But his appeal was one which could not fail, and, as a concession to himself, his friend had consented to look with favour upon Crauford, should he return bringing the letter she demanded.

Having disposed of one difficulty, Fullarton found that his good offices were not to end; he was allowed no rest until he sat down with his pen to bring his sister, Lady Fordyce, to a more reasonable point of view and a suitable expression of it. As he had expected, she proved far more obdurate than Lady Eliza; for her there was no glamour round him to ornament his requests. "God gave you friends, and the devil gave you relations," says the proverb, but it does not go on to say which power gave a man the woman who loves him. Perhaps it is sometimes one and sometimes the other. Be that as it may, though Robert returned successful from Morphie, it took him more time and pains to deal with Lady Fordyce than he had ever thought to expend on anybody.

He sat down upon the bench while Lady Eliza drew off her gloves and began to break the seal with her tapered fingers. He wondered, as he had done many times, at their whiteness and the beauty of their shape.

"You have the most lovely hands in the world, my

lady," he said at last; "some of the hands in Vandyke's portraits are like them, but no others."

He was much relieved by having finished his share in a business which had begun to weary him, and his spirits were happily attuned. She blushed up to the edge of her wig; in all her life he had never said such a thing to her. Her fingers shook so that she could hardly open the letter. She gave it to him.

"Open it," she said; "my hands are stiff with picking fruit."

He took it complacently and spread it out before her.

It was Crauford's distressed appeals rather than her brother's counsels which had moved Lady Fordyce. She was really fond of her son, and, in company with almost every mother who has children of both sexes, reserved her daughters as receptacles for the overflowings of her temper; they were the hills that attract the thunderstorms from the plain. Crauford was the plain, and Sir Thomas represented sometimes one of these natural objects and sometimes the other. Of late the whole household had been one long chain of mountains.

She was unaware of what had happened to her former letter; uncle and nephew had agreed that it was unnecessary to inform her of it, and Robert had merely explained that Crauford would not be suffered by Lady Eliza to approach his divinity without the recommendation of her special approval. It was a happy way of putting it.

"MY DEAR CRAUFORD,

"I trust that I, *of all people*, understand that it is not *wealth and riches* which *make true happiness*, and I shall be glad if you will assure Lady Eliza Lamont that you have *my consent in addressing* the young lady who is *under her protection*. I shall hope to become acquainted with her before she *enters our family*, and also with her ladyship.   I remain, my dear Crauford,

"Your affectionate mother,
"LOUISA CHARLOTTE FORDYCE.

"P.S.—When do you *intend to return home?*"

She ran her eyes over the paper and returned it to Fullarton.

"From my sister that is a great deal," he observed; "more than you can imagine She has always been a difficulty. As children we suffered from her, for she was the eldest, and my life was made hard by her when I was a little boy. Thomas Fordyce has had some experiences, I fancy."

"And this is what you propose for Cecilia?" exclaimed Lady Eliza.

"My dear friend, they would not live together; Crauford will take care of that."

"And Cecilia too. She will never marry him, Fullarton. She has told me so already. I should like to see Lady Fordyce's face when she hears that he has been refused!" she burst out.

Fullarton stared.

"I think your ladyship might have spared me all this trouble," he said, frowning; "you are making me look like a fool!"

"But I only asked her to-day," replied she, her warmth fading, "not an hour ago—not five minutes I had meant to say nothing, and let him be refused, but you can tell him, Fullarton—tell him it is no use."

A peculiar smile was on his face.

"My dear Eliza," he said, "Crauford is probably on his way here now. I undertook to bring you the letter and he is to follow it. I left him choosing a waistcoat to propose in."

"I am sorry," said Lady Eliza, too much cast down by his frown to be amused at this picture.

"Well, what of it?" he said, rather sourly. "He must learn his hard lessons like the rest of the world; there are enough of them and to spare for everyone."

"You are right," she replied, "terribly right."

He looked at her critically.

"What can you have to complain of? If anyone is fortunate, surely you are. You are your own mistress, you are well enough off to lead the life you choose, you have a charming companion, many friends——"

"Have I? I did not know that. Who are they?"

"Well, if there are few, it is your own choice. Those you possess are devoted to you. Look at myself, for instance; have I not been your firm friend for years?"

"You have indeed," she said huskily.

"There are experiences in life which mercifully have been spared you, Eliza. These are the things which make the real tragedies, the things which may go on before the eyes of our neighbours without their seeing anything of them. I would rather die to-morrow than live my life over again. You know I speak truly; I know that you know; you made me understand that one day."

She had turned away during his speech, for she could not trust her face, but at these last words she looked round.

"I have never forgiven myself for the pain I caused you," she said; "I have never got over that. I am so rough—I know it—have you forgiven me, Robert?"

"It took me a little time, but I have done it," replied he, with an approving glance at the generosity he saw in his own heart.

"I behaved cruelly—cruelly," she said.

"Forget it," said Fullarton; "let us only remember what has been pleasant in our companionship. Do you know, my lady, years ago I was fool enough to imagine myself in love with you? You never knew it, and I soon saw my folly; mercifully, before you discovered it We should have been as wretched in marriage as we have been happy in friendship. We should never have suited each other."

"What brought you to your senses?" inquired Lady Eliza with a laugh. She was in such agony of heart that speech or silence, tears or laughter, seemed all immaterial, all component parts of one overwhelming moment.

He looked as a man looks who finds himself driven into a *cul-de-sac*.

"It was—she," said Lady Eliza. "Don't think I blame you, Fullarton."

She could say that to him, but, as she thought of the woman in her grave, she pressed her hands together till the nails cut through the skin.

At this moment Crauford, in the waistcoat he had selected, came through the garden door.

As he stood before Lady Eliza the repressed feeling upon her face was so strong that he did not fail to notice it, but his observation was due to the fact that he saw his mother's letter in Fullarton's hand; that, of course, was the cause of her agitation, he told himself. But where was Cecilia? He looked round the garden.

His civil, shadeless presence irritated Lady Eliza unspeakably as he stood talking to her, evidently deterred by his uncle's proximity from mentioning the subject uppermost in his mind. He possessed the fell, talent for silently emphasising any slight moment of embarrassment. Robert watched him with grim amusement, too indolent to move away. Fordyce was like a picture-book to him.

The little group was broken up by Cecilia's return, Crauford went forward to meet her, and pompously relieved her of the two garden baskets she carried. This act of politeness was tinged with distress at the sight of the future Lady Fordyce burdened with such things.

"Let us go to the house," exclaimed Lady Eliza, rising from her bench. If something were not done to facilitate Crauford's proposal she would never be rid of him, never at leisure to reason with her aching heart in solitude. When would the afternoon end? She even longed for Fullarton to go. What he had said to her

was no new thing; she had known it all, all before. But
the words had fallen like blows, and, like an animal hurt,
she longed to slink away and hide her pain.

"Put the baskets in the tool-house, Cecilia. Fullarton, come away; we will go in."

The tool-house stood at the further end of the garden,
outside the ivy-covered wall, and Crauford was glad of
the chance given him of accompanying Cecilia, though
he felt the difficulty of approaching affairs of the heart
with a garden basket in either hand. He walked humbly
beside her. She put the baskets away and turned the
key on them.

"May I ask for a few minutes, Miss Raeburn?" he
began, "I have come here for a serious purpose. My
uncle is the bearer of a letter to her ladyship. It is from
my mother, and is written in corroboration of one which
I lately received from my father. I had written to ask
their approval of a step—a very important step—which
I contemplate. Miss Raeburn—or may I say Cecilia?—
it concerns yourself."

"Really, sir?" said Cecilia, the cheerfulness of despair
in her voice.

"Yes, yourself. No young lady I have ever seen has
so roused my admiration—my affection, I may say. I
have made up my mind on that subject. Do not turn
away, Miss Raeburn; it is quite true, believe me. My
happiness is involved. To-morrow I shall hope to inform
my parents that you will be my wife."

He stopped in the path and would have taken her hand.
She stepped back.

"I cannot," she said. "I am sorry, but I cannot."

"You cannot!" he exclaimed. "Why?"

"It is impossible, sir, really."

"But you have Lady Eliza's permission. She told me
so herself. This is absurd, Miss Raeburn, and you are
distressing me infinitely."

"Please put it out of your head, Mr. Fordyce. I cannot do it; there is no use in thinking of it. I do not want to hurt you, but it is quite impossible—quite."

"But why—why?" he exclaimed. He looked bewildered.

Cecilia's brows drew together imperceptibly.

"I do not care for you," she said; "you force me to speak in this way. I do not love you in the least."

"But what is there that you object to in me?" he cried. "Surely you understand that my father, in consenting, is ready to establish me very well. I am the eldest son, Miss Raeburn."

Cecilia's pale face was set, and her chin rose a little higher at each word

"That is nothing to me," she replied; "it does not concern me. I do not care what your prospects are. I thank you very much for your—civility, but I refuse."

He was at a loss for words; he felt like a man dealing with a mad person, one to whom the very rudiments of reason and conduct seemed to convey nothing. But the flagrant absurdity of her attitude gave him hope; there were some things too monstrous for reality.

"I will give you time to think it over," he said at last.

"That is quite useless. My answer is ready now."

"But what can be your objection?" he broke out. "What do you want, what do you expect, that I cannot give you?"

"I want a husband whom I can love," she replied sharply. "I have told you that I do not care for you, sir. Let that be the end."

"But love would come after, Miss Raeburn; I have heard that often. It always does with a woman; you would learn to love me."

He stopped and looked at her. Through her growing exasperation his very fatuity, as he stood there, almost touched her. To her mind he was so unfit an object for the love he spoke of, parrot-fashion, so ignorant of realities. A man cannot understand things for which he has been denied the capacity; like Lady Eliza, in the midst of her anger, she could see the piteous side of him and be broad-minded enough to realise the pathos of limitation.

"Don't think I wish to hurt you," she said gently, "but do not allow yourself to hope for anything. I could never love you—not then any more than now. I am honestly sorry to give you pain."

"Then why do you do so?" he asked pettishly.

She almost laughed; his attitude was invincible.

"You will regret it some day," he said.

"But _you_ never will; you will be very happy one day with someone else who finds importance in the same things as you do. I should never suit you."

"Not suit me? Why not? You do yourself injustice."

"But it is true, sir."

"You are fitted for the very highest position," he said, with solemnity.

That night Cecilia sat in her room at the open window. Her dark hair fell in a long, thick rope almost to the ground as she leaned her arms on the sill and looked out over the dew. High in the sky the moon sailed, the irresponsible face on her disc set above the trailing fragments of cloud. From fields near the coast the low whistle of plover talking came through the silence, and a night-jar shrieked suddenly from the belt of trees near the dovecote. She turned her face toward the sound, and saw in its shadow a piece of stonework glimmering in the white light. To her mind's eye appeared the whole wall in a flare of torchlight, and a figure standing in front of it, panting, straight and tense, with a red stain on brow and cheek. She had told Crauford Fordyce that she could not marry him because she did not love him, and, assuredly, she had not lied. She had spoken the truth, but was it the whole truth?

Out there, far over the woods, lay Whanland, with the

roar of the incoming sea sending its never-ceasing voice across the sandhills, and the roll of its white foam crawling round the skirts of the land. It was as though that sea-voice, which she could not hear, but had known for years, were crying to her from the distant coast. It troubled her; why, she knew not. In all the space of night she was so small, and life was vast. She had been completely capable of dealing with her own difficulties during the day, of choosing her path, of taking or leaving what she chose. Now she felt suddenly weak in spirit. A sense of misgiving took her, surrounded as she was by the repose of mighty forces greater than herself, greater, more eternal, more changeless than humanity. She laid her head upon her arms, and rested so till the sound of midnight rang from the tongue of the stable-clock across the sleeping house. The plover had ceased their talking.

She drew down the blind and stretched herself among the dim curtains of the bed, but, though she closed her eyes, she lay in a kind of waking trance till morning; and when, at last, she fell asleep, her consciousness was filled by the monotony of rolling waters and the roar of the seas by Whanland.

CHAPTER XIV

STORM AND BROWN SILK

AGNETA and Mary Fordyce were in the drawing-room of Fordyce Castle, an immensely solemn apartment rendered more so by the blinds which were drawn half-mast high in obedience to an order from Lady Fordyce. She was economical, and the carpet was much too expensive to be looked upon by the sun. In the semi-darkness which this induced the two girls were busy, one with her singing, which she was practising, and the other with the tambour-work she loved. Mary, the worker, was obliged to sit as close as possible to the window in order to get light by which to ply her needle. Agneta's voice rose in those desolate screams which are the exclusive privilege of the singer practising, and for the emitting of which any other person would justly be punished. Though thin, she was very like Crauford, with the same fresh colour and the same large front teeth, now liberally displayed by her occupation. Mary was short-sighted and a little round-shouldered from much stooping over her work-frame.

"I am afraid from what mamma has heard that Lady Eliza Lamont is not a very nice person; so eccentric and unfeminine, she said," observed Mary.

"Perhaps Miss Raeburn is the same. I am afraid poor Crauford is throwing himself away. A-a-ah-ah!" replied Agneta, leaping an octave as though it were a fence.

"He has never answered your letter, Agneta. I really wonder what she is like. Mamma only hopes she is presentable; one can never trust a young man's description of the person he is in love with, she says."

"Oh-h-h-oh! A-a-a-ah! I shall be very curious to see her, shan't you, Mary?"

"I suppose she will be invited here soon. It would be funny if she were here with Lady Maria, would it not?"

"Mamma says it is all Uncle Fullarton's doing, because he is so much mixed up with that dreadful Lady Eliza. Ah-a-a-a-ah!"

"I know; she has always thought that very undesirable, she says. I wonder how she has consented to write; I am sure she would never have done it for anyone but Crauford."

"I wonder what it is like to have a sister-in-law?" said Agneta, pausing in her shrieks.

"It would depend very much what kind of person she is," replied her sister, with some show of sense.

"Yes, but should we be allowed to go anywhere with her? Perhaps she would take us out," said Agneta.

Lady Fordyce was one of those mothers who find it unnecessary to take their daughters into society, and yet confidently expect them to marry well. Though Agneta, the youngest, was twenty-five, and Mary was past thirty, Lady Maria Milwright was the only young person who had ever stayed in the house. A couple of stiff parties were given every year, and, when there was a county ball, the Misses Fordyce were duly driven to it, each in a new dress made for the occasion, to stand one on either side of their mother's chair during the greater part of the evening. Had anyone suggested to Lady Fordyce that Mary was an old maid and that Agneta would soon become one, she would have been immoderately angry. "When my daughters are married I shall give up the world altogether," she would sometimes say; and her hearer would laugh in his sleeeve; first, at the thought of any connection between Lady Fordyce and the world, and secondly, at the thought of any connection between the Misses Fordyce and matrimony. Had they been houris of Paradise their chances would have been small, and unfortunately, they were rather plain.

"I should think Crauford will soon come back," continued Agneta, as she put away her music. "I shall ask him all sorts of questions."

To do Fordyce justice, he was a kind brother in an ordinary way, and had often stood between his sisters and the maternal displeasure when times were precarious. He did not consider them of much importance, save as members of his own family, but he would throw them small benefits now and again with the tolerant indulgence he might have shown in throwing a morsel to a pet animal.

"He has never said whether she is pretty," observed Mary reflectively. "He always calls her 'ladylike,' and I don't think mamma believes him; but, after all, she *may* be, Agneta."

"Mamma says she must have had a deplorable bringing-up with Lady Eliza."

"If she comes we must do what we can to polish her," rejoined Mary, who was inclined to take herself seriously; "no doubt there are a lot of little things we could show her—how to do her hair and things like that. I dare say she is not so bad."

Agneta pursed up her lips and looked severe.

"I think it is a great pity he did not choose Lady Maria. Of course, she is not at all pretty, but mamma says it is nonsense to think about such things. He has been very foolish."

"I really can hardly see this dull day," sighed Mary. "I wonder if I might pull up the blind ever so little. You see, mamma has made a pencil-mark on all the sashes to show the housemaids where the end of the blind is to come, and I am afraid to raise it."

"There is no sun," observed her sister; "I think you might do it."

Mary rose from her frame, but, as she did so, a step was heard outside which sent her flying back to her place, and her mother entered.

Lady Fordyce was a short, stout woman, whose nose and forehead made one perpendicular outline without any depression between the brows. Her eyes were prominent and rather like marbles; in her youth she had been called handsome. She had married late in life, and was now well over sixty, and her neck had shortened with advancing years; her very tight brown silk body compressed a figure almost distressingly ample for her age.

She installed herself in a chair and bade her daughter continue practising.

"I have practised an hour and my music is put away," said Agneta. "We were talking about Miss Raeburn. Will she come here, ma'am?"

"I suppose so," said Lady Fordyce; "but whether you will see much of her depends upon whether I consider her desirable company for you."

"She may be nice after all," hazarded Mary.

"I trust that I am a fit judge of what a young lady should be," replied her mother. "As Lady Eliza Lamont spends most of her time in the stable, she is hardly the person to form my daughter-in-law successfully."

"She is Lady Eliza's niece, ma'am, is she not?"

"She is a relation—a poor relation, and no doubt gets some sort of salary for attending to her ladyship. I must say a paid companion is *scarcely* the choice that I should have made for Crauford. What a chance for her!"

"She is most fortunate," echoed Agneta.

"Fortunate? A little more than fortunate, I should think! Adventuresses are more often called skilful than fortunate. Poor, poor boy!"

With this remark Lady Fordyce opened an account-book which lay on her lap, and began to look over its items. The girls were silent.

Mary stitched on, and Agneta spread out some music she was copying, the leaden cloud which hung over domestic life at Fordyce Castle had settled down upon the morning when there was a sound of arrival in the hall outside. No bell had rung; and the sisters, astonished, suspended their respective employments and opened their mouths. Though there were things they proposed to teach Cecilia, their ways were not always decorative. Lady Fordyce, who was a little deaf, read her account-book undisturbed, and, when the door opened to admit Crauford, it slid off her brown silk knee like an avalanche.

"I hardly expected you would take my hint so quickly," she said graciously, when the necessary embraces were over.

Crauford's face, not usually complicated in expression, was a curious study; solemnity, regret, a sense of injury, a sense of importance, struggled on it, and he cleared his throat faintly now and then, as some people will when they are ill at ease.

"I am sorry to tell you, ma'am, that your trouble has been useless I have had a great disappointment—a very great one: Miss Raeburn has refused my offer."

He looked round at his sisters as though appealing to them to expostulate with Providence.

"What?" cried his mother.

"She has refused," repeated Crauford.

"Refused? Oh, my dear boy, it is impossible! I refuse—I refuse to believe it! Nonsense, my dear Crauford! It is unheard of!"

Mary, who had never taken her eyes off her brother's face, laid down her needle and came forward.

"Sit down!" thundered her mother. "Sit down, and go on with your work! Or you can leave the room, you and Agneta. There is nothing so detestable as curiosity. Leave the room this moment!"

Dreadfully disappointed, they obeyed. Though it

was safer in the hall, the other side of the door was far more entertaining.

Crauford moved uneasily about; he certainly was not to blame for what had happened, but the two lightning-conductors had gone, and the clouds looked black around him. Also he had no tact.

"You need not be annoyed, ma'am," he began; "you did not approve of my choice."

"Happy as I am to see you deterred from such a fatal step, I cannot submit to the indignity to which you—and we all—have been subjected," said his mother. "That a *paid companion* should have refused *my son* is one of those things I find it hard to accept."

"She may yet change," he replied. "I told her I should give her time."

Lady Fordyce's prominent eyes were fixed. "Do you mean to tell me that you will ask her again? That you will so far degrade yourself as to make another offer?"

He made a sign of assent.

She threw up her hands. "What have I done?" she exclaimed, addressing an imaginary listener—"what have I done that my own children should turn against me? When have I failed in my duty toward them? Have I ever thought of myself? Have I ever failed to sacrifice myself where their interests were concerned?"

She turned suddenly on Crauford.

"No, never," he murmured.

During her life Lady Fordyce had seldom bestirred herself for anyone, but habit had made everybody in the house perjure themselves at moments like the present. Declamation was one of her trump-cards; besides, her doctor had once hinted that apoplexy was not an impossible event.

"As a mother, I have surely *some* right to consideration. I do not say much—I trust I understand these modern times too well for that—but I beg you will spare us further mortification. Are there no young ladies of

suitable position that you must set your heart upon this
charity-girl of Lady Eliza Lamont's?"

"I don't understand why you should be so much set
against her, ma'am; if you only saw Miss Raeburn you
would be surprised."

"I have *no doubt* that I should!" exclaimed his mother
in a sarcastic voice; "indeed, I have no doubt that I
should!"

Like violin playing, sarcasm is a thing which must be
either masterly or deplorable, but she was one of the
many from whom this truth is hidden.

"It would be a good thing if my sisters had one half
of her looks or manners," retorted he, goaded by her
tone. "Beside her, Agneta and Mary would look like
dairy-maids."

"Am I to sit here and hear my own daughters abused
and vilified?" exclaimed Lady Fordyce, rising and walking about. "You have indeed profited by your stay
among those people! I hope you are satisfied. I hope
you have done enough to pain me. I hope you will
never live to repent the way in which you have insulted
me."

"My dear mother, pray, be calmer. What am I doing
that you should be in this state?"

"You have called your sisters dairy-maids—*servants!*
You are throwing yourself away upon this worthless
creature who has been trying all the time to entrap you."

"How can you say such a thing, ma'am, when I tell
you that she has refused me? Not that I mean to
accept it."

"Refused you, indeed! I tell you I do not believe it;
she merely wants to draw you on. I ask you, *is it likely*
that a girl who has not a penny in the world would refuse
such prospects? Pshaw!" cried Lady Fordyce, with all
the cheap sense of one who knows nothing of the varieties
of human character.

"I wish you could see her," sighed her son.

"If you persist in your folly I shall no doubt have that felicity in time."

"My father has not taken this view," said Crauford. "You are very hard upon me, ma'am."

"Let me remind you that you have shown no consideration *for me* throughout the whole matter," she replied. "I, of course, come last. I ask you again, will you be guided by one who is more fitted to judge than you can be, and put this unjustifiable marriage out of your head?"

She stood waiting; their eyes met, and he cast his down.

"I must try again," he said with ineffective tenacity.

She turned from him and left the room, brown silk, account-book, and all.

He was accustomed to scenes like the one he had just experienced, but generally it was someone else who played the part of victim, not himself. For a week or more the world had used him very badly; his visit to Lady Eliza had been startling, his interview with Cecilia humiliating, and his reception by his mother terrific; even his uncle had maintained an attitude toward him that he could not understand. His thoughts went back to Barclay, the one person who seemed to see him in his true colours, and he longed for him as a man who has had an accident longs for the surgeon to come and bind his wounds. He had left Fullarton hurriedly and now he was sorry for what he had done.

He was certainly not going to accept Cecilia's mad folly as final; his mother had rated him for his want of pride in not abandoning his suit, but, had she understood him, she would have known that it was his pride which forbade him to relinquish it, and his vanity which assured him that he must be successful in the end. Each man's pride is a differently constructed article, while each man is certain that his private possession is the only genuine kind existing.

Lady Fordyce's own pride had received a rude blow, and she looked upon her brother as the director of it; he it was who had thrown her son into the society of the adventuress, he it was who had persuaded her to give unwilling countenance to what she disapproved. From their very infancy he had gone contrary to her. As a little boy he had roused her impatience over every game or task that they had shared. There had always been something in him which she disliked and which eluded her, and one of her greatest grievances against him had been her own inability to upset his temper. She was anything but a clever woman, and she knew that, though his character was weaker than her own, his understanding was stronger. Brother and sister, never alike, had grown more unlike with the years; his inner life had bred a semi-cynical and indolent toleration in him, and her ceaseless worldly prosperity had brought out the arrogance of her nature and developed a vulgarity which revolted Robert.

As her brown silk dress rustled up the staircase, her son, driven into an unwonted rebellion, made up his mind that, having seen his father, he would depart as soon as he could decide where to go. He hankered after Kaims. He had written to Barclay, bidding his ally farewell and telling him of Cecilia's refusal, and the ally had written a soothing reply. He praised his determination to continue his suit, assured him of his willingness to keep him acquainted with anything bearing on his interests, and, finally, begged him to remember that, at any time or season, however unpropitious, a room in his house would be at his disposal. 'Protestations of an admiring friendship closed the letter.

When the rustling was over, and he heard his mother's door close, he left the drawing-room with the determination of accepting the lawyer's offer; while he had sense enough to see that there was something undignified in such a swift return to the neighbourhood of Morphie, he yet so longed for the balm in Gilead that he made up his mind to brave the opinion of Fullarton, should he meet him. He would only spend a few quiet days in Kaims and then betake himself in some other direction. Fordyce Castle had grown intolerable.

While he pondered these things, Agneta, at her mother's dictation, was writing to Lady Milborough to ask if her daughter Maria might hasten her promised visit, and pay it as soon as possible, instead of waiting until the autumn.

"The girls were so impatient," said Lady Fordyce; "and it would be such a kindness on Lady Milborough's part if she could be prevailed upon to spare her dear Maria."

Thus two letters were dispatched; one by Crauford unknown to his mother, and one by his mother unknown to Crauford. It chanced that the two answers arrived each on the same day.

Lady Fordyce's serenity was somewhat restored by the one which found its way into her hands. Her correspondent expressed herself much gratified by the appreciation shown of her Maria. Her daughter, under the care of an elderly maid, should start immediately.

"We shall all we pleased to welcome Lady Maria, shall we not, Crauford?" said Lady Fordyce, as the family were gathered round the dinner table.

"I shall not be here, ma'am," replied her son, looking up from his veal pie. "I am starting on a visit the day after to-morrow."

CHAPTER XV

SPEID stood at the corner of a field, in the place from which he had looked up the river with Barclay on the day of his arrival. His steps were now often turned in that direction, for the line of the Morphie woods acted as a magnet to his gaze. Since the day he had spoken so freely to Granny Stirk he had not once met Cecilia, and he was weary. It was since he had last seen her that he had discovered his own heart.

Away where the Lour lost itself in the rich land, was the casket that held the jewel he coveted. He put his hand up to his cheek-bone. He was glad that he would carry that scar on it to his death, for it was an eternal reminder of the night when he had first beheld her under the branches, as they walked in the torchlight to Morphie House. He had not been able to examine her face till it looked into his own in the mirror as she put the plaster on his cheek. That was a moment which he had gone over, again and again, in his mind. It is one of the strangest things in life that we do not recognise its turning points till we have passed them.

The white cottage which Barclay had pointed out to him as the march of his own property, was a light spot in the afternoon sunshine, and the shadows were creeping from under the high wooded banks across the river's bed. Beyond it the Morphie water began. By reason of the wide curves made by the road, the way to Morphie House was longer on the turnpike than by the path at the waterside. He crossed the fence and went down to the

159

Lour, striking it just above the bridge. To follow its
bank up to those woods would bring him nearer to her,
even if he could not see her. It was some weeks since
he had been to Morphie, and he had not arrived at such
terms with Lady Eliza as should, to his mind, warrant
his going there uninvited. Many and many times he
had thought of writing to Cecilia and ending the strain of
suspense in which he lived, once and for all; but he had
lacked courage, and he was afraid; afraid of what his
own state of mind would be when he had sent the letter
and was awaiting its answer. How could he convince
her of all he felt in a letter? He could not risk it.

He looked round at the great, eight-spanned bridge
which carried the road high over his head, and down,
between the arches, to the ribbon of water winding out
to sea; to the cliffs above that grave lying in the corner
of the kirkyard-wall; to the beeches of Whanland
covering the bank a hundred yards from where he stood.
He had come to love them all. All that had seemed
uncouth, uncongenial to him, had fallen into its place,
and an affinity with the woods and the wide fields, with
the grey sea-line and the sand-hills, had entered into
him. He had thought to miss the glory of the South
when he left Spain, months ago, but now he cared no
more for Spain. This misty angle of the East Coast,
conveying nothing to the casual eye in search of more
obvious beauty, had laid its iron hand on him, as it will
lay it on all sojourners, and blinded him to everything
but its enduring and melancholy charm. There are
many, since Gilbert's day, who have come to the country
in which he lived and loved and wandered, driven by
some outside circumstance and bewailing their heavy
fate, who have asked nothing better than to die in it.
And now, for him, from this mist of association, from
this atmosphere of spirit-haunted land and sea, had
risen the star of life.

He crossed the march of Whanland by green places

where cattle stood flicking the flies, and went onwards, admiring the swaying heads of mauve scabious and the tall, cream-pink valerian that brushed him as he passed. He did not so much as know their names, but he knew that the world grew more beautiful with each step that brought him nearer to Morphie.

The sun was beginning to decline as he stood half a mile below the house, and the woods were dark above his head. A few moss-covered boulders lay in the path and the alders which grew, with their roots almost in the water, seemed to have stepped ashore to form a thicket through which his way ran. The twigs touched his face as he pushed through them.

On the further side stood Cecilia, a few paces in front of him, at the edge of the river. She had heard the footsteps, and was looking straight at him as he emerged. At the sight of her face he knew, as surely as if he had been told it, that she was thinking of him.

They stood side by side in a pregnant silence through which that third voice, present with every pair of lovers who meet alone, cried aloud to both.

"I did not expect to see you here, sir," she began.

("He has come because he cannot keep away; he has come because the very sight of the trees that surround your home have a glamour for him; because there is no peace any more for him, day nor night," said the voice to her.)

("She has come here to think of you, to calm her heart, to tell herself that you are not, and never can be, anything to her, and then to contradict her own words," it cried to him.)

He could not reply; the third voice was too loud.

"Let us go on a little way," said Cecilia.

Her lips would scarcely move, and the voice and the beating of her heart was stopping her breath.

Gilbert turned, and they went through the alders, he holding back the twigs for her to pass.

("He loves you! he loves you! he loves you!" cried the voice.)

As she brushed past him through the narrow way her nearness seemed to make the scar on his face throb, and bring again the thrill of her fingers upon his cheek. He could bear it no more. They were at the end of the thicket, and, as she stepped out of it in front of him, he sprang after her, catching her in his arms.

"Cecilia!" he said, almost in a whisper.

He had grown white.

She drew herself away with an impulse which her womanhood made natural. He followed her fiercely, on his face the set look of a man in a trance.

There are some things in a woman stronger than training, stronger than anything that may have hedged her in from her birth, and they await but the striking of an hour and the touch of one man. As he stretched out his arms anew she turned towards him and threw herself into them. Their lips met, again—again. He held her close in silence.

"Ah, I am happy," she exclaimed at last.

"And I have been afraid to tell you, torturing myself to think that you would repulse me. Cecilia, you understand what you are saying—you will never repent this?"

"Never," she said. "I shall love you all my life."

He touched the dark hair that rested against his shoulder.

"I am not worthy of it," he said. "My only claim to you is that I adore you. I cannot think why the whole world is not in love with you."

She laughed softly.

"I have been half mad," he went on, "but I am cured now. I can do nothing by halves, Cecilia."

"I hope you may never love me by halves."

"Say Gilbert."

"Gilbert."

"How perfect it sounds on your lips! I never thought of admiring my name before."

"Gilbert Speid," repeated she. "It is beautiful."

"Cecilia Speid is better," he whispered.

She disengaged herself gently, and stood looking over the water. The shadow lay across it and halfway up the opposite bank. He watched her.

"I have lived more than thirty years without you," he said "I cannot wait long."

She made no reply.

"We must speak to my aunt," she said, after a pause. "We cannot tell what she may think. At least, I shall not be going far from her."

"I cannot offer you what many others might," said he, coming closer "I am not a rich man. But, thank God, I can give you everything you have had at Morphie. Nothing is good enough for you, Cecilia; but you shall come first in everything. You know that."

"If you were a beggar, I would marry you," she said.

Honesty, in those days, was not supposed to be a lady's accomplishment, but, to Cecilia, this moment, the most sacred she had ever known, was not one for concealment of what lay in the very depths of truth. She had been unconscious of it at the time, but she now knew that that first moment at the dovecote had sealed the fate of her heart Looking back, she wondered why she had not understood.

"May God punish me if I do not make you happy," said Gilbert, his eyes set upon her. "A woman is beyond my understanding. How can you risk so much for a man like me? How can you know that you are not spoiling your life?"

"I think I have always known," said she.

He stood, neither speaking nor approaching her. The miracle of her love was too great for him to grasp. In spite of the gallant personality he carried through life, in spite of the glory of his youth and strength, he was humble-hearted, and, before this woman, he felt himself less than the dust. In the old life in Spain which had slipped from him he had been the prominent figure of the circle in which he lived. His men friends had admired and envied him, and, to the younger ones, Gilbert Speid, who kept so much to himself, who looked so quiet and could do so many things better than they, was a model which they were inclined to copy. To women, the paradox of his personal attraction and irregular face, and the fact that he only occasionally cared to profit by his own advantages, made him consistently interesting. He had left all that and come to a world which took little heed of him, to find in it this peerless thing of snow and flame, of truth and full womanhood, and she was giving her life and herself into his hand. He was shaken through and through by the charm of her eyes, her hands, her hair, her slim whiteness, the movements of her figure, the detachment which made approach so intoxicating. He could have knelt down on the river-bank.

The sun had gone from the sky when the two parted and Cecilia went up through the trees to Morphie. He left her at the edge of the woods, standing to watch her out of sight. Above his head the heavens were transfigured by the evening, and two golden wings were spread like a fan across the west. The heart in his breast was transfigured too. As he neared Whanland and looked at the white walls of the palace that was to contain his queen, the significance of what had happened struck him afresh. She would be there, in these rooms, going in and out of these doors; her voice and her step would be on the stair, in the hall. He entered in and sat down, his elbows on the table, his face hidden in his hands, and the tears came into his eyes.

When the lights were lit, and Macquean's interminable comings-in and goings-out on various pretexts were over, he gave himself up to his dreams of the coming time.

In his mind he turned the house upside down. She
liked windows that looked westward; he would go out
of his own room, which faced that point, and make it
into a boudoir for her. She liked jessamine, and
jessamine should clothe every gate and wall. She had
once admired some French tapestry, and he would ruin
himself in tapestry. She should have everything
that her heart or taste could desire.

He would buy her a horse the like of which had never
been seen in the country, and he would go to England to
choose him; to London, to the large provincial sales and
fairs, until he should come upon the animal he had in
his mind. He must have a mouth like velvet, matchless
manners and paces, the temper of an angel, perfect
beauty. He thought of a liver-chestnut, mottled on
the flank, with burnished gold hidden in the shades of
his coat. But that would not do. Chestnuts, children
of the sun, were hot, and he shivered at the bare idea
of risking her precious body on the back of some creature
all nerves and sudden terrors and caprices. He would
not have a chestnut. He lost himself in contemplation
of a review of imaginary horses.

She must have jewels, too. He had passed them over
in his dreams, and he remembered, with vivid pleasure,
that he need not wait to gratify his eyes with the sight
of something fit to offer her. In a room near the cellar
was a strong box which Barclay had delivered to him on
his arrival, and which had lain at Mr. Speid's bankers
all the years of his life in Spain. He had never opened
it, although he kept the key in the desk at his elbow,
but he knew that it contained jewels which had belonged
to his mother. He sprang up and rang for a light;
then, with the key in his hand, he went down to the
basement, carried up the box, and set it on the table
before him.

He found that it was made in two divisions, the upper
being a shelf in which all kinds of small things and a few

rings were lying; the lower part was full of cases, some wooden and some made of faded leather. He opened the largest and discovered a necklace, each link of which was a pink topaz set in diamonds. The stones were clear set, for the artificer had not foiled them at the back, as so many of his trade were apt to do, and the light flowed through them like sunlight through roses. Gilbert was pleased, and laid it again in its leather case feeling that this, his first discovery, was fit even for Cecilia.

The next thing that he opened was a polished oval wooden box, tied round and round with a piece of embroidery silk, and having a painted wreath of laurel-leaves encircling the "C. L." on the top of the lid. It was a pretty, dainty little object, preëminently a woman's intimate property; a little thing which might lie on a dressing-table among laces and fans, or be found tossed into the recesses of some frivolous, scented cushion close to its owner. It did not look as though made to hold jewels. Inside lay the finest and thinnest of gold chains, long enough to go round a slender throat, and made with no clasp nor fastening. It was evidently intended to be crossed over and knotted in front, with the ends left hanging down, for each terminated in a pear-shaped stone—one an emerald set in diamonds, and one a diamond set in emeralds. The exquisite thing charmed him, and he sat looking at it, and turning it this way and that to catch the light. He loved emeralds, because they reminded him of the little brooch he had often seen on Cecilia's bosom. It should be his first gift to her.

He next came upon the shagreen case containing the pearl necklace which Mr. Speid had carried with him when he went to fetch his bride, and which had adorned his mother's neck as she drove up in the family chariot to Whanland. He did not know its history, but he admired the pearls and their perfect uniformity and shape,

and he pictured Cecilia wearing them. He would have
her painted in them.

Instinctively he glanced up to the wall where Clementina Speid's portrait hung. By his orders it had been
taken from the garret, cleaned, and brought down to the
room in which he generally sat. She had always
fascinated him, and the discovery of her brilliant,
wayward face hidden in the dust, put away like a forgotten thing in gloom and oblivion, had produced an
unfading impression on his mind. What a contrast
between her smiling lips, her dancing eyes, her mass of
curling chestnut hair, and the forlorn isolation of her
grave on the shore with the remorseless inscription
chosen for it by the man he remembered! Those
words were not meant to apply to her, but to him who
had laid her there. Gilbert had no right to think
of her as aught but an evil thing, but, for all that,
he could not judge her. Surely, surely, she had
been judged.

And this was her little box, her own private, intimate
little toy, for a toy it was, with its tiny, finely finished
wreath of laurel, and its interlaced gilt monogram in the
centre. He took the candle and went up close to the
wall to look at her. The rings he had found in the
jewel-box were so small that he wondered if the painted
fingers corresponded to their size. The picture hung
rather high, and though he was tall, he could not clearly
see the hands, which were in shadow. He brought a
chair and stood upon it, holding the light. The portrait
had been cleaned and put up while he was absent for
a few days from Whanland, and he had not examined it
closely since that time. Yes, the fingers were very
slender, and they were clasped round a small, dark
object. He pulled out his silk handkerchief and rubbed
the canvas carefully. What she held was the laurel-
wreathed box.

He took it up from the table again with an added

interest, for he had made sure that she prized it, and it pleased him to find he was right. On the great day on which he should bring Cecilia to Whanland he would show her what he had discovered.

He replaced all the other cases and boxes, locking them up, but the painted one with the emerald and diamond drops inside it he put into a drawer of his desk—he would need it so soon. As he laid it away there flashed across him the question of whether Cecilia knew his history. 'It had never occurred to him before. He sat down on the edge of his writing-table, looking into space. In his intoxication he had not remembered that little cloud in the background of his life.

That it would make any difference to Cecilia's feelings for him he did not insult her by supposing, but how would it affect Lady Eliza? Like a breath of poison came the thought that it might influence her approval of the marriage. He needed but to look back to be certain that the shadow over his birth was a dark one. Whether the outer world were aware of it he did not know.

Any knowledge which had reached the ears of the neighbourhood could only have been carried by the gossip of servants, and officially, there was no stain resting upon him. He had been acknowledged as a son by the man whom he had called father, he had inherited his property, he had been received in the county as the representative of the family whose name he bore. Lady Eliza herself had accepted him under it, and invited him to her house. For all he knew, she might never have heard anything about the matter. But, whether she had or whether she had not, it was his plain duty, as an honourable man, to put the case before her, and when he went to Morphie to ask formally for Cecilia he would do it.

But he could not believe that it would really go against

him. From Lady Eliza's point of view, there was so much in his favour. She need scarcely part with the girl who was to her as her own child. Besides which, the idea was too hideous.

CHAPTER XVI

BETWEEN LADY ELIZA AND CECILIA

LADY ELIZA LAMONT was like a person who has walked in the dark and been struck to the ground by some familiar object, the existence and position of which he has been foolish enough to forget. Straight from her lover, Cecilia had sought her, and put what had happened plainly before her; she did not know what view her aunt might take, but she was not prepared for the effect of her news. She sat calm under the torrent of excited words, her happiness dying within her, watching with miserable eyes the changes of her companion's face. Lady Eliza was shaken to the depths; she had not forseen the contingency which might take her nearest and dearest, and set her in the very midst of the enemy's camp.

Though she forced herself to be civil to Gilbert Speid, and felt no actual enmity towards him, everything to do with him was hateful to her. Cecilia, whom she loved as a daughter, and to whom she clung more closely with each passing year, would be cut off from her, not in love nor in gratitude, as she knew well enough, but by the barrier of such surroundings as she, Lady Eliza, could never induce herself to penetrate. That house from which, as she passed its gates, she was wont to avert her face, would be Cecilia's home. For some time she had been schooling herself to the idea of their parting. When Crauford's laborious courtship had ended in failure, she had been glad; but, in comparison to this new suitor, she would have welcomed him with open arms. He had a blameless character, an even temper, excellent prospects, and no distance to which he could have transported Cecilia would divide them so surely as the few miles which separated Morphie from Whanland. She would hear her called "Mrs Speid"; she would probably see her the mother of children in whose veins ran the blood of the woman she abhorred. The tempest of her feelings stifled all justice and all reason.

"Why did you not take Crauford Fordyce, if your heart was set on leaving me?" she cried.

The thrust pierced Cecilia like a knife, but she knew that it was not the real Lady Eliza who had dealt it.

"I did not care for him," she replied, "and I love Gilbert Speid."

"He is not Gilbert Speid!" burst out her companion; "he is no more Speid than you are! He is nothing of the sort; he is an impostor—a man of no name!"

"An impostor, ma'am?"

"His mother was a bad woman. I would rather see you dead than married to him! If you wanted to break my heart, Cecilia, you could not have taken a better way of doing it."

"Do you mean that he is not Mr. Speid's son?" said Cecilia, her face the colour of a sheet of paper.

"Yes, I do. He has no business in that house; he has no right to be here; his whole position is a shameful pretence and a lie."

"But Whanland is his. He has every right to be there, ma'am."

"Mr. Speid must have been mad to leave it to him. You would not care to be the wife of an interloper! That is what he is."

"All that can change nothing," said Cecilia, after a moment. "The man is the same; he has done no wrong."

"His very existence is a wrong," cried Lady Eliza, her

hand shutting tightly on the gloves she held; "it is a wrong done by an infamous woman!"

"I love him," said Cecilia: "nothing can alter that. You received him, and you told me nothing, and the thing is done—not that I would undo it if I could. How could I know that you would be so much against it?"

"I had rather anything in the world than this!" exclaimed the other—"anyone but this man! What has driven you to make such a choice?"

"Does it seem so hard to understand why anyone should love Gilbert Speid?"

"It is a calamity that you should; think of it again—to please me—to make me happy. I can scarcely bear the thought, child; you do not know the whole of this miserable business."

"And I hoped that you would be so pleased!"

The tears were starting to Cecilia's eyes; her nerves, strained to the utmost by the emotions of the day, were beginning to give way.

"Whanland is so near," she said; "we should scarcely have to part, dear aunt."

She was longing to know more, to ask for complete enlightenment, but her pride struggled hard, and she shrank from the mere semblance of misgiving about Gilbert. She had none in her heart.

"Is this that you have told me generally known?" she said at last.

"No one knows as much as I do," answered the elder woman, turning her head away.

"Does Mr. Fullarton know?" asked Cecilia.

Lady Eliza did not reply for a moment, and when she did her head was still turned from the girl.

"I know his real history—his whole history," she replied in a thick voice; "other people may guess at it, but they know nothing."

"You will not tell me more?"

"I cannot!" cried Lady Eliza, getting up and turning upon her almost fiercely; "there is no more to be said. If you want to marry him, I suppose you will marry him; I cannot stop you. What is it to you if my heart breaks? What is it to you if all my love for you is forgotten?"

"Aunt! Dear, dear aunt!" cried Cecilia, "you have never spoken to me like this in all your life!"

She threw her arms round Lady Eliza, holding her tightly. For some time they stood clinging to each other without speaking, and the tears in Cecilia's eyes dropped and fell upon the shoulder that leaned against her; now and then she stroked it softly with her fingers.

They started apart as a servant entered, and Lady Eliza went out of the room and out of the house, disappearing among the trees. Though her heart was smiting her for her harshness, a power like the force of instinct in an animal fought against the idea of connecting all she loved with Whanland. She had called Gilbert an interloper, and an interloper he was, come to poison the last days of her life. She hurried on among the trees, impervious to the balm of the evening air which played on her brow; tenderness and fierceness dragged her in two directions, and the consciousness of having raised a barrier between herself and Cecilia was grievous. She seemed to be warring against everything. Of what use was it to her to have been given such powers of love and sympathy? They had recoiled upon her all her life, as curses are said to recoil, and merely increased the power to suffer.

She had come to the outskirts of the trees, and, from the place in which she stood, she could see over the wall into the road. The sound of a horse's trotting feet was approaching from the direction of Kaims, and she remembered that it was Friday, the day on which the weekly market was held, and on which those of the county men who were agriculturally inclined made a point of meeting in the town for business purposes. The rider was probably Fullarton. He often stopped at Morphie on his way home, and it was likely he would do so now. She went quickly down to a gate in the wall to intercept him.

Yes, it was Robert trotting evenly homewards, a fine figure of a man on his sixteen-hand black. For one moment she started as he came into sight round the bend, for she took him for Speid. The faces of the two men were not alike, but, for the first time, and for an instant only, the two figures seemed to her almost identical. As he neared her the likeness faded; Fullarton was the taller of the two, and he had lost the distinctive lines of youth. She went out and stood on the road; he pulled up as he saw her, and dismounted, and they walked on side by side towards the large gate of Morphie.

"Crauford has come back," he began, "and I have just seen him in Kaims. He is staying with Barclay; they seemed rather friendly when he was with me, but I am surprised. Why he should have come back I can't think, for Cecilia gave him no doubt of her want of appreciation of him. In any case, it is too soon. You don't like Barclay, I know, my lady."

"I can't bear him," said Lady Eliza.

"I have tolerated him for years, so I suppose I shall go on doing so. Sometimes it is as much trouble to lay down one's load as to go on with it."

"I wish I could think as you do," said she.

"Not that Barclay is exactly a load," he continued, pursuing his own train of thought, "but he is a common, pushing fellow, and I think it a pity that Crauford should stay with him."

Lady Eliza walked on in silence, longing to unburden her mind to her companion, and shrinking from the mention of Gilbert's name. He thought her dull company, and perhaps a little out of temper, and he was not inclined to go up to the house. She stood, as he prepared to remount his horse, laying an ungloved hand upon the shining neck of the black; his allusion to its beauty had made her doubly and trebly careful of it. Had he noticed her act, with its little bit of feminine vanity, he might have thought it ridiculous; but it was so natural—a little green sprig from stunted nature which had flowered out of season.

"Fullarton, Gilbert Speid has proposed to Cecilia," she said.

"And do you expect me to be astonished?" he inquired, pausing with his foot in the stirrup-iron.

"It came like a thunder-clap; I never thought of it!" she exclaimed.

"Pshaw, Eliza! Why, I told Crauford long ago that he had a pretty formidable rival in him," said he, from the saddle.

"She wants to marry him," said Lady Eliza, looking up at him, and restraining the quivering of her lips with an effort.

"Well, if she won't take Crauford, she had better take him; he'll be the more interesting husband of the two. Good-night, my lady."

She went back to the house, her heart like lead, her excitement calmed into dull misery. Fullarton did not understand, and, while she was thankful that he did not, the fact hurt her in an unreasonable way.

The evening was a very quiet one, for, as neither of the two women could speak of what she felt, both took refuge in silence. It was the first shadow that had come between them, and that thought added to the weight of Lady Eliza's grief. She sat in the deep window-seat, looking out at the long light which makes northern summer nights so short, seeming to notice nothing that went on in the room. The sight was torture to Cecilia, for a certain protectiveness which mingled with her love for her aunt made her feel as though she had wounded some trusting child to death.

Her anticipations of a few hours ago had been so different from the reality she had found, and she could not bear to think of her lover sitting in his solitary home, happy in the false belief that all was well. If ever she had seen happiness on a human face, she had seen it on his as they parted. To-morrow Lady Eliza would receive his letter.

"Cecilia," she said, turning suddenly towards the girl, "I said things I did not mean to you to-day; God knows I did not mean them. You must forgive me because I am almost beside myself to-night. You don't understand, child, and you never will. Oh, Cecilia, life has gone so hard with me! I am a miserable old woman with rancour in her heart, who has made a sorry business of this world; but it is not my fault—it is not all my fault—and it shall never divide you from me. But have patience with me, darling; my trouble is so great."

As they parted for the night, she looked back from the threshold of her room.

"To-morrow I shall feel better," she said; "I will try to be different to-morrow."

Cecilia lay sleepless, thinking of many things. She recalled herself, a little, thin girl, weak from a long illness, arriving at Morphie more than a dozen years ago. She had been tired and shy, dreading to get out of the carriage to face the unknown cousin with whom she was to stay until the change had recruited her. Life, since the death of her parents, who had gone down together in the wreck of an East Indiaman, had been a succession of changes, and she had been bandied about from one relation to another, at home nowhere, and weary of learning new ways; the learning had been rough as well as smooth, and she did not know what might await her at Morphie. Lady Eliza had come out to receive her in a shabby riding-habit, much like the plum-coloured one she wore now and in much the same state of repair, and she had looked with misgiving at the determined face under the red wig. She had cried a little, from fatigue of the long journey and strangeness, and the formidable lady had petted her and fed her with soup, and finally almost carried her upstairs to bed. Well could she recall the candlelight in the room, and Lady Eliza sitting at her bedside holding her hand until she fell asleep. She had not been accustomed to such things.

She remembered how, next day, she had been coaxed to talk and to amuse herself, and how surprised she had been at the wonderful things her new friend could do— how she could take horses by the ears as though they were puppies, and, undaunted, slap the backs of cows who stood in their path as they went together to search for new entertainment in the fields. She had been shown the stable, and the great creatures, stamping and rattling their head-ropes through the rings of their mangers, had filled her with awe. How familiar she had been with them since and how different life had been since that day! One by one she recalled the little episodes of the following years—some joyful, some pathetic, some absurd; as she had grown old enough to understand the character beside which she lived, her attitude toward it had changed in many ways, and, unconsciously, she had come to know herself the stronger of the two. With the growth of strength had come also the growth of comprehension and sympathy. She had half divined the secret of Lady Eliza's life, and only a knowledge of a few facts was needed to show her the deeps of the soul whose worth was so plain to her. She was standing very near to them now.

She fell into a restless sleep troublous with dreams. Personalities, scenes, chased each other through her wearied brain, which could not distinguish the false from the true, but which was conscious of an unvarying background of distress. Toward morning she woke and set her door open, for she was feverish with tossing and greedy of air.   As she stood a moment on the landing a subdued noise in her aunt's room made her go quickly towards it and stand listening at the door. It was the terrible sound of Lady Eliza sobbing in the dawn.

CHAPTER XVII

CECILIA PAYS HER DEBTS

CECILIA rose to meet a new day, each moment of which the coming years failed to obliterate from her memory. In the first light hours she had taken her happiness in her two hands and killed it, deliberately, for the sake of the woman she loved. She had decided to part with Gilbert Speid.

She hid nothing from herself and made no concealment. She did not pretend that she could offer herself up willingly, or with any glow of the emotional flame of renunciation, for she had not that temperament which can make the sacrificial altar a bed of inverted luxury. She neither fell on her knees, nor prayed, nor called upon Heaven to witness her deed, because there was only one thing which she cared it should witness, and that was Lady Eliza's peace of mind. Nor, while purchasing this, did she omit to count the cost. The price was a higher one than she could afford, for, when it was paid, there would be nothing left.

The thing which had culminated but yesterday had been growing for many months, and only those who wait for an official stamp to be put upon events before admitting their existence will suppose that Cecilia was parting with what she had scarcely had time to find necessary. She was parting with everything, and she knew it. The piteousness of her aunt's unquestionably real suffering was such that she determined it must end. That someone should suffer was inevitable, and the great gallantry in her rose up and told her that she could bear more than could Lady Eliza.

What she could scarcely endure to contemplate was Gilbert's trouble, and his almost certain disbelief in the genuineness of her love. In the eyes of the ordinary person her position was correct enough. Her engagement had been disapproved of by her natural guardian, and she had, in consequence, broken it. This did not affect her in any way, for she was one to whom more than the exterior of things was necessary. What did affect her was that, without so much as the excuse of being forbidden to marry her lover, she was giving him his heart's desire and then snatching it away. But, as either he or Lady Eliza had to be sacrificed, she determined that it should be Speid, though she never hesitated to admit that she loved him infinitely the better of the two. He was young, and could mend his life again, whereas, for her aunt, there was no future which could pay her for any present loss. And she had had so little. She understood that there was more wrapped up in Lady Eliza's misery than she could fathom, and that, whatever the cause of the enigma might be, it was something vital to her peace.

The hours of the day dragged on. She did not know whether to dread their striking or to long for the sound, for she had told her aunt that she wished to see her lover, and tell him the truth with her own lips, and a message had been sent to Whanland to summon him to Morphie in the afternoon. There had been a curious interview between the two women, and Lady Eliza had struggled between her love for her niece and her hatred of the marriage she contemplated. She, also, had chastened her soul in the night-season, and told herself that she would let no antipathy of her own stand in the way of her happiness; but her resolution had been half-hearted, and, unable to school her features or her words, she had but presented a more vivid picture of distress. She had not deceived Cecilia, nor, to tell the truth, had Cecilia entirely succeeded in deceiving her; but her own

feelings had made the temptation to shut her eyes too
great for her complete honesty of purpose.

Cecilia had given her reasons for her change of intention very simply, saying merely that, since their
discussion of yesterday, she had seen the inadvisability
of the marriage. To all questions she held as brave a
front as she could, only demanding that she should see
Gilbert alone, and tell him her decision with no intervention on the part of Lady Eliza. To be in a position
to demand anything was an unusual case for a girl of
those days, but the conditions of life at Morphie were
unusual, both outwardly and inwardly, and the two
women had been for years as nearly equal as any two
can be, where, though both are rich in character, one is
complicated in temperament and the other primitive.
It was on Cecilia's side that the real balance of power
dipped, however unconsciously to herself the scale went
down.

The task before her almost took her courage away, for
she had, first, to combat Speid, when her whole heart was
on his side, and then to part from him—not perhaps,
finally, in body, for she was likely to meet him at any
time, but in soul and in heart. One part of her work
she would try, Heaven helping her, to do, but the other
was beyond her. Though she would never again feel
the clasp of his arm, nor hear from his lips the words
that had made yesterday the crown of her life, she
would be his till her pulses ceased to beat. Much
and terribly as she longed to see him, dread of their
parting was almost stronger than the desire; but fear
lest he should suppose her decision rested on anything
about his parentage which Lady Eliza had told her kept
her strong. Never should he think that. Whatever
reasons she had given her aunt, he should not go without
understanding her completely, and knowing the truth
down to the very bed-rock. She shed no tears. There
would be plenty of time for tears afterward, she knew,

when there would be nothing for her to do, no crisis to meet, and nothing to be faced but daily life.

Gilbert started for Morphie carrying the note she had sent him in his pocket. He had read and re-read it many times since its arrival that morning had filled his whole being with gloom. The idea of his presenting himself, full of hope, to meet the decree which awaited him was so dreadful that she added to her summons a few sentences telling him that he must be prepared for bad news. She had written no word of love, for she felt that, until she had explained her position to him, such words could only be a mockery.

He stood waiting in the room into which he had been ushered, listening for her step. He suspected that he had been summoned to meet Lady Eliza, but he did not mean to leave Morphie without an endeavour to see Cecilia herself. When she entered he was standing quietly by the mantelpiece. She looked like a ghost in her white dress, and under her eyes the fingers of sleeplessness had traced dark marks. He sprang forward, and drew her towards him.

"No, no!" she cried, throwing out her hands in front of her.

Then, as she saw his look, she faltered and dropped them, letting his arms encircle her. The intoxication of his nearness was over her, and the very touch of his coat against her face was rest, after the struggle of the hours since she had seen him.

She drew herself away at last.

"What does that message mean?" he asked, as he let her go.

She had thought of so many things to say to him, she had meant to tell him gently, to choose her words; but, now he was beside her, she found that everything took flight, and only the voice of her own sorrow remained.

"Oh, Gilbert—Gilbert!" she sighed, "there are stronger things than you or I! Yesterday we were so happy, but it is over, and we must not think of each other any more!"

"Cecilia!" he cried, aghast.

"It is true."

"What are you saying?" he exclaimed, almost roughly. "What did you promise me? You said that nothing should change you, and I believed it!"

"Nothing has—nothing can—but, for all that, you must give me up. It is for my aunt's sake, Gilbert. If you only saw her you would understand what I have gone through. It is no choice of mine. How can you think it is anything to me but despair?"

Speid's heart sank, and the thing whose shadow had risen as he locked up the jewels and looked at his mother's face on the wall loomed large again. He guessed the undercurrent of her words.

"She has not forbidden me to marry you," continued Cecilia, "but she has told me it will break her heart if I do, and I believe it is true. What is the use of hiding anything from you? There is something in the background that I did not know; but if you imagine that it can make any difference to me, you are not the man I love, not the man I thought. You believe me? You understand?"

"I understand—I believe," he said, turning away his head. "Ah, my God!"

"But you do not doubt me—myself?" she cried, her heart wrung with fear.

He turned and looked at her. Reproach, suffering, pain unutterable, were in his eyes; but there was absolute faith too.

"But must it be, Cecilia? I am no passive boy to let my life slip between my fingers without an effort. Let me see Lady Eliza. Let me make her understand what she is doing in dividing you and me. I tell you I *will* see her!"

"She will not forbid it, for she has told me to act for

myself and leave her out of my thoughts; but she is broken-hearted. It is piteous to see her face. There is something more than I know at the root of this trouble about you—and it concerns her. I have asked her, and though she admitted I was right, she forbade me to speak of it. You would have pitied her if you had seen her. I cannot make her suffer—I cannot, even for you."

"And have you no pity for me?" he broke out.

The tears she had repressed all day rushed to her eyes. She sat down and hid her face. There was a silence as she drew out her handkerchief, pressing it against her wet eyelashes.

"Think of what I owe her," she continued, forcing her voice into its natural tone—"think what she has done for me! Everything in my life that has been good has come from her, and I am the only creature she has. How can I injure her? I thought that, at Whanland, we should hardly have been divided, but it seems that we could never meet if I were there. She has told me that."

He struck the back of the chair by which he stood with his clenched fist.

"And so it is all over, and I am to go?" he cried "I cannot, Cecilia—I will not accept it! I will not give you up! You may push me away now, but I will wait for ever, for you are mine, and I shall get you in the end!"

She smiled sadly.

"You may waste your life in thinking of that," she answered. "To make it afresh is the wisest thing for you to do, and you can do it. There is the difference between you and my aunt. It is nearly over for her, and she has had nothing; but you are young—you can remake it in time, if you will."

"I will not. I will wait."

He gazed at her, seeing into her heart and finding only truth there

"You will learn to forget me," says the flirt and jilt, raising chaste eyes to heaven, and laying a sisterly hand on the shoulder of the man she is torturing, while she listens, with satisfaction, to his hot and miserable denial.

The only comfort in such cases is that he generally does so. But with Cecilia there was no false sentiment, nor angling for words to minister to her vanity. He knew that well. Thoroughly did he understand the worth of what he was losing. He thought of the plans he had made only last night, of the flowers to be planted, of the rooms to be transformed, of the horse to be bought, of the jewels he had chosen for her from the iron box. One was lying now in a drawer of his writing-table, ready to be brought to her, and last night he had dreamed that he was fastening it round her neck. That visionary act would have to suffice him.

He came across the room and sat down by her, putting his arm about her. They were silent for a few moments, looking together into the gulf of separation before them. Life had played both of them an evil trick, but there was one thing she had been unable to do, and that was to shake their faith in each other. Cecilia had told her lover that he should make his own afresh, and had spoken in all honesty, knowing that, could she prevent his acting on her words by the holding up of her finger, she would not raise it an inch; but for all that, she did not believe he would obey her. Something in herself, which also had its counterpart in him, could foretell that.

To struggle against her decision was, as Speid knew, hopeless, for it was based upon what it would lower him in her eyes to oppose. To a certain extent he saw its force, but he would not have been the man he was, nor, indeed, a man of any kind, had he not felt hostile to Lady Eliza. He paid small attention to the assurance that, behind her obvious objection to his own history, there lurked a hidden personal complication, for the details of such an all-pervading ill as the ruin she had made for him were, to him, indifferent. He would wait determinedly. Crauford Fordyce ran through his mind, for, though his trust in Cecilia was complete, it had annoyed him to hear that he was in Kaims. Evidently the young man was of a persevering nature, and, however little worldly advantages might impress her, he knew that these things had an almost absolute power over parents and guardians.

"You told me to remake my life," he said, "and I have answered that I will not." Oh, Cecilia! I cannot tell you to do that! Do you know it makes me wretched to think that Fordyce is here again. Forgive me for saying it. Tell me that you can never care for him. I do not ask to know anything more. Darling, do not be angry."

He raised her face and looked into it. There was no anger, but a little wan of ray amusement played round her mouth.

"You need not be afraid; there is nothing in him to care for. His only merits are his prospects, and Heaven knows they do not attract me," she replied.

The clock on the mantelpiece struck, and the two looked up. Outside on the grass the shadows of the grazing sheep were long. His arm tightened round her.

"I cannot go yet," he said. "A little longer, Cecilia —a few minutes—and then the sooner it is over the better."

The room grew very still, and, through the open window, came the long fluting of a blackbird straying in the dew. All her life the sound carried Cecilia back to that hour. There seemed nothing more to be spoken but that last word that both were dreading.

"This is only torment," she said at last—"go now."

An overpowering longing rushed through her to break the web that circumstances had woven between them, to take what she had renounced, to bid him stay, to trust to chance that time would make all well. How could she let him go when it lay in her hands to stave off the moment that was coming? She had reached the turning-point, the last piece of her road at which she could touch hands with happiness.

He was holding her fast.

"I am going," he said, in a voice like the voice of a stranger—someone a long way off.

She could not speak. There were a thousand things which, when he was gone, she knew that she must blame herself for not saying, but they would not stay with her till her lips could frame them.

"Perhaps we shall sometimes see each other," he whispered, "but God knows if I could bear it."

They clung together in a maze of kisses and incoherent words. When they separated, she stood trembling in the middle of the room. He looked back at her from the threshold, and turned again.

"Gilbert! Gilbert!" she cried, throwing her arms round his neck.

Then they tore themselves apart, and the door closed between them and upon everything that each had come to value in life.

When the sound of his horse's feet had died, she stayed on where he had left her. One who is gone is never quite gone while we retain the fresh impression of his presence She knew that, and she was loth to leave a place which seemed still to hold his personality. She sat on, unconscious of time, until a servant came in to shut the windows, and then she went downstairs and stood outside the front-door upon the flags. The black-bird was still on the grass whistling, but at the sudden appearance of her figure in the doorway, he flew, shriek-ing in rich gutturals, into cover.

CHAPTER XVIII

THE BOX WITH THE LAUREL-WREATH

SPEID rode home without seeing a step of the way, though he never put his horse out of a walk; he was like a man inheriting a fortune which has vanished before he has had time to do more than sign his name to the document that makes it his. But, in spite of the misery of their parting, he could not and would not realise that it was final. He was hot and tingling with the determination to wear down Lady Eliza's opposition; for he had decided, with Cecilia's concurrence or without it, to see her himself, and to do what he could to bring home to her the ruin she was making of two lives.

He could not find any justice in her standpoint; if she had refused to admit him to her house or her acquaintance, there might have been some reason in her act, but she had acknowledged him as a neighbour, invited him to Morphie, and had at times been on the verge of friendliness She knew that, in spite of any talk that was afloat, he had been well received by the people of the county, for the fact that he had not mixed much with them was due to his own want of inclination for the company offered him. He was quite man of the world enough to see that his presence was more than welcome wherever mothers congregated who had daughters to dispose of, and, on one or two occasions of the sort, he remembered that Lady Eliza had been present, and knew she must have seen it too.

As he had no false pride, he had also no false humility, for the two are so much alike that it is only by the

artificial light of special occasions that their difference
can be seen.   He had believed that Lady Eliza would be
glad to give him Cecilia.   He knew very well that the
girl had no fortune, for it was a truth which the female
part of the community were not likely to let a young
bachelor of means forget; and he had supposed that a
man who could provide for her, without taking her four
miles from the gates of Morphie, would have been a desirable suitor in Lady Eliza's eyes.   Her opposition must,
as he had been told, be rooted in an unknown obstacle;
but, more ruthless than Cecilia, he was not going to let
the hidden thing rest   He would drag it to the light,
and deal with it as he would deal with anything which
stood in his way to her.   Few of us are perfect; Gilbert
certainly was not, and he did not care what Lady Eliza
felt.   It was not often that he had set his heart upon a
woman, and he had never set his heart and soul upon one
before.   If he had not been accustomed to turn back
when there was no soul in the affair, he was not going to
do so now that it was a deeper question.

The curious thing was that, though it went against
himself, he admired Cecilia's attitude enormously; at the
same time, the feeling stopped short of imitation.   While
with her he had been unable to go against her, and the
creeping shadow of their imminent parting had wrought
a feeling of exaltation in him which prevented him from
thinking clearly.   But that moment had passed.   He
understood her feelings and respected them, but they
were not his, and he was going to the root of the matter
without scruple.

For all that, it was with a heavy heart that he stood
at his own door and saw Macquean, who looked upon
every horse as a dangerous wild beast, leading the roan
to the stable at the full stretch of his arm.   With a
heavier one still he sat, when the household had gone to
bed, contrasting to-night with yesterday.   Last night
Whanland had been filled with dreams; to-night it was

filled with forebodings. To-morrow he must collect his ideas, and send his urgent request for an interview with Lady Eliza Lamont; and, if she refused to see him, he would put all he meant to ask into writing and despatch the letter by hand to Morphie.

In his writing-table drawer was the chain with the emerald and diamond ends, which he had left there in readiness to give to Cecilia, and he sighed as he took it out, meaning to return it to its iron resting-place in the room by the cellar. What if it should have to rest there for years? He opened the little laurel-wreathed box and drew out the jewel; the drop of green fire lay in his hand like a splash of magic. Though he had no heart for its beauty to-night, all precious gems fascinated Gilbert, this one almost more than any he had ever seen. Emeralds are stones for enchantresses, speaking as they do of velvet, of poison, of serpents, of forests, of things buried in enchanted seas, rising and falling under the green moonlight of dream-countries beyond the bounds of the world. But all he could think of was that he must hide it away into the dark, when it ought to be lying on Cecilia's bosom.

He replaced it in its box, shutting the lid, and went to the writing-table behind him to close the drawer; as he turned back quickly, his coat-tail swept the whole thing off the polished mahogany, and sent it spinning into the darkness. He saw the lid open as it went and the chain flash into a corner of the room, like a snake with glittering eyes. He sprang after it, and brought it back to the light to find it unhurt, then went to recover the box. This was not easy to do, for the lid had rolled under one piece of furniture and the lower part under another; but, with the help of a stick, he raked both out of the shadows, and carried them, one in either hand, to examine them under the candle. It struck him that, for an object of its size, the lower half was curiously heavy, and he weighed it up and down, considering it. As he did so, it rattled, showing that the fall must have loosened something in its construction. It was a deep box, and its oval shape did not give the idea that it had been originally made to hold the chain he had found in it. It was lined with silk which had faded to a nondescript colour, and he guessed, from the presence of a tiny knob which he could feel under the thin stuff, that it had a false bottom and that the protuberance was the spring which opened it. This had either got out of repair from long disuse, or else its leap across the floor had injured it, for, press as he might, sideways or downward, he could produce no effect. He turned the box upside down, and the false bottom fell out, broken, upon the table, exposing a miniature which fitted closely into the real one behind it.

It was the carefully executed likeness of a young man, whose face set some fugitive note of association vibrating in him, and made him pause as he looked, while he mentally reviewed the various ancestors on his walls. The portrait had been taken full face, which prevented the actual outline of the features from being revealed, but it was the expression which puzzled Gilbert by its familiarity. The character of the eyebrows, drooping at the outer corner of the eyes, gave a certain look of petulance that had nothing transient and was evidently natural to the face. He had seen something like it quite lately, though whether on a human countenance or a painted one he could not tell. The young man's dress was of a fashion which had long died out. Under the glass was a lock of hair, tied with a twist of gold thread and not unlike his own colour, and the gold rim which formed the frame was engraved with letters so fine as to be almost illegible. He tried to take out the miniature, but he could not do so, for it was fixed firmly into the bottom of the box, with the evident purpose of making its concealment certain. He drew the light close. The sentence running round the band was

"*Addio, anima mia*," and, in a circle just below the hair, was engraved in a smaller size these words: "*To C. L. from R. F.*, 1765."

He was face to face with the secret of his own life, and, in an instant, he understood the impression of familiarity produced upon him by the picture, for the "*R. F.*" told him all that he had not known. There was no drop in his veins of the blood of the race whose name he bore, for he was no Speid. Now all was plain. He was Robert Fullarton's illegitimate son.

He sat in the sleeping house looking at the little box which had wrecked his hopes more effectually than anything he had experienced that day. Now he understood Lady Eliza; now he realized how justifiable was her opposition. How could he, knowing what he knew, and what no doubt every soul around him knew, stand up before his neighbours and take Cecilia by the hand? how ask her to share the name which everyone could say was not his own? how endure that she should face with him a state of affairs which, for the first time, he clearly understood? He had been morally certain, before, that the bar sinister shadowed him, but, though he could have asked her to live under it with him when its existence was only known to herself and to him, the question being a social, not an ethical one, it would be an impossibility when the whole world was aware of it; when the father who could not acknowledge him was his neighbour. Never should she spend her life in a place where she might be pointed at as the wife of a nameless man. Ah, how well he understood Lady Eliza!

But, thoroughly as he believed himself able to appreciate her motives, he had no idea of the extraordinary mixture of personal feeling in which they were founded, and he credited her with the sole desire to save Cecilia from an intolerable position. Though he never doubted that those among whom he lived were as enlightened as he himself now was, the substance of the posthumous revival of rumours, attributed by many to gossip arising from Mr. Speid's actions after his wife's death, was, in reality, the only clue possessed by anyone.

By an act the generosity of which he admired with all his soul, his so-called father had legitimised him as far as lay in his power. No person could bring any proof against him of being other than he appeared, and in the eyes of the law he was as much Speid of Whanland as the man he had succeeded. He admired him all the more when he remembered that it was not an overwhelming affection for himself which had led him to take the step, but pure, abstract justice to a human being, who, through no fault of his own, had come into the world at a disadvantage. Nevertheless, whatever his legal position, he was an interloper, a pretender. He had identified himself with Whanland and loved every stick and stone it in, but he had been masquerading, for all that. What a trick she had played him, that beautiful creature upon the wall!

That the initials painted on the box and engraved on the frame inside were C. L. and not C. S. proved one thing. However guilty she had been, it was no transient influence which had ruined Clementina. Had any chance revealed the miniature's existence to Mr. Speid, it would have explained the letter he had received from her father after his own refusal by her, and it would have shown him an everyday tragedy upon which he had unwittingly intruded, to his own undoing and to hers. Like many another, she had given her affections to a younger son— for Robert, in inheriting Fullarton, had succeeded a brother—and, her parents being ambitious, the obstacle which has sundered so many since the world began had sundered these two also. Mr. Lauder was a violent and determined man, and his daughter, through fear of him, had kept secret the engagement which she knew must be a forlorn hope so soon as he should discover it. When chance, which played traitor to the couple, brought it to

light, the sword fell, and Robert, banished from the
presence of the Lauder family, returned to Fullarton and
to the society of his devoted elder brother, who asked
no more than that the younger, so much cleverer than
himself, should share all he had.   The miniature, which
he had gone to Edinburgh to sit for, and for which he
had caused the little box to be contrived, was conveyed
to Clementina with much difficulty and some bribery.
He had chosen Italian words to surround it, for he had
made the "grand tour" with his brother, and had some
knowledge of that language.   There is a fashion, even
in sentiment, and, in those days, Italian was as acceptable a vehicle for it to the polite world as French would
be now.   She yielded to circumstances which she had
no more strength to fight and married Mr. Speid a couple
of years later; and she kept the relic locked away among
her most cherished treasures.   She had not changed,
not one whit, and when, at her husband's desire, she sat
for her portrait to David Martin, then in the zenith of
his work in the Scottish capital, she held the little box
in her hand, telling the painter it was too pretty to go
down to oblivion, and must be immortalised also.   Martin, vastly admiring his sitter, replied gallantly, and
poor Clementina, who never allowed her dangerous treas-
ure to leave her hand, sat in agony till it was painted,
and she could return it to the locked drawer in which it
was kept.   There was a vague hope in her mind that the
man she had not ceased to love might, one day, see the
portrait and understand the silent message it contained.

Meanwhile, at Fullarton, Robert, who had been absent
when Clementina came to Whanland as a bride, was
trying to cure his grief, and, superficially, succeeding
well enough to make him think himself a sounder man
than he was.

He went about among the neighbours far and near,
plunged into the field-sports he loved, and, in so doing,
saw a great deal of Mr. Lamont, of Morphie, and his sis-

ter, a rather peculiar but companionable young woman, whose very absence of feminine charm made him feel an additional freedom in her society.

At this time his elder brother, who had a delicate heart, quitted this world quietly one morning, leaving the household awestruck and Robert half frantic with grief. In this second sorrow he clung more closely to his friends, and was more than ever thrown into the company of Lady Eliza. To her, this period was the halcyon time of her life, and to him, there is no knowing what it might have become if Clementina Speid had not returned from the tour she was making with her husband, to find her old lover installed a few miles from her door. Was ever woman so conspired against by the caprices of fate?

Afterward, when her short life ended in that stirring of conscience which opened her lips, she confessed all. She had now lain for years expiating her sin upon the shore by Garviekirk.

And that sin had risen to shadow her son; he remembered how he had been moved to a certain comprehension on first seeing her pictured face, without even knowing the sum of the forces against her. Little had he thought how sorely the price of her misdoing was to fall upon himself. It would be a heavy price, involving more than the loss of Cecilia, for it would involve banishment too. He could not stay at Whanland In time, possibly, when she had married—he ground his teeth as he told himself this—when she was the wife of some thrice-fortunate man whose name was his own, he might return to the things he loved and finish his life quietly among them. But not this year nor the next, not in five years nor in ten He had no more heart for pretence. This was not his true place; he should never have come to take up a part which the very gods must have laughed to see him assume What a dupe, what a fool he had been !

He would not try to see Cecilia again, but he would

write to her, and she should know how little he had understood his real position when he had asked for her love—how he had believed himself secure against the stirring-up of a past which no one was sufficiently certain of to bring against him; which was even indefinite to himself. She should hear that he had meant to tell her all he knew, and that he believed in her so firmly as never to doubt what the result would have been. He would bid her good-bye, irrevocably this time; for she should understand that, whatever her own feelings, he would not permit her to share his false position before a world which might try to make her feel it. He thought of the lady in the Leghorn bonnet, who had sat on the red sofa at the Miss Robertsons' house, and whose chance words had first made him realise the place Cecilia had in his heart. How she and her like would delight to exercise their clacking tongues in wounding her! How they would welcome such an opportunity for the commonplace ill-nature which was as meat and drink to them! But it was an opportunity he would not give them.

So he sat on, determining to sacrifice the greater to the less, and, in the manliness of his soul, preparing to break the heart of the woman he loved—to whose mind the approval or disapproval of many ladies in Leghorn bonnets would be unremarkable, could she but call herself his.

In less than a week he had left the country, and, following an instinct which led him back to the times before he had known Scotland, was on his way to Spain.

END OF BOOK I

BOOK II

CHAPTER XIX

SIX MONTHS

It was six months since Gilbert Speid had gone from Whanland. Summer, who often lingers in the north, had stayed late into September, to be scared away by the forest fires of her successor, Autumn. The leaves had dropped, and the ice-green light which spreads above the horizon after sunset on the east coast had ushered in the winter.

Christmas, little observed in Scotland, was over; the New Year had brought its yearly rioting and its general flavour of whisky, goodwill, and demoralisation. Many of the county people had resorted to their "town-houses" in Kaims, where card-parties again held their sway, and Mrs. Somerville, prominent among local hostesses, dispensed a genteel hospitality.

The friendship between Barclay and Fordyce was well established, for the young gentleman had paid the lawyer a second visit, even more soothing to his feelings than the first. In the minds of these allies Gilbert's departure had caused a great stir, for Crauford was still at Kaims when his rival summoned Barclay, and informed him that he was leaving Whanland for an indefinite time. But, though Fordyce had no difficulty in deciding that Speid's action was the result of his being refused by Cecilia Raeburn, Kaims fitted a new and more elaborate explanation to the event each time it was mentioned. The matter had nothing to do with the young lady, said some. Mr. Speid was ruined. Anyone who did not know of his disastrous West Indian speculations must have kept his ears very tight shut. And this school of opinion—a male one—closed its hands on the top of its cane, and assumed an aspect of mingled caution and integrity. This view was generally expressed in the street.

In the drawing-rooms more luscious theories throve. Miss Raeburn, as everyone must have seen, had made a perfect fool of poor Mr. Speid. All the time she had been flirting—to call it by no worse a name—with that rich young Fordyce, and had even enticed him back, when his uncle at last succeeded in getting him out of her way. It was incredible that Mr. Speid had only now discovered how the land lay! He had taken it very hard, but surely, he ought to have known what she was! It was difficult to pity those very blind people. It was also opined that Mr. Speid's departure was but another proof of the depravity of those who set themselves up and were over-nice in their airs. He was already a married man, and justice, in the shape of an incensed Spanish lady—the mother of five children— had overtaken him while dangling after Miss Raeburn. With the greatest trouble, the stranger had been got out of the country unseen. It was a lesson.

Among the few who had any suspicions of the truth, or, at least, of a part of it, was Barclay; for he had been a young clerk in his father's office at the time when the first Mr. Speid left Whanland in much the same way. He could not help suspecting that something connected with the mystery he remembered was now driving Gilbert from Scotland, for he scorned no means of inquiry, and had heard, through channels he was not ashamed to employ, of a demeanour in Cecilia which proved it impossible that she had sent her lover away willingly. Some obstacle had come between them which was not money; the lawyer had good reasons for

knowing that there was enough of that. He also knew
how devoted Lady Eliza was to the young woman, and
how welcome it would be to her to have her settled
within such easy reach. He did not believe that any
personal dislike on her part had set her against the
marriage, for, however little he liked Gilbert himself,
he knew him for a type of man which does not generally
find its enemies among women. He was certain, in his
own mind, that she had stood in the way, and his suspicion of her reasons for doing so he duly confided to
Fordyce, bidding him pluck up heart; he was willing,
he said, to take a heavy bet that a year hence would
see Cecilia at the head of his table. Thus he expressed
himself.

"And I hope it may often see you at it too," rejoined
Crauford, with what he considered a particularly happy
turn of phrase. Barclay certainly found no fault with
it.

Though Crauford's vanity had made the part of
rejected one insupportable, and therefore spurred him
forward, he probably had less true appreciation of
Cecilia than any person who knew her, and in the
satisfactory word "ladylike" he had sunk all her
wonderful charm and unobvious, but very certain,
beauty; he would have to be a new man before they
could appeal to him as they appealed to Gilbert. What
had really captivated him was her eminent suitability
to great-ladyhood, for the position of being Mrs. Crauford
Fordyce was such an important one in his eyes that he
felt it behoved him to offer it immediately, on finding
anyone who could so markedly adorn it.

But, under the manipulation of Barclay, his feelings
were growing more intense, and he lashed himself into
a far more ardent state of mind The lawyer hated
Gilbert with all his heart, and therefore spared no pains
in urging on his rival. His desire to stand well with
Fordyce and his pleasure in frustrating his client jumped

the same way, and he had roused his new friend's jealousy until he was almost as bitter against Speid as himself. Crauford, left alone, would probably have recovered from his disappointment and betaken himself elsewhere, had he not been stung by Barclay into a consistent pursuit of his object; and, as it was upon his worst qualities that the lawyer worked, his character was beginning to suffer. For all the elder man's vulgarity, he had a great share of cleverness in dealing with those who had less brains than himself, and Fordyce was being flattered into an unscrupulousness of which no one would have believed him capable. He would have done anything to worst Gilbert.

Meantime, there was consternation at Fordyce Castle. Crauford had no wish to be more at home than was necessary, and it was only towards the end of Lady Maria Milwright's sojourn there that he returned, to find his mother torn between wrath at his defection and fear lest he should escape anew. The latter feeling forced her into an acid compliance towards him, strange to see. But he was impervious to it, and, to the innocent admiration of Lady Maria, in whose eyes he was something of a hero, he made no acknowledgment; his mind was elsewhere. Mary and Agneta looked on timidly, well aware of a volcanic element working under their feet; and Agneta, who felt rebellion in the air and had some perception of expediency, made quite a little harvest, obtaining concessions she had scarce hoped for through her brother, to whom Lady Fordyce saw herself unable to deny anything in reason. It was a self-conscious household, and poor Lady Maria, upon whom the whole situation turned, was the only really peaceful person in it.

Macquean was again in charge of Whanland and of such things as remained in the house; the stable was empty, the picture which had so influenced Gilbert was put away with its fellows, and the iron box of jewels had returned to the bankers. The place was silent, the gates closed.

Before leaving, Speid had gone to Kaims to bid his cousins good-bye, and had remained closeted with Miss Hersey for over an hour. He said nothing of his discovery, and made no allusion to the barrier which had arisen between him and the woman he loved. He only told her that Cecilia had refused him at Lady Eliza's wish, and that, in consequence, he meant to leave a place where he was continually reminded of her and take his trouble to Spain, that he might fight it alone. At Miss Hersey's age there are few violent griefs, though there may be many regrets, but it was a real sorrow to her to part with her kinsman, so great was her pride in him. To her, Lady Eliza's folly was inexplicable, and the "ill-talk" on account of which she no longer visited Mrs. Somerville did not so much as enter her mind. Relations are the last to hear gossip of their kinsfolk, and the rumours of thirty years back had only reached her in the vaguest form, to be looked upon by her with the scorn which scurrilous report merits. That they had the slightest foundation was an idea which had simply never presented itself. Very few ideas of any kind presented themselves to Miss Caroline, and to Miss Hersey, none derogatory to her own family.

"Her ladyship is very wrong, and she will be punished for it," said the old lady, holding her gray head very high. "Mr. Speid of Whanland is a match for any young lady, I can assure her."

He looked away. Evidently "Speid of Whanland" sounded differently to himself and to her. He wondered why she did not understand what had gone against him, but he could not talk about it, even to Miss Hersey.

"You will find plenty as good as Miss Raeburn," she continued. "You should show her ladyship that others know what is to their advantage better than herself."

Gilbert sighed, seeing that his point of view and hers

could never meet. Granny Stirk would have understood him, he knew, for she had tasted life; but this frail, gentle creature had reached that sexless femininity of mind which comes after an existence spent apart from men. And he loved her none the less for her lack of comprehension, knowing the loyalty of her heart.

"You will come back," she said, "and, maybe, bring a wife who will put the like of Miss Raeburn out of your head. I would like to see it, Gilbert; but Caroline and I are very old, and I think you will have to look for news of us on the stone in the churchyard. There are just the two names to come. But, while we are here, you must tell me anything that I can do for you after you have gone."

"I will write to you, ma'am," said Speid, his voice a little thick; "and, in any case, I mean to ask you a favour before I go."

She looked at him with loving eyes.

"I am going to give you my address," he said, "or, at least, an address that will eventually find me. I am going to ask you to send me word of anything that happens to Miss Raeburn."

"You should forget her, Gilbert, my dear."

"Oh, ma'am! you surely cannot refuse me? I have no one but you of whom I can ask it."

"I will do it, Gilbert."

It was with this understanding that they parted.

To Jimmy Stirk and his grandmother his absence made a blank which nothing could fill. The old woman missed his visits and his talk, his voice and his step, his friendship which had bridged the gulf between age and youth, between rich and poor. She was hardly consoled by the occasional visits of Macquean, who would drop in now and then to recapitulate to her the circumstances of a departure which had never ceased to surprise him. He was not cut after her pattern, but she tolerated him for his master's sake.

From Morphie bits of information had trickled; on the day of his last visit the servants had let nothing escape them, and Lady Eliza's face, as she went about the house, was enough to convince the dullest that there was tragedy afoot. A maid had been in the passage, who had seen Gilbert as he left Cecilia.

"Ye'll no have gotten any word o' the laird?" inquired Granny on one of the first days of the young year, as Macquean stopped at her door.

"Na, na."

The old woman sighed, but made no gesture of invitation. From behind her, through the open half of the door, Macquean heard the sound of a pot boiling propitiously, and a comfortable smell reached him where he stood.

"A' was saying that a' hadna heard just very muckle," continued he, his nostrils wide—"just a sma' word——"

"Come away in-by," interrupted the Queen of the Cadgers, standing back, and holding the door generously open. "Maybe ye'll take a suppie brose; they're just newly made. Bide till a' gie ye spune to them."

It was warm inside the cottage, and he entered, and felt the contrast between its temperature and that of the sharp January air with satisfaction. Granny tipped some of the savoury contents of the black pot into a basin.

"What was it ye was hearin' about the laird?" she asked, as she added a horn spoon to the concoction, and held it out to him.

"Aw! it was just Wullie Nicol. He was sayin' that he was thinkin' the laird was clean awa' now. It's a piecie cauld, d'ye no think?" replied Macquean, as well as he could for the pleasures of his occupation.

"But what else was ye to tell me?" she said, coming nearer.

"There was nae mair nor that. Yon's grand brose."

With the exception of the old ladies in the close, no

one but Barclay had heard anything of Speid. Macquean received his wages from the lawyer, and everything went on as it had done before Gilbert's return, now more than a year since. Business letters came to Barclay at intervals, giving no address and containing no news of their writer, which were answered by him to a mail office in Madrid. To any communication which he made outside the matter in hand there was no reply. Miss Hersey had written twice, and whatever she heard in return from Speid she confided only to her sister. It was almost as though he had never been among them. The little roan hack and the cabriolet with the iron-gray mare were sold. As Wullie Nicol had said, he was "clean awa' now."

Gilbert's one thought, when he found himself again on Spanish soil, was to obliterate each trace and remembrance of his life in Scotland, and he set his face to Madrid. On arriving, he began to gather round him everything which could help him to re-constitute life as it had been in Mr. Speid's days, and, though he could not get back the house in which he had formerly lived, he settled not far from it with a couple of Spanish servants and began to wonder what he should do with his time. Nothing interested him, nothing held him. Old friends came flocking round him and he forced himself to respond to their cordiality; but he had no heart for them or their interests, for he had gone too far on that journey from which no one ever returns the same, the road to the knowledge of the strength of fate. Señor Gilbert was changed, said everyone; it was that cold north which had done it. The only wonder was that it had not killed him outright. And, after a time, they let him alone.

Miss Hersey's letters did not tell him much; she heeded little of what took place outside her own house and less since he had gone; only when Sunday brought its weekly concourse to her drawing-room did she come into touch with the people round her. Of Lady Eliza, whose Presbyterian devotions were sheltered by Morphie kirk and who made no visits, she saw nothing. Now and then the news would reach Spain that "Miss Raeburn was well" or that "Miss Raeburn had ridden into Kaims with her ladyship," but that was all Gilbert had wished to cut himself completely adrift and he had his desire. The talk made by his departure subsided as the circles subside when a stone has been dropped in a duckpond; only Captain Somerville, seeing Cecilia's face, longed to pursue him to the uttermost parts of the earth, and, with oaths and blows, if need be, to bring him back.

CHAPTER XX

THE January morning was moist and fresh as Lady Eliza and Cecilia Raeburn, with a groom following them, rode towards that part of the country where the spacious pasture-land began. The sun was at their backs and their shadows were shortening in front of them as it rose higher. The plum-coloured riding-habit was still in existence, a little more weather-stained, and holding together with a tenacity that provoked Cecilia, who had pronounced it unfit for human wear and been disregarded.

Rocket, the bay mare, was pulling at her rider and sidling along the road, taking no count of remonstrance, for she had not been out for several days.

"I wish you had taken Mayfly, aunt," remarked Cecilia, whose horse walked soberly beside his fidgeting companion.

"And why, pray?" inquired the other, testily.

"Rocket has never seen hounds and I am afraid she will give you some trouble when she does. At any rate, she will tire you out."

"Pshaw!" replied Lady Eliza.

Six months had passed Cecilia, bringing little outward change, though, thinking of them, she felt as though six years had gone by in their stead; her spirits were apparently as even, her participation in her aunt's interests apparently the same, for she was one who, undertaking a resolve, did not split it into two and fulfil the half she liked best. Each of our acts is made of two parts, the

spirit and the letter, and it is wonderful how nominally
honest people will divide them.   Not that there is aught
wrong in the division; the mistake lies in taking credit
for the whole.   She had resolved to pay for her aunt's
peace of mind with her own happiness, as it seemed that
it could be bought at no other price, and she was determined that that peace of mind should be complete.   She
gave full measure and the irrevocableness of her gift
helped her to go on with her life.   It was curious that a
stranger, lately introduced to her, and hearing that she
lived with Lady Eliza Lamont, had called her "Mrs.
Raeburn," in the belief that she was a widow.   It was
not an unnatural mistake, for there was something about
her that suggested it.   Her one day's engagement to
her lover was a subject never touched upon by the two
women.   Once, Lady Eliza had suspected that all was
not well with her and had spoken; once in her life Cecilia
had fostered a misunderstanding.

"I could not have married him," she had replied; "I
have thought over it well."

No tone in her voice had hinted at two interpretations,
and the elder woman had read the answer by the light of
her own feelings.

The laird with whose harriers they were to hunt that
day lived at a considerable distance.   It was not often,
in those times before railways and horse-boxes were
invented, that there was hunting of any sort within
reach of Morphie.   There were no foxhounds in the
county and no other harriers, though Lady Eliza had,
for years, urged Fullarton to keep them; but the discussion had always ended in his saying that he could
not afford such an expense and in her declaring that
she would keep a pack herself.   But things had gone
on as they were, and a dozen or so of days in a season
was all that either could generally get.   This year she
had only been out twice.

The meet was at a group of houses too small to be

called a village, but distinguished by the presence of a public-house and the remains of an ancient stone cross. A handful of gentlemen, among whom was Robert Fullarton, had assembled on horseback when they arrived, and these, with a few farmers, made up the field. Cecilia and her aunt were the only females in the little crowd, except a drunken old woman whose remarks were of so unbridled a nature that she had to be taken away with some despatch, and the wife of the master, who, drawn up decorously in a chaise at a decent distance from the public-house, cast scathing looks upon Lady Eliza's costume. Urchins, ploughmen, and a few nondescript men who meant to follow on foot, made a background to the hounds swarming round the foot of the stone cross and in and out between the legs of the whips' horses. The pack, a private one, consisted of about fifteen couple.

Rocket, who expressed her astonishment at the sight of hounds by lashing out at them whenever occasion served, was very troublesome and her rider was obliged to keep her pacing about outside the fringe of bystanders until they moved off; she could not help wishing she had done as Cecilia suggested. The mare was always hot, and now she bid fair to weary her out, snatching continually at her bit and never standing for a moment.

"Her ladyship is very fond of that mare," observed Robert, as he and Cecilia found themselves near each other. "Personally, good-looking as she is, I could never put up with her. She has no vice, though."

"It is her first sight of hounds," said his companion, "and no other person would have the patience to keep her as quiet as she is. My aunt's saddle could so easily be changed on to Mayfly. She will be worn out before the day is over."

"He will be a bold man who suggests it," said he, with a smile which irritated her unreasonably.

"If he were yourself, sir, he might succeed. There's

Mayfly behind that tree with James.   It could be done in a moment."

"It is not my affair, my dear young lady," said he.

They were in a part of the country where they could no longer see the Grampians as they looked into the eastern end of the Vale of Strathmore.   Brown squares of plough-land were beginning to vary the pastures, and, instead of the stone walls—or "dykes," as they are called on the coast—the fields were divided by thorn hedges, planted thick, and, in some cases, strengthened with fencing.   On their right, the ground ran up to a fringe of scrub and whins under which dew was still grey round the roots; the spiders' webs, threading innumerable tiny drops, looked like pieces of frosted wool, as they spread their pigmy awnings between the dried black pods of the broom and the hips of the rose briers.

The rank grass and the bracken had been beaten almost flat by the storms of winter, and they could get glimpses of the pack moving about among the bare stems and the tussocks.   Fullarton and Cecilia stood in the lower ground with Lady Eliza, whose mare had quieted down a good deal as the little handful of riders spread further apart.

As the three looked up, from the outer edge of the undergrowth a brown form emerged and sped like a silent arrow down the slope toward the fields in front of them; a quiver of sound came from the whins as a hound's head appeared from the scrub.   Then, in an instant, the air was alive with music, and the pack, like a white ribbon, streamed down the hillside.   The whip came slithering and sliding down the steepest part of the bank, dispersing that portion of the field which had injudiciously taken up its position close to its base, right and left.   The two women and Fullarton, who were well clear of the rising ground, took their horses by the head, and Robert's wise old horse, with nostrils

dilated and ears pointing directly on the hounds, gave
an appreciative shiver; Rocket lifted her forefeet, then,
as she felt the touch of Lady Eliza's heel, bounded forward through the plough.

They were almost in line as they came to the low
fence which stretched across their front, and, beyond
which, the hounds were running in a compact body.
Rocket, who had been schooled at Morphie, jumped well
in the paddock, and, though Cecilia turned rather
anxiously in her saddle when she had landed on the
further side of the fence, she saw, with satisfaction, that
Lady Eliza was going evenly along some forty yards
wide of her. They had got a better start than anyone
else, but the rest of the field was coming up and there
seemed likely to be a crush at a gate ahead of them
which was being opened by a small boy. Fullarton
ignored it and went over the hedge; his horse, who
knew many things, and, among them, how to take care
of himself, measuring the jump to an inch and putting
himself to no inconvenience. In those days few women
really rode to hounds, and, to those present who had
come from a distance, Lady Eliza and her niece were
objects of some astonishment.

"Gosh me!" exclaimed a rough old man on a still
rougher pony, as he came abreast of Cecilia, "I'll no
say but ye can ride bonnie! Wha learned ye?"

"My aunt," replied she.

"Will yon be her?" he inquired, shifting his ash plant
into his left hand and pointing with his thumb.

She assented.

"Gosh!" said he again, as he dropped behind.

They were running straight down the strath along the
arable land; the fields were large and Cecilia was relieved
to see that Rocket was settling down, and that, though
she jumped big, she was carrying Lady Eliza well. The
horse she herself was riding had a good mouth, and
liked hounds; and when they turned aside up a drain, and,

crossing the high road, were running through more
broken ground, she found herself almost the only person
with them, except the master, the first whip, and
Fullarton, who was coming up behind. They were
heading rather north-west and were in sight of the
Grampians again, and dykes began to intersect the landscape Now and then, patches of heather and bits
of swamp intruded themselves on the cultivation.
Though they had really only come a very few miles, they
had got into a different part of the world, and she was
beginning to think they would have a long ride home,
considering how far they had come to the meet and how
steadily they had been running inland, when the hounds
checked in a small birch plantation. The fresh air blew
from the hills through the leafless silver stems and the
heavy clouds which hung over them seemed laden with
coming rain. The ground had been rising all the way
and some of the horses were rather blown, for, though
the ascent was gradual, they had come fast. The old
man on the rough pony got off and stood, the rein over
his arm, on the outskirts of the trees; though he weighed
fifteen stone he had the rudiments of humanity, and his
beast's rough coat was dripping.

"I'm thinking I'll awa' hame," he remarked to an
acquaintance.

Cecilia was just looking round for Lady Eliza when
an old hound's tongue announced his discovery, and the
pack made once more, with their heads down, for the
lower ground

"Down again to the fields, I do believe," said Fullarton's voice. "That horse of yours carries you perfectly,
Cecilia."

"Do you know anything of my aunt?" said she, as the
hounds turned into a muddy lane between high banks.

"She was going well when I saw her," he replied. "I
think she wants to save Rocket, as it is her first day. It
does not do to sicken a horse with hounds at the be-

ginning. Yes, there they go—westward again—down to the strath. I doubt but they changed their hare in the birches."

In the first quarter of an hour he had observed how Rocket's vehemence was giving way to the persuasion of Lady Eliza's excellent hands, and how well the mare carried her over the fences they met. It was a pleasure to see her enjoying herself, he thought; of late, he had feared she was ageing, but to-day she might be twenty-five, as far as nerve or spirits were concerned. What a wonderful woman she was, how fine a horsewoman, how loyal a friend! It did him good to see her happy. It was a pity she had never married, though he could not imagine her in such a situation, and he smiled at the idea. But it *was* a pity. It looked as if Cecilia would go the same way, though he could imagine her married well enough. Two suitors in a year, both young, both well-off, both well-looking and both sent about their business—one even as far as Spain! The girl was a fool.

But, meanwhile, in spite of Fullarton's satisfaction, Lady Eliza had not got much good out of her day. It was when she was crossing the road that she felt the mare going short, she was a little behind her companions, and, by the time she had pulled up and dismounted, they were galloping down the further side of the hedge which bounded it. Though Rocket was resting her near foreleg, she would hardly stand for a moment; with staring eyes and head in the air she looked after the vanishing field, and Lady Eliza could hardly get near her to examine the foot which, she suspected, had picked up a stone. She twisted round and round, chafing and snatching at the reins; she had not had enough to tire her in the least degree, and her blood was up at the unwonted excitement and hot with the love of what she had seen. Lady Eliza had given orders to the groom who was riding Mayfly to keep the direction of the hounds in his eye and to have the horse waiting, as near to where they finished as possible, for her to ride home; as Fullarton had said, she did not want to give Rocket a long day, and she meant, unless the hounds were actually running, to leave them in the early afternoon. Probably he was not far off at this moment; but, looking up and down the road, she could see no one, not even a labourer nor a tramp. She stood exasperated by the short-sighted stupidity of the beast. Again and again she tried to take the foot up, but Rocket persisted in swerving whenever she came near; of all created beings, a horse can be the most enraging.

At last she got in front of her, and, slipping the reins over her arm, bent down, raising the foot almost by main force; wedged tightly between the frog and the shoe was a three-cornered flint.

She straightened herself with a sigh, for she felt that there was no chance of seeing hounds again that day. The stone was firm and it would take some time to dislodge it. She led the mare to a sign-post which stood at the roadside with all the officious, pseudo-human air of such objects, and tied her silly head short to it; then, having wedged her knee between her own knees, after the manner of smiths, began to hammer the flint with another she had picked up on a stone-heap. The thing was as tightly fixed in the foot as if it had grown there.

When, at last, she had succeeded in getting it out, her back was so stiff that she sat down on a milestone which stood close by, offering information to the world, and began to clean her gloves, which her occupation had made very dirty. There was no use in galloping, for the whole field must be miles away by this time, and her only chance of coming up with it was the possibility of the hounds doubling back on the road. She determined to stay about the place where she was and listen. She mounted from her mile-stone, after endless frustrated attempts, and walked Rocket as quietly along the road as she could prevail upon her to go; luck was undoubtedly against her.

Has any reader of mine ever ridden in the pitch-dark, unwitting that there is another horse near, and been silently apprized of the fact by the manner of going of the one under him? If so, he will know the exact sensations which Rocket communicated to her rider. Lady Eliza's attention was centered in the distance in front of her, but she became aware, through the mare, that an unseen horse was not far off. In another moment, she saw the rough pony and the rough old man who had accosted Cecilia emerging from a thicket half-way up the slope above her.

"What ails ye?" he enquired, as he reached the road and observed, from her looks, that she had been struggling with something.

"Have you seen the hounds?" she cried, ignoring his question.

"I'm awa' hame," replied he, on the same principle.

"But which way have the hounds gone? God bless me! can't you hear?" she cried, raising her voice louder.

"Awa' there!" he shouted, waving his arm in the direction in which she was going. "A' saw them coming doon again as a' cam' ower the brae; they'll be doon across the road by this. Awa' ye go!"

Before the words were well out of his mouth she was off, scattering a shower of liquid mud over him.

"Fiech! ye auld limmer!" he exclaimed, as he rubbed his face, watching her angrily out of sight.

As she came to a bit of road where the land sloped away gently to her left, she saw the hounds—who, as Fullarton guessed, had changed their hare—in the fields below her. They had checked again, as they crossed the highway, and just where she stood, there was a broken rail in the fence. She could tell by the marks in the mud that they had gone over it at that spot. She had an excellent chance of seeing something of the sport yet, for Rocket was as fresh as when she had come out and the land between her and the hounds was all good grass.

She turned her at the broken rail, riding quietly down the slope; then, once on the level ground of the strath, she set her going.

She put field after field behind her; for though, on the flat, she could not see far ahead, the ground was wet and the hoof-prints were deep enough to guide her. Rocket could gallop, and, in spite of her recent sins, she began to think that she liked her better than ever. She had bought her on her own initiative, having taken a fancy to her at a sale, and had ridden her for more than a year. It was from her back that she had first seen Gilbert Speid at Garviekirk. Fullarton, while admitting her good looks, had not been enthusiastic, and Cecilia had said that she was too hot and tried to dissuade her from the purchase; she remembered that she had been very much put out with the girl at the time and had asked her whether she supposed her to be made of anything breakable. Her niece had said "no," but added that she probably would be when she had ridden the mare. Cecilia could be vastly impudent when she chose; her aunt wondered if she had been impudent to Fordyce. She did not pursue the speculation, for, as she sailed through an open gate, she found herself in the same field with the tail end of the hunt and observed that some of the horses looked as though they had had enough. There must have been a sharp burst, she suspected, while she was struggling with Rocket near the sign-post. Evidently Fullarton and Cecilia were in front.

She passed the stragglers, and saw Robert's old black horse labouring heavily in a strip of plough on the near side of a stout thickset hedge which hid the hounds from her view. Rocket saw him too and began to pull like a fiend; her stall at Morphie was next to the one in which he invariably stood when his master rode there; that being frequently, she knew him as well as she did her regular stable companions. Lady Eliza let her go, rejoicing to have recovered the ground she had lost, and to be likely, after all her difficulties, to see the end of her morning's sport.

Fullarton was making for a thin place in the hedge, for his horse was getting tired and he was a heavy man; besides which, he knew that there was a deep drop on the other side. She resolved to take it at the same gap and began to hold Rocket hard, in order to give him time to get over before she was upon him.

But Rocket did not understand. The wisdom of the old hunter was not hers, and she only knew that the woman on her back meant to baulk her of the glories in front. Her rider tried to pull her wide of the black horse, but in vain; she would have the same place. Robert was about twenty yards from her when he jumped and she gathered herself together for a rush. Lady Eliza could not hold her.

To her unutterable horror, just as the mare was about to take off, she saw that Robert's horse had stumbled in landing and was there, in front of her—below her—recovering his feet on the grass.

With an effort of strength which those who witnessed it never forgot, she wrenched Rocket's head aside, almost in mid-air. As they fell headlong, she had time, before her senses went, to see that she had attained her object.

For Fullarton stood, unhurt, not five paces from where she lay.

CHAPTER XXI

THE BROKEN LINK

In an upper room, whose window looked into a mass of bare branches, Lady Eliza lay dying. This last act she was accomplishing with a deliberation which she had given to nothing else in her life; for it was two days since the little knot of horrified sportsmen had lifted her on to the hurdle which someone had run to fetch from a neighbouring farm. Rocket, unhurt but for a scratch or two, had rolled over her twice and she had not fallen clear.

The hounds had just killed when Cecilia, summoned by a stranger who had pursued her for nearly half a mile, came galloping back to find her unconscious figure laid upon the grass. The men who stood round made way for her as she sprang from her horse. She went down on her knees beside her aunt and took one of her helpless hands.

"She is not dead?" she said, looking at Fullarton with wild eyes.

She was not dead, and, but for a few bruises, there were no marks to show what had happened; for her injuries were internal, and, when, at last, the endless journey home was over and the two doctors from Kaims had made their examination, Cecilia had heard the truth. The plum-coloured habit might be put away, for its disreputable career was done and Lady Eliza would not need it again. She had had her last ride. In a few days she would come out of the house; but, for the first time, perhaps, since it had known her, she would pass the stable door without going in.

She had been carried every step of the way home, Cecilia and Fullarton riding one on either side, and, while someone had gone to Kaims for a doctor, another had pushed his tired horse forward to Morphie to get a carriage. But, when it met them a few miles from the end of their march, it had been found impossible to transfer her to it, for consciousness was returning and each moment was agony. The men had expressed their willingness to go on, and Robert, though stiff from his fall, had taken his turn manfully. A mattress had been spread on the large dining-room table and on it they had laid the hurdle with its load. Another doctor had been brought from the town to assist his partner in the examination he thought fit to make before risking the difficult transport upstairs. Fullarton, when it was over, had taken one of the men apart. It might be hours, it might even be a couple of days, he was told. It was likely that there would be suffering, but there would be no pain at the end, he thought. The spine, as well as other organs, was injured.

And so, at last, they had carried her up to her own room. Cecilia was anxious to have one on the ground-floor made ready, but she had prayed to be taken to the familiar place, and the doctors, knowing that nothing could avail now, one way or the other, had let her have her will.

She had never had any doubts about her own condition. Before Cecilia nerved herself to tell her the verdict that had been passed, she had spoken.

"Cecilia, my little girl," she had said, "what will become of you? What will you do? If it were not for you, child, God knows I should not mind going. But I can do nothing for you."

"If I could only go with you," whispered Cecilia, laying her face down on the sheet.

"Perhaps I was wrong," continued Lady Eliza, "perhaps I have done harm. I knew how little I could

leave you; there were others who would have taken
you And you were such a nice little girl, Cecilia, but
so thin and shy . . . and I shall not see you for a
long time . . . we went to see the horses . . .
look, child! . . . tell James to come here. Can't
you see that the mare's head-collar is coming off? . . .
Run, Cecilia, I tell you!"

In the intervals between the pain and delirium which
tortured her for the first few nights and days, her
one cry was about Cecilia—what would become of
Cecilia?

Through the dark hours the girl sat soothing her and
holding the feverish hand as she listened to the rambling
talk. Now she was with the horses, now back in the old
days when her brother was alive, now talking to Fullarton, now straying among the events of the past months;
but always returning again to what weighed on her
mind, Cecilia's future. Occasionally she would speak
to her as though she were Fullarton, or Fordyce, or
even James the groom. Worst of all were the times
when her pain was almost more than she could bear.

A woman had been got from the town to help in
nursing her, a good enough soul, but, with one of those
strange whims which torment the sick, Lady Eliza
could not endure her in the room, and she sat in the
dressing-room, waiting to do anything that was wanted.
Trained nurses were unknown outside hospitals in those
days.

Robert had remained all night at Morphie after the
accident and had sat by the bedside while she was conscious of his presence.

"I owe you my life," he said to her; "oh, Eliza! why
did you do that? My worthless existence could have
so well been spared!"

He went home in the morning, to return again later,
and Cecilia, who had been resting, went back to her post.
The doctor now said that his patient might linger for

days 'and departed to his business in Kaims for a few hours.

"Robert!" said Lady Eliza, suddenly.

"It is I, ma'am; here I am," answered the girl, laying her fingers upon her arm; there was no recognition in the eyes which stared, with unnatural brilliance, into her face.

"Robert," said the voice from the bed, "I can never go to Whanland; you shall not try to take me there . . . she is not there—I know that very well—she is out on the sands—dead and buried under the sand—— But she can't marry him . . . I could never see her if she went to Whanland. . . . How can I part with her? Cecilia, you will not go?"

"Here I am, dearest aunt, here I am." She leaned over Lady Eliza. "You can see me; I am close to you."

"Is that impostor gone?" asked Lady Eliza.

"Yes, yes, he has gone," answered Cecilia, in a choked voice.

A look came into Lady Eliza's face as though her true mind were battling, like a swimmer, with the waves of delirium.

"I have never told Cecilia that he is Fullarton's son," she said, "I have never told anyone. . . . She was a bad woman—she has taken him from me and now her son will take my little girl. . . . Mr. Speid, your face is cut—come away—come away. Cecilia, we will go to the house. . . . But that is Fullarton standing there. Robert, I want to say something to you. Robert, you know I did not mean to speak like that! Dear Robert, have you forgiven me? . . . But what can I do about my little girl? What can I do for her, Fullarton?"

She held Cecilia's fingers convulsively. The girl kept her hand closed round the feeble one on the bed-cover, as though she would put her own life and strength into it with her grasp; she fancied sometimes that it quieted

the sick woman in some strange way. She sat behind
the curtain like a stone; there was little time to think
over what she had just heard, for the wheels of the
doctor's gig were sounding in the avenue and she must
collect herself to meet him. He was to stay for the
night. But now everything that had been dark was
plain to her. Her lover was Fullarton's son! Down
to the very depths she saw into her aunt's heart, and
tears, as hot as any she had shed for her own griefs, fell
from her eyes.

"Thank God, I did what I could for her," she said.

The night that followed was quieter than the one
preceding it and she sat up, having had a long rest,
insisting that the doctor should go to bed; while her
aunt's mind ran on things which were for her ears alone,
she did not wish for his presence. Towards morning
he came in and forced her to leave the bedside, and, worn
out, she slept on till it was almost noon. She awoke to
find him standing over her.

"Lady Eliza is conscious," he said, "and she is not
suffering—at least, not in body. But she is very uneasy
and anxious to see you. I fancy there is something on
her mind. Do what you can to soothe her, Miss Raeburn, for I doubt if she will last the day; all we can hope
for her now is an easy death."

Lady Eliza lay with her eyes closed; as Cecilia entered
she opened them and smiled. She went to the bed.

"How tired you look," said Lady Eliza. "It will
soon be over, my dear, and we shall have parted at last.
Don't cry, child. What a good girl you have been!
Ah, my dear, I could die happy if it were not for you.
I have nothing to leave you but a few pounds a year and
my own belongings and the horses. Morphie will go
to relations I have never seen. What am I to do for
you? What are you to do? Oh, Cecilia! I should have
laid by more. But I never thought of this—of dying
like this—and I looked to your marrying. I have been

a bad friend to you—I see that now that I come to lie here."

"If you speak in that way you will break my heart," said Cecilia, covering her face with her hands.

"Come close; come where I can see you. You must make me a promise," said Lady Eliza; "you must promise me that you will marry. Crauford Fordyce will come back—I know that he will, for Fullarton has told me so. I said it was useless, but that is different now. Cecilia, I can't leave you like this, with no one to protect you and no money—promise me when he comes that you will say yes."

"Oh, aunt! oh, dear aunt!" cried Cecilia. "Oh, not that, not that!"

"Promise me," urged Lady Eliza.

"Oh, anything but that—do not ask me that! There is only one man in the world I can ever love. It is the same now as on the day he left."

"Love is not for everybody," said Lady Eliza, slowly. "Some have to do without it all their lives."

There was no sound in the room for a little time.

"The world looks different now," began Lady Eliza again. "I don't know if I was right to do as I did about Gilbert Sp—about Whanland. I am a wicked woman, my dear, and I cannot forgive—but you don't know about that."

"If he comes back, aunt—if he comes back?"

"But you cannot wait all your life for that. He is gone and he has said he will not come back. Put that away from you; I am thinking only of you—believe me, my darling. I beg of you, Cecilia, I pray you. You know I shall never be able to ask anything again, soon."

"Give me time," she sobbed, terribly moved.

"In a year, Cecilia—in a year?"

Cecilia rose and went to the window. Outside, over the bare boughs, some pigeons from the dovecote were whirling in the air. Her heart was tortured within her.

Crauford was almost abhorrent to her, but it seemed as though the relentless driving of fate were forcing her towards him. She saw no escape. Why had Gilbert gone! His letter had made no mention of Fullarton's name, and he had only written that he could not ask her to share with him a position which, as he now knew, was thoroughly understood by the world and which she would find unbearable. In his honesty, he had said nothing that should make her think of him as anything but a bygone episode in her life, no vow of love, none of remembrance. Even if she knew where he had gone she could not appeal to him after that. She looked back at Lady Eliza's face on the pillow, now so white, with the shadow of coming death traced on it. She had thought that she had given up all to buy her peace, but it seemed as if there were still a higher price to be paid As she thought of Crauford, of his dull vanity, of his slow perceptions, of his all-sufficing egotism, she shuddered. His personality was odious to her. She hated his heavy, smooth, coarse face and his heavier manner, never so hateful as when he deemed himself most pleasant. She must think of herself, not as a woman with a soul and a body, but as a dead thing that can neither feel nor hope. What mattered it what became of her now? She had lost all, absolutely all. It only remained for her to secure a quiet end to the one creature left her for a pitiful few hours.

She went back and stood by the pillow. The dumb question that met her touched her to the heart.

"I will promise what you wish," she said, steadily. "In a year I will marry him if he asks me. But if, if"— she faltered for a moment and turned away—"not if Gilbert Speid comes back. Aunt, tell me that I have made you happy!"

"I can rest now," said Lady Eliza.

In spite of the predictions of the doctor, the days went on and still she lingered, steadily losing strength, but

with a mind at ease and a simple acceptance of her case.
She had not cared for Crauford, but he would stand
between Cecilia and a life of poverty, of even possible
hardship, and she knew that his faults were those that
could only injure himself. He would never be unkind
to his wife, she felt sure. The world was too bad a
place for a beautiful young woman to stand alone in,
and Gilbert would not come back. Why should he
when the causes of his going could not be altered?
Now, lying at the gate of another life, this one, as she
said, looked different. Cecilia had told her, months ago,
that she could never marry Speid, but her vision had
cleared enough to show her that she should not have
believed her. However, he was gone.

Her mind was generally clear now: bouts of pain there
were, and, at night, hours of wandering talk; but her
days were calm, and, as life lost its grip, suffering was
loosening its hold too.

It was late one night when Cecilia, grudging every
moment spent away from the bedside, saw that a change
had come over her. She had been sleeping, more the
sleep of exhaustion than of rest, and, as she awoke, the
girl knew that their parting must be near. The doctor
was due at any moment, for he slept at Morphie every
night, going to his other patients in the day; he was
a hard-worked man. She sat listening for his coming.

The house was very quiet as she heard his wheels roll
into the courtyard. His answer to her question was
the one she expected; there was little time left. She
ran out to the stable herself and sent a man on horseback
to Fullarton.

"Lose no time," she said, as she saw him turn away.

When she re-entered the room the doctor looked at her
with meaning eyes.

"I feel very weak," said Lady Eliza, "don't go far
from me, my dear. Cecilia, is Fullarton here?"

"I have sent for him."

She took her seat again within sight of the eyes that always sought her own; they were calm now, and she knew that the chain which had held the passing soul back from peace was broken, for she had broken it with her own hand. Whatever the consequences, whatever she might be called upon to go through, she was glad. When the time should come to face the cost, she would find courage for it.

"You do not wish to see the minister again?" she asked, in a little time. He had visited Lady Eliza once.

"There is no more to say. Cecilia, do you think I shall go before Fullarton comes?"

"I have told them to be quick. They have taken Rocket."

"Oh—Rocket. I shall not see Rocket again. She was a good mare. But I must not think of that now; perhaps I have thought too much of horses."

It was nearly an hour since her messenger had gone when Cecilia looked anxiously at the clock. The doctor had given Lady Eliza what stimulant she could swallow to keep her alive till Fullarton should come, and, though she could scarcely turn her head, her dying ears were listening for his step at the door. It came at last.

"I am here, my lady," he whispered, as he took Cecilia's place.

"I have been wearying for you, Robert," she said, "it is time to say good-bye. You have been good to me."

He slipped his arm under the pillow and raised her till her head leaned against his shoulder. She was past feeling pain. Instead of the wig she had always insisted upon wearing, a few light locks of her own grey hair strayed on her forehead from under the lace-edged scarf Cecilia had put round her, softening her face. She looked strangely young.

Robert could not speak.

"Eliza——" he began, but his voice broke.

"Be good to Cecilia, Fullarton. My little girl—if I had done differently——"

Cecilia rose from her knees and leaned over Fullarton to kiss her.

"Aunt, I have promised. All will be well with me."

"Yes, yes, I know. I am happy. Robert——"

With an effort she raised her hand, whiter, more fragile than when he had admired it as they sat in the garden; even in her death she remembered that moment. And, as, for the first and last time in her life, he laid his lips upon it, the light in her eyes went out.

*   *   *   *   *   *

It was nearing sunrise when he left Cecilia in the dark house, and daylight was beginning to look blue through the clinks of the shutter as it met the shine of the candles.

"I will come back to-day," he said; "there will be a great many things I must help you about. To-morrow you must come to Fullarton."

"And leave her?" she exclaimed.

"If her friendship for me had been less," said he, as they parted, "you and I would have been happier to-day. My God! what a sacrifice!"

"Do you call that friendship?" she cried, facing him, straight and white in the dimness of the hall. "Is *that* what you call friendship? Mr. Fullarton, have you never understood?"

*   *   *   *   *   *

Fullarton rode home in the breaking morning, his long coat buttoned high round his neck. It was chilly and the new day was rising on a world poor and grey, a world which, yesterday, had held more than he understood, and to-day, would hold less than he needed. His loss was heavy on him and he knew that he would feel it more each hour. But what bore him down was the tardy understanding of what he had done when he forged the link just broken. He had accepted a life as a gift, without thanks and without the knowledge of what he did, for he had been too intent upon himself to see the proportions of anything.

Now only was he to realise how much she had lightened for him the burden of his barren life. How often he had seen in her face the forgiveness of his ungracious words, the condoning of his little selfishness, how often known her patience with his ill-humours! She, who was so impatient, had she ever been ungentle with him? Once only. It was not so many months since she had asked his pardon for it as they sat on the garden bench. With what magnanimity he had forgiven her!

He entered the house and sat down at the pale fire which a housemaid had just lit. His heart was too worn, too numb, too old for tears; it could only ache. His butler, an Englishman who had been with him twenty years, came in and put some wine on the table, but he did not turn his head; the man poured out a glass and brought it to him.

"It will do you good, sir," he said, "and your bed is ready upstairs. You should try to sleep, sir, if you are going to see her ladyship again to-day."

Robert looked up.

"Her ladyship is dead," he said.

CHAPTER XXII

CECILIA SEES THE WILD GEESE

THERE are some periods in life when the heart, from very excess of misery, finds a spurious relief; when pain has so dulled the nerves, that, hoping nothing, fearing nothing, we sink into an endurance that is not far from peace.

Thus it was with Cecilia Raeburn. When the vault in the little cemetery between Morphie House and Morphie Kirk had been closed over Lady Eliza, Robert brought her and all her belongings to Fullarton, in accordance with a promise he had made at the bedside of his friend. She went with him passively, once that the coffin had been taken away, for the house, after the gloom and silence of its drawn blinds, was beginning to resume its original look and the sight hurt her. She had been uprooted many times since her early youth, and, like a wayfarer, she must take the road again. Her last rest had continued for fourteen happy years whose happiness made it all the harder to look forward. Her next would be Fullarton, and, after that, possibly —probably, wherever the solid heir to the house of Fordyce should pitch his tent. But a year was a respite, for who knew what might happen in a year? He might transfer his unwelcome attentions to someone else, or death, even, might step in to save her; she had just seen how near he could creep without sign or warning. She would not look forward, but, in her secret heart, she could not banish the faint hope that Gilbert might come back.

228

All the dead woman's possessions which had passed to herself she had brought to Fullarton. Necessity had compelled her to sell the furniture and the horses; and the sight of the former being carried away from its familiar place was softened to her by the fact that Robert had bought it all. He had also secured Rocket; and, although the mare's headlong impatience had dug her owner's grave, she had been so much loved by Lady Eliza that Cecilia could scarce have endured to think of her in strange hands. She had wished to give her to Fullarton, but he, knowing that each pound must be of importance to her, had refused to accept the gift. Rocket now stood in a stall next to the black horse she had followed with such fatal haste.

Among the many things for which Cecilia was grateful to Fullarton, not the least was the consideration which moved him to forbid Crauford the house. He was aware that his nephew meant to recommence his suit, and though, knowing her and being ignorant of Lady Eliza's dying desire, he did not think she would accept him now more than before, he would not allow her to be annoyed. Some weeks after the funeral Fordyce had proposed himself as his uncle's guest for a few days and been told that, for some time to come, it would be inconvenient to receive him.

During the fierce ordeal of her last days at Morphie Cecilia had had little time to turn over in her mind the startling truth which her aunt, in her delirious state, had revealed; but now, as she sat in the long spring evenings, silent while Fullarton read, she would look earnestly at him to discover, if she might, some resemblance to his son. Occasionally she fancied she could trace it, scarcely in feature, but in voice and figure. Whether rightly or wrongly, what she had learned drew her closer to him, and she took a sad satisfaction in the thought that her lover's father was, till she could settle some way of existence, playing father to her too. She loved him because he had been so much to Lady Eliza and because she now saw how profoundly the revelation of the part he had borne in her life moved him. He had become sadder, more cynical, more impervious to outer influence, but she knew what was making him so and loved him for the knowledge. Only on one point did she judge him hardly, and that was for the entire lack of interest or sympathy he had shown to Gilbert; not realising what havoc had been wrought in his life by his birth nor giving due weight to the fact that, until a year previously, he had never so much as set eyes on him. His intense desire had been to bury his past—but for one adored memory—as deep as the bottomless pit, and Gilbert's return had undone the work of years. He could never look at him without the remembrance of what he had cost. He did not know if his son were aware of the bond between them, and he was determined to check any approach, however small, which might come of his knowledge by an unchangeable indifference; though he could not banish him, at least he would ignore him as much as was consistent with civility of a purely formal kind. Lady Eliza had understood this and it had deepened her prejudice; what small attention she had given to Speid had been the outcome of her desire that Robert should appreciate her absolute neutrality; that he should know she treated him as she would treat any presentable young man who should become her neighbour; with neither hostility nor special encouragement.

And so Cecilia stayed on at Fullarton, silenced by Robert when she made any mention of leaving it, until spring merged into summer and Crauford Fordyce, making Barclay's house the base of his operations, knocked once more at his uncle's door in the propitious character of wooer. He returned in the evening to his friend with the news that Miss Raeburn had refused to listen to his proposal: while Lady Eliza had not been a year in her grave, she said, she had no wish to think of marrying.

To his emphatic assurance that he would return when that period should be over she had made no reply, and, as they parted and he reiterated his intention, she had told him to hope for nothing.

"I know what women are at when they say that!" exclaimed Barclay; "there is nothing like perseverance, Fordyce. If you don't get her next time you may laugh at me for a fool. She got nothing by her ladyship's death, and she will find out what that means when she leaves Fullarton. Keep up heart and trust Alexander Barclay."

Crauford's visit shook Cecilia out of the surface composure that her unmolested life had induced, and brought home to her the truth that every day was lessening her chance of escape. Apparently, his mind was the same, and, meanwhile, no word of the man she would never cease to love came to her from any source. Once she had gone to Kaims and paid a visit to the Miss Robertsons, hoping for news of him, however meagre, but she had been stiffly received. A woman who had driven away Gilbert Speid by her cold refusal was scarcely a guest appreciated by Miss Hersey, nor was the old lady one to detect anything showing another side of the situation. She looked with some disdain upon her visitor and longed very heartily to assure her that such a fine young fellow as her kinsman was not likely to go solitary about the world for lack of a wife. She reported the visit duly when she wrote to him, but without comment.

When winter came hope died in Cecilia; there was no one to stay her up, no one to whom she could go for a touch of sympathy, and, should Fordyce carry out his threat of returning in January, the time would have come when she must redeem her word. She had felt the strength of a lion when she saw her promise bring content to Lady Eliza; now, her heart was beginning to fail. But, fail or not, there was but one end to it.

Sometimes she would go out alone and walk through

the wet fields toward the river—for the higher reaches of
the Lour were almost within sight of the windows of
Fullarton—and look at its waters rolling seaward past
that bit of country which had held so much for her. She
loved it the more fiercely for the thought that she must
soon turn her back on it. Once, a skein of wild geese
passed over her head on their flight to the tidal marshes
beyond Kaims, and the far-away scream in the air held
her spellbound. High up, pushing their way to the sea,
their necks outstretched as though drawn by a magnet
to their goal, they held on their course; and their cry
rang with the voice of the north—the voice of the soul
of the coast. She leaned her head against a tree and
wept unrestrainedly with the relief of one not commonly
given to tears. Once more, she told herself, before leaving Fullarton, she would ride to Morphie and look at the
old house from the road; so far, she had never had courage to turn her horse in that direction, though she now
rode almost daily. Once, too, she would go and stand by
the Lour bridge where she could see the white walls of
Whanland.

· While Cecilia, at Fullarton, was trying to nerve herself
to the part she must play, Crauford, at Fordyce, was
spending a more peaceful time than he had experienced
since he first confided the state of his heart to his family.
Lady Fordyce's suspicions were lulled by his demeanour
and by a fact, which, to a person of more acumen, would
have been alarming; namely, that he never, by any
chance, mentioned Miss Raeburn's name nor the name
of anything connected with her. He had said nothing
about his fruitless visit to Barclay, and Fullarton, whose
inclination it was to let sleeping dogs lie, did not supple-
ment the omission. His nephew no longer honoured
him with his confidence and he had no desire to provoke
another correspondence with his sister. To Cecilia also
he said nothing; while he realised that to settle herself
so well would be a good thing from a worldly point of

view, his contempt for Crauford gave him a liberal notion
of her feelings when she refused him.   He knew what
had happened, but he dismissed the episode without
comment.

Autumn had again brought Lady Maria Milwright as a
guest to Fordyce, and the prodigal son, having temporarily finished with his husks and being inwardly stayed
up by Cecilia's half-implied permission to address her
again, had time for the distractions of home life.   Fordyce Castle blossomed as the rose, and Mary and Agneta
would, no doubt, have done the same thing, had it not
been a little late for such an experience.   Lady Fordyce
went so far as to give a dinner-party and a school feast.

Crauford kept his own counsel strictly, and, though he
had the honesty to make no advances to Lady Maria, her
appreciation of him made her an agreeable companion;
his sisters looked on with keen interest and Agneta was
emboldened to congratulate him on his return to the
paths of wisdom

"Admit, brother," she began one day as they found
themselves alone together, "that Lady Maria is vastly
superior to Miss Raeburn, after all."

"Nonsense !" exclaimed he, taken aback.

"But why is it nonsense?" continued his sister, "what
is amiss with Lady Maria?"

"Her face," said Crauford shortly.

"But Mama says it is absurd to think of that; I heard
her say so to Papa—quite lately too."

"And what did he answer?" enquired her brother,
thinking of a sentiment in the memorable letter Sir
Thomas had written him.

"I think he said that he supposed all cats were grey
in the dark. He could not quite understood what
Mama said; it seemed such an odd answer, for they had
not been talking about cats. It made her rather angry
too."

Crauford said nothing and the two walked on.   They

were on the lawn, watching Sir Thomas and the local
minister playing bowls in the shower of dead horse-
chestnut leaves, which fell, periodically, like so many
yellow fans, to the ground

"Did Miss Raeburn play the harp?" asked Agneta, at
last.

"No; at least I have never heard her," he replied.

"Lady Maria does; did she sing?"

"No."

"Lady Maria sings. She has had lessons from an
Italian master; I saw a little drawing of him that is in
her work-box. What could Miss Raeburn do that you
thought her so wonderful?" persisted Agneta.

Crauford knit his brows. Cecilia's general mastery of
life was difficult to explain, nor, indeed, did he quite
understand it himself.

"She is so—so ladylike," he said.

"Why do you always say that? Miss Raeburn was
only a companion; now Lady Maria has a title."

People were much more outwardly snobbish in those
days than they are now that the disease has become
internal; at present, it would scarcely be possible to
make such a speech and survive it.

"You know nothing about it. Miss Raeburn was
Lady Eliza's relation and she called her her niece. And
why do you say 'was'? She is not dead."

"I don't know; I suppose, because we need not trouble
about her any more. Do tell me what she was like,
Crauford, I have so often wanted to know. Do, do,
dear Crauford!"

"If I tell you a great many things, will you promise
to keep them entirely to yourself?" he enquired, in an
access of gracious elder brotherhood. He longed for a
confidant.

"Oh, yes! yes!" cried Agneta, running her arm through
his, "I will not even tell Mary."

"I think she has seen the folly of her refusal," said he,

gravely. "I saw her a few weeks ago; in fact, I renewed my offer, but she said she could not listen to me so soon after her aunt's death. I am going back next January, and I have reason to suppose, in fact, Barc—— I am almost sure she will accept me then. I trust you will receive her kindly, Agneta. I shall look to you."

Between gratification at his words and apprehension for the future his sister was almost struck dumb.

"What will Mama say?" she exclaimed when she found her tongue.

"I am afraid it does not much matter what Mama says," replied Crauford, with playful intrepidity.

He knew very well that he would not be at Fordyce to hear.

But there was no use in meeting troubles half-way and Agneta was dying to know more.

"Is she tall, brother?"

"Rather tall," he replied. "She has a beautiful figure—very slender."

"As thin as Lady Maria?"

"Good gracious, no!" exclaimed Crauford.

"And what is her hair like, dark or fair?"

"Rather dark, but not black."

"And her eyes?"

"Remarkable eyes—in fact, rather too extraordinary. Not quite usual."

"She does not squint?" cried Agneta, seized with horror.

"Should I wish for a wife who squinted?" asked he, rather huffily.

"No, no, of course not; don't be angry, Crauford. Why do you not like her eyes?"

"Oh, I do like them; only I wish they were more like other people's, wider open and bluer; you will see her for yourself, Agneta. There was another man who wanted to marry her not long ago, a sulky-looking fellow called Speid; but she soon sent him away and he has gone off to Spain."

"Because of her? Did he really?" exclaimed Agneta, taking a long breath as she recognised the desperate matters life could contain.

Lady Maria's parasol, which was seen advancing in the distance between the laurel bushes, put an end to further confidences, for Lady Maria's eyes, round enough and blue enough to satisfy anybody, had discovered the brother and sister and she was coming toward them.

Crauford, having been absent from the breakfast table, had not met the young lady that morning. He made a stiff, serio-comic bow, laying his hand on his heart. He could unbend sometimes.

"I hope your ladyship is well to-day," he observed.

She blushed awkwardly, not knowng how to take his pleasantries. She looked good and modest, and, in feature, rather as if she had changed faces with a pea-hen. Agneta surveyed her from head to heel, earnestly and covertly; she did not look as if she would drive any-one to Spain. She was rather impressed by the idea of a sister-in-law who could so ruffle her brother and his sex, for, though she was over twenty-six years old, she had only read of such things in books; she had an over-whelming respect for men, and it scarcely occurred to her that women whom one might meet every day, and who were not constitutionally wicked, could deal with them so high-handedly. The possibilities of woman-hood had never dawned on her, any more than they dawn on hundreds of others, both well and ill-favored, who live contentedly, marry early, have children frequently, and, finally, die lamented, knowing as much of the enthralling trade of being a woman as they did on the day they were born.

But Agneta was groping along the edge of a world of strange discoveries, as she stood by the bowling-green and mechanically watched the figures of her father and the Reverend Samuel Mackay straddling as they appraised their shots. Crauford and Lady Maria had long vanished into the house by the time she turned to look after them, and the bowl-players had finished their game, discussed it, and begun another. She felt that being in her brother's confidence had given her a great stride in life.

Four months later, she stood in the same place by the bowling-green and saw him drive up the avenue to the Castle; he had been at Fullarton for nearly a week and she went round to the front door to meet him.

"My news is important, Agneta," he said, as he greeted her. "Miss Raeburn has consented; I have come to fetch some clothes I want and am going away again to-morrow. Say nothing."

"Oh!" said his sister. "I——"

The sentence was never completed, for Lady Fordyce appeared in the hall.

CHAPTER XXIII

When the decisive step had been taken and Crauford's perseverance was at last crowned with success, he straightway informed his uncle of his good fortune; also, he begged him to say nothing of the matter till he should have gone to Fordyce Castle to announce his news. As we have seen, he did not mean to announce it in person, but he wished to see Agneta before retiring to a safe distance and writing to Sir Thomas, of whose consent the past had made him sure; from his sister he counted on hearing how soon it would be wise for him to face Lady Fordyce. Before he left Fullarton he had allowed himself one day to be spent with Cecilia.

"You cannot expect me to go to-morrow," he said to her, with solemn gallantry, as he emerged from Fullarton's study, where he had been to declare the engagement.

"Do you not think your parents might be offended if you delay?" she suggested faintly.

"Let them!" exclaimed Crauford.

All next day she had clung to Fullarton's proximity, hating to be alone with the man with whom she was to pass her life, and feeling half desperate when Robert closeted himself with a tenant who had come to see him on business. Crauford's blunt lack of perception made him difficult to keep at a distance, and she had now no right to hurt his feelings. On her finger was the ring he had, with much forethought, brought with him; and, had it been an iron chain on her neck, it could not have

238

galled her more. When, at last, he had driven away, she rushed to her room and pulled it off; then she dipped her handkerchief in rosewater and dabbed her face and lips; for, though she had tried to say good-bye to him in Fullarton's presence, she had not succeeded and she had paid heavily for her failure.

For whatever motive she was accepting his name, his protection, and the ease of life he would give her, she must treat him fairly; she felt this strongly. She had not hid from him a truth which she would have liked him better for finding more unpalatable; namely, that she did not love him.

"You will learn to, in time," he had observed, complacently.

If he had said that he loved her well enough for two, or some such trite folly as men will say in like circumstances, it would have been less hateful. · But he had merely changed the subject with a commonplace reflection. For all that, she felt that she was cheating him.

To play her part with any attempt at propriety, she must have time to bring her mind to it without the strain of his presence. He might appear at Fullarton at any moment, with the intention of staying for days, and Cecilia decided that she must escape from a position which became hourly more difficult. While she racked her brain in thinking how this might be effected, like a message from the skies came a letter from her friend and Fullarton's cousin, the Lord Advocate's widow. "Though I know Mr. Crauford Fordyce very slightly," she wrote, "he is still related to me, and I have to thank him warmly for being the means of bringing my dearest Miss Raeburn into the family. Would that I could see you to offer you my sincerest good wishes! I do not know whether the day is yet fixed, but should you have time to spare me a visit, or inclination to consult the Edinburgh mantua-makers, I should receive you with a pleasure of whose reality you know me well enough to be assured."

She had still nearly eight weeks' respite. The wedding which was to take place upon the tenth of April, was, at her earnest request, to be at Morphie Kirk, for she wanted to begin her new life near the scenes of the old one. She was to be married from Fullarton; Robert, having constituted himself her guardian, would give her away, and Crauford, according to time-honoured etiquette, would be lodged in Kaims; Mr. Barclay had offered his house. In justice to the bridegroom, she must not fall short of the ordinary standard of bridal appearance, and she showed Robert his cousin's letter, saying that, with his permission, she would go to Edinburgh to buy her wedding gown. On the plea of ill-health Lady Fordyce had refused to be present at the ceremony, and it was only the joint pressure brought to bear on her by brother and husband which forced from her a reluctant consent that Mary and Agneta should go to Fullarton and play the part of bridesmaids. Sir Thomas had shown unusual decision.

It was on the day before her departure that Cecilia rode out to take a last look at Morphie. Though there was, as yet, no hint of coming spring in the air, in a month the thrushes and blackbirds would be proclaiming their belief in its approach, and a haze, like a red veil, would be touching the ends of the boughs. As she stopped on the highroad and looked across the wall at Morphie House, she felt like a returned ghost. Its new owners had left it uninhabited and the white blinds were drawn down like the eyelids of a dead face; her life there seemed sometimes so real and sometimes so incredible—as if it had never been. She saw herself going through the rooms, loitering in the garden, and performing the hundred and one duties and behests she had done so willingly. She smiled, though her heart ached, as she remembered her aunt's short figure leaning out of a window above the

stable-yard, watching the horses being brought out for
exercise and calling out her orders to the men. How
silent it all was now; the only moving things were the
pigeons which had always haunted Morphie, the descend-
ants of those for which Gilbert had fought two years ago.
She turned away and took the road that followed the
river's course to Whanland.

Here, too, everything was still, though the entrance
gate was standing open. She had never yet been inside
it; long before it had acquired special interest for her
she had felt a curiosity about the untenanted place; but
Lady Eliza had always driven by quickly, giving unsatis-
factory answers to any questions she had put. She rode
in, unable to resist her impulse, and sat on horseback
looking up at the harled walls. The front door was
ajar, and, seeing this, she was just about to ride away,
when there were footsteps behind her and Granny Stirk,
her arms loaded with fresh-cut sticks, came round a corner of the house. She let her bundle fall in a clattering
shower and came up to Cecilia. Since Gilbert had left she
had not seen the woman who, she was sure, had been the
cause of his departure, and her heart was as hard against
her as the heart of Miss Hersey Robertson.

"Do you take care of the house?" asked Cecilia, when
they had exchanged a few words

"Ay; whiles a' come in-by an' put on a bittie fire.
The Laird asket me. But Macquean's no verra canny
to work wi'."

"Oh, Granny, let me come in!" cried Cecilia. "I want
so much to see this place. I shall never see it again—I
am going away, you know."

The Queen of the Cadgers eyed her like an accusing
angel.

"And what for are ye no here—you that sent the Laird
awa'?" she cried. "Puir lad! He cam' in-by to me,
and says he, "Ye've been aye fine to me, Granny," says
he. And a' just asket him, for a' kenned him verra well,

"Whaur is she?" says I. "It's a' done, Granny," says he, "it's a' done!" An' he sat down to the fire just wearied-like. "An' are ye no to get her?" says I. "Na," says he. "*Aweel, ye'll get better,*" says I. A' tell't him that, Miss Raeburn—but he wadna believe it, puir lad."

Cecilia had not spoken to one living creature who had met Gilbert Speid since they parted, and her eyes filled with tears; she slid from her horse and stood weeping before the old woman. Her long self-control gave way, for the picture raised by Granny's tongue unnerved her so completely that she seemed to be losing hold of everything but her own despair. She had not wept since the day she had heard the wild geese.

"Ay! ye may greet," said the Queen of the Cadgers, "ye've plenty to greet for! Was there ever a lad like Whanland?"

Cecilia could not speak for sobs; when the barriers of such a nature as hers are broken down there is no power that can stay the flood.

"He thocht the world o' you," continued Granny, folding her arms; "there was naething braw eneuch for you wi' him. There wasna mony that kent him as weel as a' kent him. He didna say verra muckle, but it was sair to see him."

"Granny! Granny! have pity!" cried Cecilia. "I cannot bear this! Oh, you don't understand! I love him with all my heart and I shall never see him again. You are so cruel, Granny Stirk—where are the reins? I am going now."

Blind with her tears, she groped about in the horse's mane.

"What ailed ye to let him awa' then?" exclaimed the old woman, laying her hand on the bridle.

"I could not help it. I cannot tell you, Granny, but I had to give him up. Don't ask me—I was obliged to give him up, though I loved him better than anything in the world. It was not my fault; he knew it. I am so miserable—so miserable !"

"An' you that's to be married to the Laird o' Fullarton's nephew !" cried Granny Stirk.

"I wish I were dead," sobbed Cecilia.

Though Granny knew nothing of the tangle in which her companion was held, she knew something of life, and she knew real trouble when she saw it. Her fierceness against her was turned into a dawning pity. How any woman could give up a man she loved was a mystery to her, and how any woman could give up the Laird of Whanland, incomprehensible. But the ways of the gentry were past finding out.

"Come awa' in," she said, as Cecilia dried her eyes, "and a'll cry on Macquean to tak' the horse. Jimmy's at the stable an' he'll mind it; 'twas him brocht me here i' the cairt."

She took the rein from her and walked round the house, leading the animal

"Macquean, ye thrawn brute !" she cried, as she went, "tak' yon horse to Jimmy. He'll no touch ye, man !"

Cecilia entered, and, through a passage window, she could see Macquean in a rusty black coat, sitting on a stone-heap outside.

"Come here, a' tell ye !" cried the Queen of the Cadgers.

Cecilia saw him shake his head.

"Ye'd be mair use as a golloch* than a man," said Granny, throwing the reins to her grandson, who was coming toward them.

Cecilia went into a room and sat down on a windowseat; most of the furniture was put away, and what was left had been covered up carefully by Granny and Macquean. Clementina's portrait was gone from the wall, as well as that of the bay coach-horse, and the alcoves by the fireplace were empty of books. She sat and gazed at the bare beech-trees and the fields between

* Blackbeetle.

Whanland and the sand-hills. He must have looked out at that view every day, and her eyes drank it in, the garden wall and the stable buildings broke its flat lines. Being on the ground floor, she could not see the sea; but the heaven above, with its long-drawn, fine clouds, wore the green-gray which suggests an ocean-sky. She was quite calm by the time Granny came in and stood beside her.

The old woman, though softened and puzzled, was yet in an inquisitorial mind; she stood before the window-seat, her arms akimbo, and her skirt turned up and drawn through the placket-hole, for she had been cleaning.

"An' what gar'd ye put Whanland awa' if ye liket him sae weel?" she asked again. "Dod, that wasna the gait a' wad hae gaed when a' was a lassie!"

"I cannot speak about it," answered Cecilia, rising, her face set; "there is no use in asking me. I was forced to do it. God knows I have no heart left. Oh, Granny! if he could but come back! In two months I shall be married."

The Queen of the Cadgers stood silent; there was so much more in the matter than she had suspected; Cecilia might be a fool, but she was not the cold-hearted flirt whom she had pictured torturing Gilbert for her own entertainment.

"It's ill work mendin' ae man's breeks when yer hairt's in anither ane's pocket," she said.

Though mirth was far, indeed, from her, Cecilia could not help smiling at this crusty cutting from the loaf of wisdom.

"Ah! ye may lauch now," exclaimed Granny solemnly, "but what 'll ye do when he comes hame, an' you married? Ye'll need to mind yersel' then."

Neither of the women knew on how appropriate a spot the warning was offered, as they stood within a few feet of Clementina Speid's empty place upon the wall.

"I shall be gone," answered Cecilia. "I pray that I may never see his face again."

"Wad ye tak' him, syne he was hame?"

"Do you mean if he were to come now?" asked Cecilia.

"Ay."

"Oh, Granny, stop—there is no use in thinking or hoping."

"Wad ye gang wi' him?" persisted the old woman.

"What do you think?" cried Cecilia, facing her suddenly, "do you think anything could keep me back? Do you think I have ever ceased hoping or praying? Don't torment me—I have enough to bear. Come, let me see Whanland Show me everything, dear Granny, before I go. I shall look at it and never forget it; all my life I shall remember it. Come."

The two went from room to room, Granny leading the way. Cecilia's eyes devoured everything, trying to stamp each detail on her mind. They went through the lower rooms, and upstairs, their steps echoing in the carpetless passages. There was little to see but the heavy four-post beds, a few high-backed chairs which still stood in their places, and the mantelpieces carved with festoon and thyrsus. They went up to the attics and into the garret; the pictures had come back to the place in which Gilbert had first found them.

"Yon's the Laird's mother," said Granny, turning Clementina's portrait to the light, "she's bonnie, puir thing.'"

"Was that like her?"

"The very marrows of her," replied she.

The mother Gilbert had never seen and the bride he had never married were come face to face. The living woman looked at the painted one, searching for some trace of resemblance to the man from whom she had divided her; it was too dark for her to see the little box in Clementina's hand There was something in her bearing which recalled Gilbert, something in the brows and the carriage of the head.

"Come away," she said at last, "I must go home now. I shall always thank you for showing me Whanland."

They went downstairs and she stood on the doorstep while Granny went to the stable for her horse; the light was beginning to change; she would have to ride fast to reach Fullarton before it went. To-morrow she was to leave for Edinburgh, and her return would only take place a few days before the wedding. A page in her life was turning down. She was to go to London with her husband, and, in a few months, they were to come back to settle in a place in Roxburghshire belonging to Sir Thomas Fordyce. The east coast would soon fade away from her like one of its own mists; the voice of the North Sea, which came faintly from the shore, was booming a farewell, for the tide was coming in beyond the bents.

Before she turned away she leaned down from her saddle.

"Some day," she said, "when—if—Mr. Speid comes back, tell him that I came here and that——"

But she could not go on and rode down the short approach without ending her sentence. "Good-bye!" she called at the gate, waving her hand.

Cecilia had reached Fullarton by the time Granny Stirk had finished her cleaning, for her visit had taken a good piece out of the afternoon. Though she generally was a steady worker, the old woman paused many times and laid down her duster. She took particular care of the room in which Gilbert slept, but, as she shook and beat the heavy curtains of his bed, her mind was not in her task. She was willing to admit that his passion was not altogether indefensible. As women went, Cecilia was more than very well, and, like nearly everyone who had once spoken to her, she did not deny her beauty. She pitied her too; though, it is to be feared, had her dead body been of any use to Speid, she would have stood by and seen her murdered. But, as he preferred her living, he should have her, if she, Joann Stirk, could get him home in time. Once let him come back and she would tell him what to do.

"Ye'll hae to drive me to Kaims i' the cairt the morn's morn," she observed to her grandson, as they bowled homeward.

"I'm for Blackport," said Jimmy, laconically.

"Ye'll do as ye're bid," replied the Queen of the Cadgers.

CHAPTER XXIV

A ROYAL VISIT

WHILE Granny had shaken the curtains in Gilbert's bedroom her mind had worked as hard as her hands; there was no doubt in it of one thing; namely, that, by hook or by crook, he must be brought home. It was a large idea for her to have conceived, because she scarcely knew where he was and had no idea how he might be reached. She understood that Barclay had means of communication with him, but, since the visit he had paid her, ostensibly to examine her mended roof, and, really, to pry into Speid's affairs, she had distrusted him fundamentally. The matter was intimate and needed the intervention of someone upon whom she could depend. As the Laird of Fullarton was uncle to the person she wished to circumvent, he also was an impossible adviser. The Miss Robertsons, under any aspect but that of being Gilbert's relations, she looked upon as futile. "Twa doited auld bodies wha's lives is nae object to them," as she had described them, were not worth consideration in such a case. In her strait she suddenly bethought herself of Captain Somerville. He had three special advantages; he was her idol's friend, he was exceedingly civil to herself, and she had once seen him in uniform. This last qualification gave him something of the weight and security of a public character. Also, a person who had fought the French—all foreigners were French to her—in every quarter of the world, must surely be able to put his hand on any part of it at a moment's notice.

248

As a matter of fact, she could hardly have made a better choice. The sailor, who bore a most human love to
his kind, had appraised many men and women in his
time, and he had a vast admiration for Granny. Gallant
himself to the core of his simple soul, he loved the quality in others, and the story of her fight with circumstances and final mastery of them had struck him in a
sensitive place. On that memorable day on which she
had seen him in uniform he was returning from Aberdeen,
where he had gone to meet an official person, and his
chaise passed her cottage. As he drove by, he saw the
little upright figure standing on the doorstep, and,
remembering her history, with a sudden impulse he
raised his hand and saluted her.

Though he was not, perhaps, so renowned a warrior as
the Queen of the Cadgers supposed, Captain Somerville
had seen a good deal of service, and had lost his leg, not
in the doing of any melodramatic act, but in the ordinary
course of a very steadily and efficiently performed duty.
As a boy, he had gone to sea when the sea was a harder
profession than it is now and when parents had had to
think, not twice, but many times, before committing
their sons to it. He had run away and smuggled himself upon a merchantman lying in the harbour near his
home, and before she sailed he had been discovered by
the first mate. His irate father, to whom he was
returned, thinking to cure him of an infatuation he could
not, himself, understand, arranged with the captain
that he should be taken on the voyage—which was a
short one—and made to work hard. "It would show
the young fool," he said, "that the Church"—for which
he was destined—"was a more comfortable place than
a ship." But the treatment produced an exactly contrary result. Finally, the family three-decker received
the person of a younger brother, and, after much discussion, His Majesty's Navy that of a new midshipman.
More than fifteen years afterward he got into a young

man's scrape in an obscure seaport, and emerged from it with Mrs. Somerville in tow. It was one from which a less honourable man would have escaped more fortunately. The lady was accustomed to say, in after times, that she had been "married from the schoolroom," but many who heard her suspected that there had never been a schoolroom in the matter. He had now been Coastguard Inspector at Kaims for over seven years.

The sailor was sitting at the breakfast-table next morning opposite to his wife, portions of whose figure were visible behind the urn; Miss Lucilla was away on a visit. The house stood a little back from the High Street, and, though the room was quiet, a cart which had stopped at the foot of the strip of garden was unnoticed by the pair.

"If ye please," said the parlour-maid, looking in, "there's a fishwife wad like to speak wi' you."

"We require nothing to-day," said Mrs. Somerville.

"She's no sellin'. She's just needin' a word wi' the Captain. It's Mrs. Stirk—her that bides out by Garvie-kirk."

"It's Her Majesty of the Cadgers, my dear," said the Inspector; "we must ask her to come in."

The parlor-maid smiled.

"She says she wad like to see ye alone, sir. 'It'll no keep,' she says."

"Impertinent woman!" exclaimed Mrs. Somerville, "what can she have to say that I am not supposed to hear?"

"I would do a good deal to oblige her," said Somerville, dragging himself up. "Show her into the next room."

Granny Stirk had put on her pebble brooch; the little woollen shawl, crossed over her chest with its long ends tied behind the waist, was of a bright red and black check; her head was bare and her thick iron-gray hair held by a black net; her gold earrings shone. An

indefinable rush of fresh air, brine, and tar came in with
her.

"Sit down, Mrs. Stirk," said Somerville, as he stumped
in. "What can I do for you?"

"Sir," said she, "could ye tell me what's come of the
Laird o' Whanland?"

"God bless me!" exclaimed the astonished sailor, "I
think he's in Spain.

"Does he no write ye? A' mind he was aye billies*
wi' you."

"I have heard nothing of him since he left."

She made a gesture of dismay.

"Mr. Barclay must know where he is," said he. "I
could get his direction for you, I dare say, if it was anything urgent."

"Fie, na!" she exclaimed. "Lord's sake! dinna say
a word to the like o' him!"

"But what is the trouble, my good woman?"

Before replying, Granny drew her chair close to his,
throwing a searching look round the room and at the
door, unfortunately, she could not see through the
latter, but had she been able to do so she would have
noticed Mrs. Somerville standing on the door-mat.

She plunged into her tale

"Did ye no ken that the Laird was just deein' for yon
lassie o' her ladyship's? A' ken't it fine, but he tell't me
no to speak a word, and, dod! a' didna. Well, he cam'
in-by to me and tell't me he was gangin' awa' for she
wadna tak' him. That was the way o't; that was what
gar'd the puir lad gang. Did ye ken that, sir?"

"I guessed it," said the Inspector, enormously surprised at this beginning.

"Well," continued the Queen of the Cadgers, leaning
forward and solemnly shaking his knee to compel attention, "well, she's to be married in April month an' she's
greetin' hersel' to death for the Laird."

* Friends.

"How do you know that?" asked Somerville.

"A' was puttin' on a bittie fire at Whanland yesterday —a' do that, whiles—an' she cam' ridin' up. 'Oh, Granny, let me come in-by!' says she. 'What way are ye no here?' says I. 'What way did ye let the Laird gang?' An' she just began greetin' till I was near feared at her; it was aye the Laird—the Laird. I wager she canna thole yon lad she's to get. Says I, 'Wad ye tak' him if he was to come back i' the now?' 'Oh!' says she, 'div ye think I wadna? Oh! if he was hame! If he was hame!' A' could hae greetit mysel', Captain."

"But why did she not marry him at the beginning?"

"I askit her that. 'Granny,' says she, 'a' canna tell ye; a' couldna help mysel'. There's things a' canna speak o'. A' wish a' was dead,' she says.—An' there's Whanland that doesna ken it!" continued the old woman. "Sir, we'll need to get him hame afore it's ower late."

Somerville was silent, feeling as though he were being invited to plunge into a torrent. He was certain that every word Granny said was true, for, though he had only seen Cecilia once since the news of her engagement was public, that once had been enough to show him that she was wretched. Some miserable tragedy was certainly brewing.

"Suppose Mr. Speid has forgotten her?" he hazarded.

"*Him* forget?" cried Granny, rising with a movement which made her earrings swing. "By Jarvit, Captain, a' didna think ye was sic a fule!"

"Perhaps I'm not," said he, rather nettled; "but what made you come to me?"

"Was a' to gang to the Laird o' Fullarton that's uncle to yon red-faced loon? Was a' to gang to yon tod Barclay that's aye wi' him an' that doesna like the Laird—a' ken fine he doesna. Was a' to gang to they twa auld maidies i' the Close that doesna understand naething? Not me!" said Granny, tossing her earrings again.

Captain Somerville put his hand on the back of his neck and ran it up over the top of his head till his nose got in the way; his hair looked like a field of oats after a rain-shower. Things did seem bad.

"Ye'll need to write him—that's what ye'll need to do. Tell him if he doesna come hame, it'll be ower late," continued Granny.

"But he may not want to come, Mrs. Stirk—he may have changed his mind. Remember, it is more than a year and a half since he left."

"Have a' no tell't ye?" cried she. "There's naebody kens the Laird as a' ken him. Gang yer ain gait, sir, but, when Whanland kens the truth, an' when yon lassie's awa' wi' the wrong lad,'you an' me'll need to think shame o' oursels!"

There was scarcely anyone who could more fitly appreciate the horror of Cecilia's position than the sailor. Long years of a companionship, whose naked uncongenialness he had decently draped with loyalty, were behind him to give point to Granny's words; also, he thought of her face as he had last seen it; and he had that highest and rarest courage, the courage that is not afraid of responsibility. The rock on which second-rate characters go to pieces had no terrors for him.

The silence now was so deep that Mrs. Somerville, on the mat outside, began to fear a move and made as quiet a retreat as she could to the breakfast-room. She had heard enough to interest her considerably. Though the talk was resumed before she was out of earshot, she did not dare to return, for she saw, looking at the clock, that the maid might come up at any moment to clear the breakfast-table.

"I will find out where to write to him," said the sailor. "We must lose no time, for the letter may take weeks to reach him. I am afraid it is a forlorn hope, Mrs. Stirk, but we'll do our best. I shall write very urgently to Miss Raeburn and tell her what I have done."

"That's you!" exclaimed the old woman.

"I must send the letter out to Fullarton to be addressed," continued he, "I have not heard where she is lodging in Edinburgh."   .

"Dinna hae ony steer wi' that Barclay," said Granny. "He's aye keekin' an' speerin' about what doesna concern him, an' makin' work wi' Mr. Fordyce."

"I will go to the Miss Robertsons this afternoon," said he, half to himself. "I know Miss Hersey writes to Speid. I suppose that, when I send my letter to him, I may say you have been here, Mrs. Stirk, and speak of your meeting with Miss Raeburn?"

"Ye can that," replied she, preparing to go, "for a'm terrible pleased a' did it. A'll awa' now, sir, an' thank ye."

Mrs. Somerville, looking out of the window, watched the Queen of the Cadgers walk down to her cart. A sneer touched the lady's face as the old woman got in beside her grandson and was driven away.

"Well," said she, as her husband entered, "what did that impudent old creature want? You were a long time listening to her."

"She was consulting me about private matters, my dear; and I don't consider Mrs. Stirk an impudent person."

"You are so fond of being mixed up with common people," rejoined his wife, "I am sure I never could understand your tastes."

Had the sailor never mixed up with common people Mrs. Somerville would not have been sitting where she was.

His feelings were stirred a good deal and he was in a mood in which pettinesses were peculiarly offensive to him. Besides that, he was inclined to think Granny's acquaintance something of an honour.

"If there were more people in the world like Mrs. Stirk, it would be a good thing for it," he said shortly. "You are an uncommon silly woman sometimes, Matilda."

CHAPTER XXV

MRS. SOMERVILLE retired from the breakfast-room in the height of ill-humour: it was not often that her husband spoke to her in so plain a manner and she was full of resentment. She was conscious that she had behaved badly in listening at the door, and, though the act did not seem to her such a heinous offense as it might have done to many others, her conscience aggravated her discomfort.

But curiosity was a tough element in her, and she was stayed up through its faint attacks by the interesting things she had overheard. Though her ears were not sharp, and the pair on the other side of the door had been sometimes indistinct, she had learned enough to gather what was afoot. Evidently, Cecilia Raeburn was now breaking her heart for Gilbert Speid, whom she had refused, and the Inspector and Mrs. Stirk had agreed that he should be told of it; so that, if he were still wearing the willow for the young woman, he might return in time to snatch her from her lawful bridegroom.

She had heard a good deal from Barclay of the checkered progress of Fordyce's wooing and she saw Speid through the lawyer's spectacles; also, the drastic rebuke she had suffered from Miss Hersey Robertson on his account had not modified her view. To add to this, he was extremely friendly with Captain Somerville, and she was of a class which is liable to resent its husband's friends. She was jealous with the dreadful jealousy of women of her breeding; not from love, of the person who is its object, but from an unsleeping fear for personal prerogative. She determined to tell Barclay of her discoveries, though she had no intention of telling him how she had come· by them; and the thought of this little secret revenge on the Inspector was sweet to her.

Throughout the morning she maintained an injured silence which he was too much preoccupied to observe, and when, in the afternoon, he took his hat and the stick he used for such journeys as were short enough for him to attempt on foot, she watched him with a sour smile. He had not told her where he was going, but she knew and felt superior in consequence. She wondered when Barclay would come to see her; if he did not arrive in the course of a day or two she must send him a note. He was accustomed to pay her a visit at least once every week, and it was now ten days since he had been inside her doors.

Captain Somerville, though he returned with his object attained, had not found that attainment easy. The Miss Robertsons had always looked favourably on him as an individual, but Miss Hersey could not forget that he was the husband of his wife; and, since the moment when she had risen in wrath and left the party at his house, there had been a change in her feelings towards him. Well did she know that such a speech as the one which had offended her could never have been uttered by the sailor; the knowledge made no difference; Miss Hersey was strictly and fundamentally illogical.

Gilbert had given his address to his cousins with the request that it should not be passed on to anyone. He wanted to have as little communication as possible with the life he had left behind, and the news of Cecilia, for which he had begged, was the only news he cared to receive; business letters passing between himself and Barclay were written and read from necessity. He wished to give himself every chance of forgetting, though, in his attempts to do so, he was nearly as illogical as Miss Hersey.

The Inspector's request for his direction was, therefore, in the old ladies' eyes, almost part and parcel of his wife's effrontery, and it was met by a stiff refusal and a silence which made it hard for him to go further. The red chintz sofa bristled. It was only his emphatic assurance that what he wished to tell Gilbert would affect him very nearly which gained his point. Even then he could not get the address, and had to content himself with Miss Hersey's promise, that, if he would write his letter, seal it and deliver it to her, she would direct and send it with all despatch. He returned, conscious of having strained relations almost to breaking point, but he did not care; his object was gained and that was what concerned him. He had become almost as earnest as Granny. The florid lady who watched his return from behind her drawing-room window-curtains observed the satisfaction in his look.

He was a slow scribe, as a rule, and it took him some time to put the whole sum of what Granny had told him before Speid; it was only when he came to the end of his letter that his pen warmed to the work and he gave him a plain slice from his opinion. "If your feelings are the same," he wrote, "then your place is here; for, if you stay away a day longer than you need, you are leaving a woman in the lurch. I do not understand this matter but I understand that much." Then he added the date of the wedding, underlined it, and assured Gilbert that he was "his sincere friend, Wm. Somerville." A few minutes later, his lady, still at the window, saw the individual who was at once coachman, errand-boy, and gardener disappear in the direction of Miss Robertson's house with a sealed packet in his hand.

It was not until evening that he sat down to think what he should say to Cecilia. The need for haste was

not so great in this case, but every hour was of value
with respect to the letter Miss Hersey was forwarding
to Gilbert.   There was no knowing where he might be,
nor how long it might take in reaching him, nor how
many obstacles might rise up on the road home, even
should he start the very day he received it.   But, here,
it was different.   The sailor bit the top of his pen as he
mused; many things had puzzled him and many things
puzzled him still.   He had received a shock on hearing
of Cecilia's intended marriage.   In his own mind he had
never doubted that she loved Speid, and this new
placing of her affections was the last thing he expected;
if there were no question of affection, then, so much the
worse, in his eyes.   He thought little of Fordyce and
imagined that she thought little of him too.   He had
never supposed that money would so influence her, and
his conclusion—a reluctant one—was that the extreme
poverty which must be her portion, now Lady Eliza
was gone, had driven her to the step.

Granny Stirk's news had opened his eyes to the probability that there were influences at work of which he
knew nothing, and he was uncommon enough to admit
such a possibility.   When most people know how
easily they could manage everybody else's business, the
astonishing thing is that they should ever be in straits
on their own account.   But it never astonishes them.
Captain Somerville had the capacity for being astonished,
both at himself and at other people; the world, social
and geographical, had taught him that there is no royal
road to the solution of anyone's difficulties.   The man
who walks about with little contemptuous panaceas in
his pocket for his friends' troubles is generally the man
whose hair turns prematurely gray with his own.   What
had Cecilia meant when she told the old woman, weeping,
that she could not help herself?   He would, at least,
give her the chance of helping herself now, and she
could take it or leave it as she chose.   He was not

going to advise her nor to make suggestions; he would merely tell her what he had done. He had no difficulty in justifying his act to his conscience; he justified it to his prudence by reflecting on what she had given the Queen of the Cadgers to understand; namely, that, if the exile should return, she would throw all to the winds for him.

"My writing-table is to be dusted to-day, and I shall leave this here," he said to his wife on the following afternoon, as he put the letter he had written on the drawing-room mantelpiece; "if you can hear of anyone going in the direction of Fullarton, I should be glad to have it carried. It is to Miss Raeburn, in Edinburgh, so Mr. Fullarton must address it for me."

The Inspector was muffled in his plaid and Mrs. Somerville knew that his duty was taking him south of Kaims; Fullarton lay north of it. As he left the house he hesitated a moment. What if Barclay should call, as he often did, on his way to Fullarton, and his wife should entrust him with the letter? Granny had been urgent in telling him to keep clear of the lawyer. But he laughed at his own doubt; for, with the worst intentions, how should Barclay know what it contained? What had he to do with it? The old woman's dislike of him made her take absurd ideas into her head.

Mrs. Somerville placed the letter where it could lean against the clock, and, when the front-door had shut behind him, she settled herself to a comfortable afternoon by the fire; beside her lay the materials for trimming a bonnet, and, within hand-stretch, a small table-cover under which she might hide them at the approach of company. As she had said to Lucilla, she "did not wish to get the name of trimming her own bonnets." Her mind was so full of the object on the mantelpiece that she did not hear a step on the stairs, and, greatly as she desired Barclay's visit, when he was ushered in, she had temporarily forgotten his existence. The bonnet disappeared with a scuffle.

"You are quite a stranger, I declare!" she exclaimed when the lawyer had seated himself.

"Of necessity, Mrs. Somerville—never of inclination. My time has been scarcely my own this week past."

"And upon whom have you bestowed it, pray?"

"Have no fear, ma'am. My own sex is entirely responsible. And I have been making a slight alteration in my house; a trifle, but necessary. I am to lodge my friend Fordyce for the wedding and his best man is coming too—at least, so he tells me. They are feather-brained, these young fellows."

Mrs. Somerville's knowledge was hot within her, and she turned over in her mind how she might begin to unfold it without committing herself.

"It will not be a large affair," continued he, "no one but myself and Mr. Fullarton and a handful of Fordyce's relatives; the bride makes as much pother about her bereavement as if it had happened yesterday. Lady Fordyce is not to be present. I think she has taken such a poor match very much to heart."

"We were invited specially by Miss Raeburn," interposed the lady, who was not averse to playing a trump card when she had one.

Cecilia had personally asked the Inspector to the kirk, and had, perforce, made up her mind to the natural consequence in the shape of his wife; he had been Gilbert's friend, and he felt that his presence would help her through the ordeal.

"Then you will be of the bride's party," observed Barclay, looking superior.

"Yes," replied Mrs. Somerville, settling herself snugly against the back of her chair, "we shall—if there is any bride at all."

He looked at her interrogatively.

"I said, *if there is any bride at all*, Mr. Barclay; and for that matter, I may add, *if there is any wedding either*."

"What is to hinder the wedding? My dear Mrs. Somerville, you puzzle me."

"Ah," she said, nodding her head slowly up and down, "you are right to ask, and I can tell you that *Mr. Speid* may hinder the wedding."

"You are speaking in riddles," said the lawyer. "I may be dull, but I cannot follow you."

"If I tell what I know, you will get me into trouble," she said, shaking her forefinger at him; "there is no trusting you men."

"Surely you will make an exception in my case! What have I done to merit your distrust?"

"Many shocking things, I have no doubt," she replied, archly.

"Ma'am, you are cruel!" he exclaimed, with a languishing look. He could have beaten her, for he was writhing with internal curiosity.

"Well, well; do not take it so to heart," said she, "and promise that you will not betray me. Yesterday, after breakfast, a disreputable person, a Mrs. Stirk, who seems to be known about here—*I* know nothing about her—asked to speak to the Captain. I was sitting at the breakfast-table, but the door was open, so what they said was forced upon me; really *forced upon me*, Mr. Barclay. Mrs. Stirk said that she had seen Miss Raeburn and that she was crying—it was a very improbable story—and that she was breaking her heart for Mr. Speid, she had the impudence to tell the Captain that he should write and bring him home."

Barclay's eyes were almost starting out of his head.

"You may well look surprised," said Mrs. Somerville, "but what will you say when I tell you he has done it? And because a fishwife told him, too! I let him know what an impudent old baggage I thought her, and I got no thanks for my pains, I assure you!"

The lady's voice had risen with each word.

"Written to Speid? Impossible! How does he know where to find him?"

"Miss Robertson is to send the letter. There will be no wedding yet, as I tell you."

"He cannot get home; at any rate, it is very doubtful," said the lawyer, counting on his fingers, "for, by the time he reaches here, Fordyce will be a married man. And he will not stop the marriage, if he comes. Miss Raeburn would never dare to give Fordyce the slip now, for all her high-and-mighty ways."

"But the Captain has written to her too, so she will have plenty of time to make up her mind Look at the letter on the mantelpiece, waiting to be taken to Fullarton. He put it there when he went out."

Barclay sat staring at the missive and arranging his ideas. He wondered how soon he could escape and send news of what he had heard to Fordyce; he hesitated to hurry away at once, for he had not been to see Mrs. Somerville for a long time, and he knew he was expected to sit with her, as he generally did, for at least an hour. One thing was certain; that letter on the mantelpiece should not reach Cecilia if he could help it. The other had gone beyond recall, but he doubted it getting into Speid's hands in time to do much harm. Meantime, there was nothing like prompt action.

"It is rather curious that I should be going to Fullarton to-day; I am on my way there at this moment. I had meant to make you a long visit to-morrow, but I could not resist the temptation of turning in as I passed this door just now. Suppose I were to carry the letter? No good will come of it, I am sure, but, if the Captain wishes it to go, go it must. Can you not persuade him to think better of it?"

"Indeed, if he heard you had been here on your way to Fullarton and I had not sent it, he would be annoyed. But how am I to forgive you for such a niggardly visit? You have hardly been here five minutes."

"By allowing me to pay you a liberal one to-morrow,"
replied the astute Barclay. "I can then assure you of
the safety of the letter. What am I to do? Give me
all directions."

"You are to hand it to Mr. Fullarton and ask him to
address it and send it to Miss Raeburn. It is a very
queer business, is it not?"

"It will smooth down. I attach no importance at all
to it," replied he.

"You are mighty cool about it, seeing that Mr.
Fordyce is such a friend."

"It can come to nothing," said he.

He was determined she should not suspect his feelings,
which were, in reality, tinged with dismay. If Speid
should baffle them still! The letter might reach him in
time and he might easily act upon it. A torrent of
silent abuse was let loose in his heart against Granny
Stirk. He had hated her roundly for some time, and
now he would have given anything to be able to turn
her off the Whanland estate altogether. He promised
himself that he would see what could be done when this
affair of Fordyce's marriage was off his mind.

"Mr. Fordyce should thank me for warning you,"
said Mrs. Somerville, "if he has any sense he will hurry
on the wedding-day after this. Whatever happens, do
not betray me!"

A look in her face suggested to him that she might, in
her heart, suspect what he had in his mind. He would
make sure.

"I suppose I dare not delay this for a day or two?"
he said, tentatively, looking from her to the letter.

"Oh, no! no!" she cried, in alarm. "Oh! what
would happen if anyone found out that I had told
you?"

"I am only joking," he laughed, much relieved,
"pray, pray don't upset yourself, ma'am."

"I really do not know whether I have not done sadly

wrong in speaking," said she, turning her eyes down.
"I have many scruples. My name must never, *never*
be mentioned."

"You insult me, Mrs Somerville, when you talk in
that way. Your name is sacred to me, as it has ever
been, and your action is most timely, most obliging.
I only regret that your own wishes forbid my telling
Fordyce of your kind interest in him—in us, I should
say, for I identify myself with my friends. I am nothing
if not true. You surely, of all people, can give me that
character."

Playfulness returned to her.

"Come, come," she said, "you may go away. I
shall not tell you what I think for fear of making you
vain!"

Barclay left the house with the precious letter in his
pocket; he had come out that afternoon with no intention of going anywhere near Fullarton. On reaching
his own front door he banged it so heartily with the
knocker that his maidservant felt her heart thump too.
She came running to answer the summons.

"Order round the chaise immediately," he cried,
"and see that the fire is kept in till I come back!"

As he stood at the door, waiting for his conveyance to
be brought, he saw the strange one belonging to Captain
Somerville enter the street on its homeward way. He
ran to the gate which opened on the yard behind his
house

"Be quick, can't you!" he roared to the man harnessing the horse.

What he feared he knew not, but the sight of the
Inspector's plaided body sitting under the retrograde
hood of his carriage, like an owl in a hollow tree, made
him long to be clear of the town.

CHAPTER XXVI

ALEXANDER BARCLAY DOES HIS BEST

THOUGH Barclay had no intention of allowing the letter he carried to reach its final destination, he could not venture to stop its course till it had passed Fullarton's hands. He was too much afraid that Somerville and Fullarton might meet within the next few days. The mail office should be responsible for its loss, if that loss were ever discovered; a contingency which he doubted strongly. He found it exceedingly annoying to be obliged to take this farcical drive on such a chilly afternoon, but Prudence demanded the sacrifice and he humoured her, like a wise man. Fordyce's obligations to him were becoming colossal.

He found Fullarton in his library and explained that he was on his way home. He had looked in in passing, he said, to ask him to address a letter which Captain Somerville had given him for Miss Raeburn. He was rather hurried, and would not send his carriage to the stables; if the letter were directed at once, he would take it with him and leave it at the mail office, should it still be open. Robert was not in the humour either for gossip or business and he was glad to be rid of Barclay so easily. He took up his pen at once. In five minutes the lawyer was on his return road to Kaims.

The mail office was closed, as he knew it would be at that time in the evening, and he brought his prize home; to-morrow, though he would take several letters there in person, it would not be among their number.

In its place would be one addressed by himself to the bride-elect and containing a formal congratulation on her marriage. Should inquiry arise, it would be found that he had despatched a letter bearing her name on that day. It was best that the track should lose itself on the further side of the mail office; the rest was in the hands of Providence. It was a badly-patched business, but it was the neatest work he could put together at such short notice.

When the servants had gone to bed and the house was quiet, the lawyer locked himself into his dining-room, where a snug little mahogany table with a suggestive load of comforts stood ready by the arm of his easy-chair. He sat down and took from his pocket the letter he had carried about all the afternoon, reading it through carefully. As he refreshed himself with the port he had poured out he counted again on his fingers. But there was no use in counting; he could come to no conclusion, for it rested purely with accident to decide how soon Captain Somerville's communication should reach Gilbert. If there were no delays, if he were at Madrid or at some place within reach of it, if he made up his mind on the spot, if he could find means to start immediately and met no obstacle on the way— it was possible he might arrive within a few days of the wedding. Then, everything would depend upon Cecilia; and it would need almost superhuman courage for a woman to draw back in such circumstances. He had done a great thing in possessing himself of the paper he held. Little as he knew her, he suspected her to be a person of some character, and there was no guessing what step she might take, were she given time to think. "Hope for the best and prepare for the worst." He was doing this thoroughly.

He emptied his glass, and, with the gold pencil on his fob-chain, made a rough note in his pocket-book of the contents of Somerville's letter; then he crushed the epistle into a ball and stuffed it into the red heart of the coals with the poker, holding it down till it was no more than a flutter of black ash. This over, he wrote Fordyce an account of what he had done. "I am not really apprehensive," he concluded, "but, hurry the wedding, if you can do so on any pretext, and never say that Alexander Barclay did not do his best for you."

Crauford was at Fordyce Castle when the news reached him and it gave him a shock. His ally seemed to be out-running all discretion in his zeal; to stop a letter was such a definitely improper thing to do that it took his breath away. Not that it was his fault, he assured himself as he pondered on it, and it was too late to make any remonstrance; besides which, as he had not personally committed the act, he had nothing with which to blame himself. Things looked serious. In a few days Speid might be on his way home. He would write to Cecilia on the spot; nay, he would go to Edinburgh himself and persuade her to hasten the wedding. He would invent a pretext. It was curious that, while Barclay's act struck him as a breach of gentlemanlike behaviour, it never struck him from Cecilia's point of view, though it was clear she did not want to marry him and that she did want to marry Speid. If it had struck him he would scarcely have understood. She was behaving most foolishly and against her own interests; she did not seem to realise that he had the warmest feelings for her, that he was prepared to make her happy and give her everything she could desire. So great was the complacency—personal and hereditary —in which he had been enveloped since his birth, that he could not see another obvious truth which stared him in the face: namely, that he whose wife has married one man and loves another stands in a place which ought to terrify a demi-god. If he hated Speid now, he might have to hate him still more in time. In his reply to Barclay he did not remonstrate with him;

what was the use of doing so now that the thing was over?

Heartily did he wish the wedding hurried on for many reasons, one of them was that his mother, who had taken to her bed on hearing of his engagement, had now arisen, though her health, she said, would not admit of her leaving Fordyce Castle or being present at the ceremony. Nor were the protests of her family very sincere. Agneta and Mary, who were to go to their uncle, were looking forward feverishly to their first taste of emancipation, and Sir Thomas, having had experience of his wife when in contact with the outer world, thought with small gusto of repeating it. He had insisted that his daughters should go to Fullarton, and no one but himself knew what he had undergone, Lady Fordyce being furious with her brother for having, as she said, arranged the marriage. Everyone agreed that her decision was a merciful one for all concerned, and, while Sir Thomas again "found it convenient" to sit up in his study till the cocks crew, the two girls were supported by the prospect of the coming excitement.

Agneta and Crauford kept much together; but, though she was the only person to whom he could speak with any freedom, he did not tell her what he had heard from Barclay. He was a hero to his sister; and a hero's bride is conventionally supposed to have eyes for no one but himself. Existing conventions were quite good enough for him.

His engagement was scarcely a blow to Lady Maria Milwright; for though, as has been said, he was a hero in her eyes also, she was so simple in character and so diffident that she had never even speculated on his notice. Ideas of the sort were foreign to her. But, as her fingers embroidered the handkerchief-case which she sent him as a wedding-gift, she was overwhelmed with Miss Cecilia Raeburn's good fortune. Agneta was

with him in his room when he unpacked the little parcel
and read the letter it contained.

"I consider that very kind of Lady Maria; very kind
indeed," he said. He did not only consider it kind, he
considered it forgiving and magnanimous.

"I wonder if you will be as happy as if you had married
her?" said his sister, suddenly. "Is Miss Raeburn
devoted to you, Crauford?".

The question took him rather unawares.

"Why do you ask?" inquired he.

"Oh, I don't know. Only she refused you twice, you
know, brother."

"Not twice," said he. "She gave me great encouragement the second time."

"I am sorry it is not to be a grand wedding with lots
of fine company. I should have enjoyed that. But,
all the same, it will be a great change for me and Mary.
Miss Raeburn said we were to choose our own dresses.
Do you know, we have never chosen anything for ourselves before?"

"I am going to Edinburgh to-morrow or the next day
to order my own clothes," said he. "I have chosen
stuffs already. I shall wear claret-coloured cloth with
a buff waistcoat and a satin stock. That ought to
look well, I think."

"We are to wear white, and white fur tippets and
Leghorn bonnets with pink rosettes. Papa gave Mary
the money to pay for what we chose, for mamma would
have nothing to do with it. It is a good thing, for she
would not have given us nearly so much. Will there
really be no one but ourselves and Uncle Fullarton at
the wedding, Crauford?"

"There will be our cousin Frederick Burnfield, who
is to be best man, and my friend Mr. Barclay of Kaims.
He is the Fullarton man of business and a mighty
pleasant fellow Frederick and I are to stay at his
house for the wedding. Then there are a Captain and

Mrs. Somerville whom Miss Raeburn"—he always spoke of Cecilia as "Miss Raeburn," even to his family—"has invited, I cannot understand why; they are dull people, and the lady is not over genteel in her connections, I believe. Morphie Kirk is a very small place for a wedding, but Miss Raeburn has made a particular point of being married there. I often accompanied her to it when Lady Eliza was alive; and I can guess (though she has not told me) that she feels the suitability of our being married there for that reason. It is a pretty feeling on her part," said Crauford.

Her fancy for Speid could not really go very deep, he reflected, as this little sentiment of hers came into his mind. The meddlesome old woman who had brought such a story to Captain Somerville might have known how hysterical women were when there was a question of weddings. Cecilia simply did not know her own mind.

He would see her in Edinburgh and do his best to persuade her to settle a new date for their marriage, even should it be only a few days earlier than the old one. And he would buy her some jewels—they would help on his request.

CHAPTER XXVII

THE SKY FALLS ON GILBERT

GILBERT SPEID sat in the house just outside Madrid, which had represented home to him for most of the eighteen months of his sojourn in Spain; he was newly returned from Granada. It had been Mr. Speid's custom to pass a part of each year there, and it was there that he had, according to his wish, been buried. Gilbert had gone to look at the grave, for the decent keeping of which he paid a man a small yearly sum, and had found his money honestly earned; then, having satisfied himself on that point, he had wandered about in haunts familiar to him in his youth and early manhood. It was not three years since he had set foot in them last, and he was not much more than thirty-two years old, but it seemed to him that he looked at them across a gulf filled with age and time. He returned to Madrid wondering why he had left it, and finding a certain feeling of home-coming in his pleasure at seeing his horses.

He made no pretence of avoiding his fellow-creatures, and no effort to meet them; and as, though he spoke perfect Spanish, he had always been a silent man, there was little difference in his demeanour. But it was universally admitted among old acquaintances that his Scottish life had spoiled him. He rode a great deal and frequented the same company; and he would often stroll down to the fencing-school, where he had learned so much, to practice with his old master or with any new light which had risen among the foils since he left

Spain.   He felt the pressing need of settling to some definite aim in life, but he put off the trouble of considering it from week to week and from month to month.

Miss Hersey wrote only occasionally, for her sight was not good, and the world did not then fly to pens and paper on the smallest pretext as it does now.   A letter was still something of a solemnity, even to the educated. Also, Miss Hersey thought that the sooner he forgot Cecilia the better it would be, and the sooner he would return.   She hoped he would bring back a wife with him—always provided she were not a Roman Catholic. She had told him of Lady Eliza's accident and death and of Cecilia's removal to Fullarton, adding that she understood Miss Raeburn was to remain there until some arrangement could be made for her future; Mr Fullarton was said to have promised Lady Eliza, on her deathbed, that he would act as guardian.

It took nearly a month for a letter from Scotland to reach Madrid, and Gilbert had asked a friend who lived near to take charge of such correspondence as might come for him within a fortnight of his return from Granada.   He had only reached home late on the previous night, and he was now expecting the packet to be brought to him.

He had slept long, being tired, and when he emerged from his room the sun was brilliant.   He walked out on the whitewashed veranda which ran round the upper story of the house, and looked out on the March landscape which the almond-blossom was already decorating. The ground sloped away before him, and, on the northwest, the Sierra de Guardarama cut into the sky.   The pomegranates had not yet begun to flower, but a bush which stood near the walls cast the shadow of its leaves and stems against the glaring white.   In Scotland, the buds would scarcely yet be formed on the trees; but the air would be full of the fresh smell of earth and that stir of life, that first invisible undercurrent of which the body is conscious through a certain sixth sense, would be vibrating. The Lour would be running hard and the spring tides setting up the coast. He stood looking, with fixed eyes, across the almond-blossom to a far-off country that he saw lying, wide and gray, in the north, with its sea-voice calling, calling. His servant's foot-step behind him on the stones made him turn; he was holding out a little packet of letters.

"These have been sent from Don Balthazar's house," said the man, in Spanish, indicating a few tied together with string. "The others were at the mail-office this morning."

Gilbert sat down on the parapet of the veranda and turned over the letters; those that had come from his friend's house must have been awaiting him a week, possibly longer. There were two which interested him, one from Miss Hersey and one directed in a hand he had seen before but could not now identify; it was writing that he connected with Scotland. Miss Robertson's letter was among those which Don Balthazar had kept, and he opened it first. The old lady generally reserved any tidings of Cecilia for the last paragraph, and he forced himself to read steadily from the beginning, for, like many high-strung people, he found an odd attraction in such little bits of self-torture.

Half-way down the last sheet he dropped the paper as though he were shot and the blood ran to his face in a wave. It contained the news of Cecilia Raeburn's engagement; she was to marry Crauford Fordyce, and the wedding was fixed for the middle of April.

He seized the letter again and glutted his eyes with the hateful words.

"You will cease to fret about her now," concluded Miss Hersey simply, "and that will be a good thing. I hear they are to live on a property which belongs to Sir Thomas Fordyce in Roxburghshire. See and get you a wife somewhere else, dear Gilbert, but not a

Papist.   Caroline and I would think very ill of that.''

It was some time before he strung up his mind to read the rest of the correspondence strewn about his feet, but, when he broke the seal of the other Scottish letter, he looked first at the end.   It was signed "Wm. Somerville," and consisted of four closely-written pages. Before he came to the last line he sprang up, feeling as though the sky had fallen on him.   He ran through his room into the passage, shouting at the top of his voice for his servant; the Spaniard came flying up three steps at a time, his dark face pale.   He found Gilbert standing in the middle of the veranda; the scattered letters were blowing about, for a sudden puff of wind had risen.

"Pack up!" he shouted; "get my things ready!   I am going to England!"

"But Señor——"

"Go on!   Begin!   I tell you I am going to England to-night—sooner, if possible!   Bring me my purse. Send to Don Balthazar and tell him that I am going in a few hours."

He took the purse from the astonished man, and in another minute was in the stable and slipping a bridle over one of the horse's heads, while the groom put on the saddle and buckled the girths.   He threw himself into it and galloped straight to the nearest inn and posting-house in the town, for the carriage which had brought him back on the previous night belonged to a small post-master in Toledo and could be taken no further than Madrid

Here he had a piece of disguised good fortune, for, though he could get neither cattle nor conveyance that day, a Spanish Government official was starting for France early on the morrow, and was anxious to hear of some gentleman who might occupy the vacant seat in the carriage he had hired and share the expenses of the road.   In those days, when people travelled armed, any

addition to a party was to be welcomed. It only remained for him to seek his friend Don Balthazar, and,
through him, to procure an introduction to the traveller.
Their ways would lie together as far as Tours.

Don Balthazar was a friend of his youth; a lean,
serious-looking young man who had turned from a
luxuriant crop of wild oats and married a woman with
whom he was in love at this moment, a year after
Gilbert had gone to Scotland. He had never seen
Speid so much excited, and he succeeded in calming
him as the two talked over the details of the journey.
They made out that it would take ten days to reach
Tours, allowing three extra ones for any mishap or
delays which the crossing of the Pyrenees might occasion
In France, the roads would be better and travelling
would improve. Twenty-three days would see him in
Scotland, setting out on the morrow, the fourteenth of
March, he could reasonably expect to get out of the
Edinburgh coach at Blackport on the sixth of April.
The wedding was not to take place until the tenth. He
did not confide in Don Balthazar; he merely spoke of ·
"urgent business."

"Of course it is a woman," said Doña Mercedes to her
husband that night.

"But he never used to care about women," replied he,
stroking his long chin; "at least——"

"Is there *any* man who does not care about women?"
exclaimed the lady, twirling the laced handkerchief she
held; "bring me one and I will give you whatever you
like!"

"That would be useless, if he had seen you," replied
Don Balthazar gallantly.

Doña Mercedes threw the handkerchief at him and
both immediately forgot Gilbert Speid.

It was as if Gilbert lived, moved, and breathed in the
centre of a whirlwind until he found himself sitting in
the carriage by the Spanish official, with Madrid drop-

ping behind him in the haze of morning. Inaction was restful while he could see the road rolling by under the wheels; every furlong was a step nearer his goal. His whole mind had been, so to speak, turned upside down by Captain Somerville's pen He was no longer the lover who had divided himself from his mistress because honour demanded it, but a man who, as the sailor said, was leaving a woman in the lurch; that woman being the one for whom he would cheerfully have died four times a day any time these last two years

The possibility of arriving too late made him shudder; he turned cold as he remembered how nearly he had stayed another ten days in Granada while this unforeseen news lay waiting for him at Don Balthazar's house. He had a margin of some days to his credit, should anything check his journey, and, once beyond the Pyrenees, progress would be quicker. If delay should occur on this side of Toulouse, he could there separate himself from his companion and drive by night as well as by day, for he would be on the main posting-road through France.

He had not written to Cecilia. He would travel nearly as fast as the mail and a letter would precede his arrival only by a very short space There had been no time, in the hurried moments of yesterday, to write anything to her which could have the weight of his spoken words; and, were his arrival expected, he feared the pressure that Fordyce, and possibly Fullarton, would bring to bear upon her before she had the support of his presence. He did not know what influences might be surrounding her, what difficulties hedging her about; his best course was simply to appear without warning, take her away and marry her. He might even bring her back to Spain. But that was a detail to be considered afterwards

He remembered the sudden admission he had made to Granny Stirk in her cottage, and told himself that some unseen divinity must have stood by, prompting him. How little did he suspect of the sequel to that day on which he had caught Lady Eliza's mare; how unconscious he was of the friend standing before him in the person of the little old woman who offered him her apron to dry his hands and said "haste ye back" as he left her door. He had written her a few lines, directing her to go to Whanland and get his room ready, and adding that he wished his return kept secret from everyone but Jimmy, who was to meet the Edinburgh coach at Blackport on the sixth of April. He had no horses in Scotland which could take him from Blackport to Whanland, but he would be able to hire some sort of conveyance from the inn, and, on the road home, he could learn as much as possible of what was happening from the lad. His letter would, in all probability, arrive a day or so in advance of himself, and Granny Stirk would have time to send her grandson to meet him and make her own preparations. Though the Queen of the Cadgers could not read, Jimmy, who had received some elementary schooling, was capable of deciphering his simple directions.

It was eight days after leaving Madrid that the fellow-travellers parted at Tours, having met with no delay beyond the repairing of a wheel, which had kept them standing in a wayside village for a couple of hours, and the almost impracticable nature of the roads in the Pyrenees. The official had called in the help of his Government in the matter of post-horses to the frontier, and these, though often miserable-looking brutes, were forthcoming at every stage Owing to the same influence, a small mounted escort awaited them as they approached the mountains; and the Spaniard's servants, who occupied a second carriage and had surfeited themselves with tales—only too well founded—of murders and robberies committed in that part of the country, breathed more freely.

It was with rising spirits that Speid bade his companion farewell, and, from the window of the inn at which they had passed the night, watched his carriage roll away on the Paris road; he had hired a decent chaise, which was being harnessed in the courtyard below to start on the first stage of its route to Havre, and he hoped to embark from that seaport in three days.

Of the future which lay beyond his arrival at Whanland he scarcely allowed himself to think, nor did he arrange any definite plan of action. Circumstances should guide him completely and what information he could get from Jimmy Stirk. He had no doubt at all of Cecilia's courage, once they should meet, and he felt that in him which must sweep away every opposition which any one could bring. He would force her to come with him. There were only two people in the world—himself and the woman he loved—and he was ready, if need be, to go to the very altar and take her from it. She had cried out and the echo of her voice had reached him in far-away Spain. Now, there was no power on earth which should stand before him.

So he went on, intent on nothing but the end of his journey; looking no further; and holding back from his brain, lest it should overwhelm him, the too-intoxicating thought that, in a couple of weeks, she might be his.

When, at last, from a point of rising ground a few miles from the seaboard, he saw the waters of the English Channel, his heart leaped. He drove into Havre just at sunset on the evening of the twenty-fifth of March. Six days later he was in London.

He had hoped to reach it earlier, but it was with the greatest difficulty that he was able to get a passage to Portsmouth; he had crossed to England in a wretched fishing-boat, and that bad weather, predicted on the French shore and only risked by the boat's owner for a large sum of money, met and delayed him.

He saw the dark mass of Edinburgh Castle rising from the lights of the town on the second evening after his departure from London; the speech which surrounded the coach, as it drew up, made him realise, with a thrill, that now, only two divisions of his journey lay between him and Blackport—Blackport where he would meet Cecilia. Next morning found him on the road to Perth, where he was to sleep that night.

The weather was cold and gusty on the last day of his travels, and the Tay, as they crossed it after leaving Perth, yellow and swollen; but the familiar wide fields and the distant wall of the Grampians stirred his heart with their promise. The road ran up the Vale of Strathmore, northeast of the Sidlaws; as their undulations fell away they would stretch to Kaims and the sea, and he would once more be in that enchanted spot of land where the North Lour ran and the woods of Morphie unrolled themselves across its seaward course.

The last change of horses was at Forfar; from there they were to run through the great moor of Monrummon into Blackport, where they would be due at eight o'clock. If he could secure anything which had wheels from one of the posting-houses, he would sleep that night at Whanland.

The passengers buttoned their coats tightly as they went forward, for the weather was growing worse and the wind came tearing in their faces. Before darkness fell, fringes of rain-cloud, which had hung all day over the Grampians, began to sweep over them. The horses laid back their ears as heavy drops, mixed with hail, struck them in sensitive places and the coachman's hands were stiff on the reins from the chill water running off his gloves. Now and again the gale raised its voice like an angry woman, and the road reflected the lamps as though it had been a pond. They had left Forfar some time when the coachman, in the darkness, turned a hard, dripping face to Gilbert, who was on the box-seat.

"D'ye hear yon?" he said, lifting his whip.

Speid leaned his head sideways and was conscious of a roar above the voice of the blast; a tossing and rolling sea of noise in the air which he thought must be like the sound of waves closing above the head of a drowning man. It was the roar of the trees in Monrummon.

As the coach plunged in, the dark ocean of wood swallowed it up, and it began to rock and sway on one of the bad roads intersecting the moor. The smell of raw earth and wet heather was mixed with the strong scent of the firs that laboured, surged, buffeted overhead in the frenzy of the wind. The burns that, in places, crossed their road had now become turgid torrents, dragging away soil and stones in their rush.

"It'll na' do to loss oursel's here," observed the coachman. "Haud up, man!"

The last exclamation was addressed to the off wheeler, who had almost slipped on a round stone laid bare by the water flaying the track. The only inside passenger, a West-country merchant on his way north, let down the window and put out his head, to draw it in promptly, outraged by finding himself in such surroundings and by the behaviour of the elements outside. Such things did not happen in Glasgow.

It was when they were on the middle of the moor that the bed of a burn, steeper than any they had yet encountered, crossed their way. It was not much wider than an ordinary ditch, but the force of the water driven through it had scored the bottom deep, for the soil was soft in its course. The coachman had his team well together as they went down the slope to it, and Gilbert watched him, roused from his abstraction by the fascinating knowledge that a man of parts was handling the reins. The feet of the leaders were clear of the water and those of the wheelers washed by the red swirl in the burn's bed, when the air seemed to rush more quickly a few yards to their left, and, with a crack like that of the sky splitting, the heavy head of a fir-tree came tearing downwards through its fellows.

The terrified horses sprang forward up the steep ground; the coach staggered like a drunkard; the pole dipped, rocking upwards, and the pole-chains flashed in the light of the swinging lamps as it snapped in two.

The traces held, for they reached the further side almost by their own impetus, and the guard was at the leaders' heads before the Glasgow merchant had time to let down his window, and, with all the righteous violence of the arm-chair man, to launch his reproaches at the driver; Gilbert climbed down and began to help the guard to take out the leaders. The coachman sat quietly in his place.

"Well, well; we'll just need to bide whaur we are," he said, as the swingle-trees were unhooked.

By the light of the lamps, the pole was found to be broken, slantwise, across the middle, and there was nothing for the passengers to do but make the best of their position and await the morning. The gale continued to rage; and, though the guard declared it possible to lash the breakage together and proceed carefully by daylight, such an attempt would be out of the question in the state of the roads, while the storm and darkness lasted. The two other outside passengers, one of whom was a minister, were an honest pair of fellows, and they accepted the situation as befitted men of sense.

The window of the coach went down and the Glasgow man's head appeared. He had tied up his face in a woollen handkerchief with large red spots. The ends rose above his head like rabbit's ears.

"You'll take me to the end of my journey or I'll ken the reason!" he shouted to the little group. "I've paid my money to get to Aberdeen and it's there I'm to go!"

Guard and coachman smiled, the former broadly and

the latter at the side of his mouth. Neither said anything.

"My name's George Anderson, and I'm very well acquaint wi' you!" roared the inside passenger in the voice of one who has discovered a conspiracy.

He had never seen any of the party till that morning, but he did not seem to mind that.

"The pole is broken, sir. You can see it for yourself if you will come out," said Gilbert, going up to the coach.

"Na, thank ye. I'm best whaur I am," said the man.

The smile now extended to the minister and his companion, and, at sight of this, the merchant burst into fresh wrath.

"Am I to be kept a' the night in this place?" he cried. "I warrant ye, I'll have the lot o' ye sorted for this when I get to Aberdeen!"

"If you like to ride one of the leaders into Blackport, you can," suggested Gilbert, with a sting in his voice; "the guard is going with the mails on the other."

"Aye, ye'd best do that. Ye'd look bonnie riding into the town wi' yon thing on your head," said the minister, who had a short temper.

The window went up.

The united efforts of Speid and his four companions succeeded in getting the coach to one side of the way, and three of the horses were tied up, its shelter between them and the weather; the Glasgow merchant remained inside while they moved it. The rain was abating and there were a few clear patches in the sky, as, with the mail-bags slung round him, the guard mounted the fourth horse and prepared to ride forward.

"If you can find a boy called Stirk at the inn," said Gilbert, "tell him to wait for me in Blackport till morning." And he put some money in the man's hand.

The guard touched his cap and disappeared.

It was a long night to Speid. The three passengers

built themselves a shelter with luggage and rolled themselves in what wraps and rugs they had; not one of them
had any desire to share the inside of the coach with its
occupant. The ground was too damp to allow a fire
to burn and what wood lay at the roadside was dripping.
In a few hours the guard returned with such tools as
he could collect; the road improved further on, he said,
and the remaining six miles of the stage could be done
at a walk after the sun rose. He had seen nothing of
Jimmy Stirk. He and the coachman joined the party
in the shelter.

Gilbert, unsleeping, lay with his eyes on the sky;
though he had been much tempted to go on with the
guard, he would have gained little by doing so; his
choice of a night's lodging must be between Blackport
or Monrummon, and, under the circumstances, one
place was intolerable as the other.

CHAPTER XXVIII

AGNETA ON THE UNEXPECTED

GILBERT was wrong in supposing he would arrive in Scotland on the very heels of his letter, for it reached Granny Stirk's hands three days before the night which ended, for him, on Monrummon Moor. Jimmy, who had brought it from Kaims in the evening, spelt it out successfully by the firelight.

The old woman sat, drowned in thought, her fiery eyes on the flame; she could not understand why Cecilia had made no response to what Captain Somerville had written, for she had seen him on the previous day and was aware that no word had come from Edinburgh. Though she knew that Barclay had carried the letter to Fullarton, she had no suspicion that he had tampered with it, imagining her action and that of the sailor unknown to anyone. How should Barclay guess its contents? Also, she had no notion to what extent he was in Fordyce's confidence, or what a leading part he had played in the arrangement of the marriage. Instinct and the remembrance of his visit to her were the only grounds for the distrust with which she looked upon him.

She had not doubted Cecilia's sincerity and she did not doubt it now; but, unlike Gilbert, she was beginning to doubt her courage. She was in this state of mind when she heard that the wedding day was changed from the tenth to the seventh of the month; Speid would only arrive on the evening before the ceremony. The matter had gone beyond her help, and she could not

285

imagine what the upshot would be. But, whatever might come of it, she was determined to play her own part to the end. Early to-morrow morning she would send Jimmy to Kaims to tell the sailor of the news she had received, and Macquean should go, later, to get a few provisions for Whanland; she, herself, would have a field-day in the laird's bedroom with mops and dusters and see that his sheets were "put to the fire."

Meanwhile, at Fordyce Castle, events, almost equal to a revolutionary movement in significance, had taken place. Like many another tyrant, Lady Fordyce, once bearded, began to lose the hold which custom had given her over the souls and bodies of her family. Sir Thomas had, for the first time, established another point of view in the house, and its inmates were now pleased and astonished to learn that they survived. That kind of knowledge is rarely wasted. One result of the new light was that Agneta was allowed to accompany Crauford to Edinburgh, where she was to try on her brides-maid's costume, report upon Mary's, and make acquaintance with her future sister-in-law.

The sight of Cecilia was a revelation to Agneta. The hide-bound standards of home had not prepared her to meet such a person on equal terms and she knew herself unable to do so creditably; the remembrance of Mary's suggestion that they might "give her hints" on the doing of her hair, and such-like details, made her feel inclined to gasp. Cecilia suggested something selected, complicated, altogether beyond her experience of life and outside her conception of it. Crauford, to whom this was evident, looked on triumphantly.

"Well?" he began, as they returned together to their lodging in George Street.

"She is *quite* different from what I expected, brother —quite different."

"Did I not tell you so?" he exclaimed.

"You did—you did; but I did not understand. No

more will Mary till she has seen her.   I am afraid she will astonish Mama dreadfully."

Fordyce chuckled.   The thought of his mother had never made him chuckle before.   But times were changing.

"I shall write to Mary to-morrow," continued Agneta. "Crauford, I can quite understand about the gentleman who went to Spain."

At this her brother's smile faded, for the words made him think of the gentleman who might be returning from Spain.   As soon as possible he must address himself to the task before him, namely, that of persuading Cecilia to make the wedding-day a fortnight earlier.

At the risk of wearying the reader, who has followed this history through letters, fragments of letters, receipts of letters, and even suppression of letters, Agneta's somewhat ungrammatical sentiments must be given.

"MY DEAR MARY" (she wrote),

"I do not know what Mama will say.   We have arrived safe and waited upon Cousin Maitland where Miss Raeburn is staying.   She is *not at all* like what we imagined.   You said we could perhaps teach her how to do her hair, but it is most *beautifully done*, and she has a lovely tortoiseshell comb handsomer than Lady Maria's. She is not at all shy, even with Crauford, but she was most obliging and polite to him and to me too.   Cousin Maitland says she thinks she likes her better than any young lady she ever saw.   I don't know what Mama will say, because I am quite sure Miss Raeburn will not be afraid of her, for she looks as if she were not afraid of anybody or cared for anybody very much, not even Crauford.   He told me she was very fond of flowers, but I think he must be mistaken, for he brought her some roses that were *ever so expensive* at this time of the year and she thanked him nicely but she never looked at them after she had put them down.   Cousin Maitland is a very odd person; her chin and nose nearly meet and she wears long earrings and said a lot of clever things I did not understand. She has an enamel snuff-box with rather a shocking picture on it. It is very nice being on a journey alone and ringing the bell when I want anything, but Jane forgot to bring my best slippers, which is tiresome, as we are to dine with Cousin Maitland to-morrow. Give my love and respects to our father and mother and also from Crauford. I send my love to you.

"Your affectionate sister,

"AGNETA FORDYCE.

"P.S.—She has the *loveliest* feet."

All the arguments and persuasions which Crauford could bring to bear on his bride did not avail to shorten the time before the marriage by a fortnight, for the dress-makers at work upon her very modest trousseau declared themselves unable to finish it by that date, and Cecilia was thankful for their objections. He had dressed up some bogey of family convenience which he held up before her, but, by aid of its ministrations, he was only able to knock off three days from the interval and fix the occasion for the seventh instead of the tenth of April. He wrote to Barclay, apprising him of the change.

When the time arrived by which some result of Somerville's letter might reasonably be expected, the lawyer was constant in his inquiries at the mail office. As no sign came, he determined to drive out to Whanland and question Macquean, for he thought that if Gilbert contemplated a sudden return the man in charge of the house would scarcely be ignorant of it.

It was on the second day preceding Speid's intended arrival that he set out for this purpose, and, at the outskirts of the town, observed the person he wished to see approaching with the vacillating but self-satisfied gait peculiar to him. Rather to his surprise, Macquean made a sign to the coachman to stop.

"Have ye heard the news?" he asked abruptly, his large mouth widening

"What news?" cried the lawyer, leaning far out of his chaise.

"The Laird's to be hame, no the morn's morn, but the morn ahint it."

"Has he written?"

"Granny got a letter a day syne. She bad' me no tell, but a' didna mind the auld witch. A' kent fine the Laird wad need to tell ye."

"Quite right!" exclaimed Barclay, with fervour. "That old she-devil is beyond endurance."

A descriptive epithet that cannot be written down broke from Macquean.

"What time do you expect Mr. Speid, late or early?"

"He'll no be at Blackport or aicht o'clock Friday first, an' gin the coach is late, it'll be nine. A'm thinking he'll likely bide a' night i' the toon an' come awa' hame i' the morn. A'm awa' now to see and get proveesions."

The lawyer had other business on hand, so, after a few more words with Macquean, he drove on; the servant continued his way into Kaims.

This was ill news. Barclay had played Crauford's game for so long that it had almost become his own, and he felt like a child who sees signs of imminent collapse in the sand-castle which has stood almost to the turn of the tide. Only three more days and baffled, probably, by an old woman's pestilent interference! If Speid had left Spain in such a hurry it was not likely that he meant to have all his trouble for nothing, and, if no delay should occur on his road, he would arrive just fifteen hours too early. It was a close business.

For all his oiled and curled appearance, his fat hands and his servility, there was something of the man of action about Barclay. Also, he was endlessly vindictive. The idea of Gilbert triumphing at the eleventh hour was as bitter as gall, and he resolved, while he sat looking

like a hairdresser's image in the chaise, that no strong
measure he could invent should be lacking to frustrate
him.   As far as Crauford was concerned he had a free
hand and he would use it freely.   Suggestions boiled in
his brain.   To delay Speid in Blackport on the night he
arrived would be advantageous, and if he could only
delay him till the following noon all would be well.

He ran mentally over every possibility.   Suppose, as
Macquean had said, the coach should not be up to time
and the traveller should come no further that night, he
would scarcely start for home before nine on the next
day.   At ten, or thereabouts, he would reach Whanland, and, by a few minutes past eleven, Fordyce would
be married to Cecilia.   Everything fitted in so nearly
that, assuming that it should arrive late—as it usually
did—the slightest delay would settle the matter.

By the time he had alighted at his own door he had
made up his mind to send a mounted messenger at once
to Blackport, and, in Fordyce's name, to secure every
post-horse to be had at the two posting-houses in the
town.   The pretext should be the conveyance of wedding
spectators to Morphie; the animals should be brought to
Kaims early next morning.   In the afternoon, the
bridegroom was to arrive as his guest, with his best man,
and he would tell him what he had done.   His approval
was a foregone conclusion.

Should the coach come in punctually, or should Gilbert hear, in Blackport, that the wedding was to take
place at once, his plan might yet miscarry.   The chances
were almost even, he told himself; there were other
horses, no doubt, which could be begged, borrowed, or
stolen by a man determined to get forward, but there
would be a delay in finding them and that delay might be
the turning-point.   Macquean had not informed Barclay
that Jimmy Stirk was to meet Gilbert, for the simple
reason that he did not know it himself; Speid had asked
Granny to say nothing to any person of his coming, so,

though obliged to tell him to make preparations at Whanland, she had entered into no details.   She had mentioned the day and hour he was expected at Blackport
and that was all.

CHAPTER XXIX

THE next day broke cold and stormy and driving rain sped past the windows of the Stirks' cottage. In the morning Jimmy set out, having decided to go afoot and to return with Gilbert in whatever vehicle he should accomplish the last stage of his way home. As the day went on the old woman's restlessness grew, and, by afternoon, her inaction, while so much was pending, grew intolerable to her. She opened the back door and looked out seaward to where a patch of ragged light broke the flying clouds. This deceitful suggestion of mending weather decided her on the action for which she was hankering. To Kaims she would go. Captain Somerville might, even now, have received some word from Cecilia, and in any case the sight of his face would soothe her agitated mind. Her heart was so deep in what was going on that she was at the mercy of her own nerves so long as she was unable to act; and to-day there was not even her grandson to distract her mind. The man's more enviable part was his.

It was seldom, now, that she drove herself, and it was years since she had harnessed a horse. She wrapped her body in her thick, gray plaid, pinning it tightly round head and shoulders, and went out to the shed where Rob Roy was dozing peacefully in the straw, in false expectation of a holiday. Almost before he had time to realise what she wanted, she got him on his legs, pushed the collar over his astonished face, and led him out across the windy yard, to where the cart stood in a sheltered corner. In a few minutes she was turning his head toward Kaims.

The rain held off as she splashed down the road, and, at the bridge, the North Lour ran hard and heavy under her; the beeches round Whanland House were swaying their upper branches when she passed, as seaweeds sway in a pool at the in-running tide. She drove straight to the Black Horse in the High Street, for, behind the inn-yard, was a tumbledown shanty, where carriers, cadgers, and such of the lower classes as went on wheels, might stable their carts when they came to the town. The grander accommodation, which had the honour of harbouring the chaises and phaëtons of the gentry, was on the inner side of the wall. When she had left Rob Roy she walked to the Inspector's house and was admitted. She was ushered straight into the Captain's presence; he sat in his study, dressed for the road, for he had duty near Garviekirk. The expression he wore was one unusual to him.

"I have made a discovery, Mrs. Stirk," he said, abruptly. "The letter I wrote to Miss Raeburn never reached her. She has not received it."

Her eyes seemed to pierce him through; he turned his face away.

"I am a good deal distressed," he continued—"I did not suppose that—those one associated with—did such things."

"It's Barclay!" exclaimed Granny.

"We cannot be quite certain," he went on, "so the less we say about it the better. He was asked to carry it to Fullarton and I have reason to know that it never reached Miss Raeburn. I have spoken quite freely to you; as you have identified yourself with this affair, I felt I should not keep anything back from you. I am sick at heart, Mrs. Stirk—sick at heart."

His expression was blurred by a dull suffering.

"Fegs! ye needna fash about the likes o' him,

sir! I warrant ye it's no the first clortie* job he's done!"

"It is painful," said he.

There was more than the Queen of the Cadgers could fathom in the honest man's trouble; more lying on his heart, as he drove away down the street, than she, looking after him, could guess. The sordid knowledge of his wife's nature had been with him for years, shut behind bars through which he would not glance, like some ignoble Caliban. That morning he had been forced to look the hateful thing in the face.

A letter had come to Mrs. Somerville from Cecilia, directing her to the private entrance at Morphie Kirk. "I hope Captain Somerville is well," was its conclusion; "with the exception of a note of congratulation from Mr. Barclay, I have heard nothing of anyone at Kaims since I left Fullarton."

Mrs. Somerville had read it aloud, stopping suddenly in the middle of the last sentence, remembering Barclay's semi-jocular suggestion of delaying the letter, and turned scarlet. She was apt, in difficulties, to lose her head.

"I'm sure it is no fault of Mr. Barclay's!" she exclaimed. "I told him how urgent it was."

"*What?*" exclaimed the Inspector, turning in his chair.

Then, seeing how she had incriminated herself, she had plunged into explanations. The door had been ajar —she had been unable to help hearing what Mrs. Stirk had said on the day when he had written to Miss Raeburn—the words had *forced* themselves on her. It was not her fault. She had never moved from where he had left her sitting at the breakfast-table.

Somerville looked squarely at his wife. The door had not been ajar, for he had fastened it carefully, as he

* Dirty.

always did before hearing private business. He remembered doing so, perfectly.

"It was not ajar," he said, in a voice she had rarely heard; "it was shut. And it is impossible to hear between the two rooms."

"I always did hate that old woman!" cried Mrs. Somerville, her face in a flame, "and why you ever let her into the house I never did know! I'm sure if Lucilla were here she would take my part. And now to be accused of——"

"What have I accused you of?" asked her husband. "I have not accused you yet. But I will. I accuse you of telling that hound, Barclay, what you heard, and, if I sit here till to-morrow, I will have every word you have betrayed."

Piece by piece he dragged from her her treachery; evasions, tears, lies, he waded through them all. Furious and frightened, what confidences of Barclay's she had, she divulged also. At the end he had risen painfully and left the room.

The sailor was a hot-headed, hot-hearted man. He had no proof against the lawyer and he knew it; but he believed him capable of anything and was prepared to maintain his belief.

"You may tell Barclay," he said, as he paused at the door, "that I have no proof against him but my own conviction If he can prove me wrong I will apologise humbly—publicly, if he pleases. But, until that day, if he ventures to enter my house while I can stand, I will turn him out of it with my cane."

When Granny Stirk had done a few matters of business in Kaims, she went down the side-street to the back premises of the Black Horse. Before her, a figure battled with the wind that rushed down the tunnel of houses, and as he turned into the yard gate she saw that this person was none other than Barclay. He went in without observing her, and called to a man who was idling among the few vehicles which stood empty about the place. She continued her way round the outside wall to the spot where she had left Rob Roy, and untied the rope by which he was tethered. Above, a large hole in the stonework let out a strong stable smell from the row of dark stalls built against its inner face. The occasional movement of horses mixed with the voices of two people who were walking along the line of animals together.

"Yon's them," said one of the unseen individuals, as a scraping of boots on the flags suggested that the pair had come to a standstill under the aperture.

"Now, how many are there exactly?" inquired the voice of Barclay.

"That'll be sax frae the Crown an' four frae the Boniton Arms—they've just got the four in now. Them's the twa grays at the end; an' other twa's up yonder, the brown, an' yon brute wi' the rat-tail."

"Are you quite certain that these are all that can be had? Mind you, I want every single beast secured that is for hire in Blackport."

His companion made a small, semi-contemptuous sound.

"That michtna be sae easy," he replied. "Whiles there may be a naig I dinna ken i' the toun—what are ye wantin' wi' sic a lot, sir?"

His tone implied more of the practical than the inquisitive, but the lawyer cut him short.

"That's my affair," he replied. "My order is plain enough, surely. I want every horse that is for hire in the town secured and brought here—*every horse*, mind you. And by eight o'clock to-night they must be out of Blackport—here, that is."

The trace which Granny was hooking slipped through her fingers, and she stood, open-mouthed, while the footsteps of the speakers died away. It did not take her a moment to draw the right inference; if the lawyer had mentioned Fordyce's name she might not have understood so easily what was going forward; but he had spoken as though the order had emanated from himself, and Granny, on the other side of the wall, had a burning lamp of wrath in her soul which illuminated his deed.

It was almost half-past five, and in less than three hours Gilbert would arrive at Blackport to find that there was no available means of getting further. She knew him well enough to be sure he would start on foot, if need be, so soon as he should learn from Jimmy of what was to happen on the morrow; but, meanwhile, here was Rob Roy, at the end of the reins she held, and what belonged to the Stirk family belonged also to the Laird of Whanland so long as she had breath to say so. She got into her place and drove carefully out of the narrow gate into the street. It was scarcely time for the light to fail, but the sky was dark with rain-cloud and the weather rolling in from a wild sea that was booming up the coast. She cared for none of these things; inland, eight miles off, lay Blackport, and, in less than an hour, she would be there with a horse.

Where the side-street met the High Street, an archway joined the inn buildings to the opposite houses, and, under it, she observed Barclay taking shelter from the sudden squall of rain which had come up in the last few minutes. Beneath its further end, across the way, stood two loafers, one of whom she recognised as a cadger whose cart was now unharnessed in the yard. Though his days in the trade had begun long after her own had ended, she knew something about him; principally, that rumour connected him with a Blackport poaching gang which had been active in the preceding year. He looked at her as she approached and sent an obscene word to meet her, but she neither heard nor heeded, for her attention was set on the lawyer whom she was about to pass.

"Where are you bound for?" called Barclay.

Her eyes flamed.

"Ah! ye deevil!" she cried, "a' heard ye! Look! Here's a horse that'll be in Blackport the nicht!"

Before she was through the arch Barclay realised that she must have been near him in the yard. By what chance she had understood his business there he knew not—had not time to guess. He turned livid.

"Stop her!" he shouted to the two men as he made a futile dash after the cart.

The cadger on the opposite pavement sprang forward.

"Go on!" roared the lawyer, "go on, man! Stop her! Stop her!"

Granny struck Rob Roy sharply and he plunged into his collar. The cadger sprang at his head, but the horse swerved, and his hand fell on the rein just behind the rings of the pad. There was a curse and a rattle; like a snake the whip-tong curled in the air and came down across his face, with a hissing cut that Barclay could hear where he stood, and, as the man fell back, his hands to his eyes, the gallant old woman swung out into the middle of the street.

"Go on! Go after her! Five pounds if you can stop her! Ten!" yelled Barclay.

"Awa' ye go and get yer cairt!" cried the friend who had been standing with the cadger.

At the mention of money the man took his hands from his face; a red wale lay across it and the water poured from his eyes.

"He's got a cairt yonder i' the yaird!" cried the friend again.

"Quick then!" shouted Barclay, seizing him. "If you stop that hell-cat getting to Blackport to-night you shall get ten pounds, and I'll see you come to no harm. Run!"

At this moment Granny, going at a smart trot, turned to look back, for she was not yet out of sight; she saw the cadger pushed toward the inn by Barclay, she saw

him run back under the arch, and she understood. She
sat down in her place, her heel against the footboard,
and let the lash float out on Rob Roy's shoulder. She
knew the value of a good start.

Showers of mud flew behind her as the little horse's
hoofs smote the earth in the fast, steady trot to which
she kept him. The east wind almost hurled her out of
her seat as she passed the fringe of the town, for she was
going north, and it came in from the sea, not half a mile
off, with a violence that blew Rob Roy's mane stiffly out
from his neck. At the further side of Kaims flowed the
South Lour, making a large tidal lake west of it; along
the north side of this estuary the Blackport road ran,
straight, but for certain indecisive bends; practically
level for eight miles. As she turned along it and found
the blast at her back she increased her pace. Not far
in front the way dipped, and a sluggish stream which
drained the fields on her right hand ran under a low,
stone bridge into the marsh which edged the "Basin of
Kaims," as the semi-salt lake was called. The wind
had whipped the water into small waves, for it was high
tide and the swirl almost invaded her path; a couple of
gulls, tilted sideways on outspread wings, were driven
over her head. The sound of the crawling water was
drowned in the gale which was growing steadily. She
pressed on, the horse well in hand, till she reached the
summit of the rise half a mile ahead and pulled up for a
moment in the shelter of a broken wall. Turning, she
strained her eyes into the dusk, and, remote from the
undercurrent of the water's voice, on the following wind
there came to her the distant beat of hoofs.

She was old, her body's strength was on the wane, but
the fire of her spirit was untouched, as it would be until
Death's hand, which alone could destroy it, should find
her out. Though she knew herself face to face with a
task which needed more than the force she could bring
to it, though her body was cold in the rain and the hands

which steered her were aching, her heart leaped in her
as she pulled Rob Roy together and cried to him in the
wind.   The Queen of the Cadgers was on the road again.

O faithful hands that have wrought here; that have
held sword, or plough, or helm!   O fighters, with souls
rising to the heavy odds, nerves steadying to the shock
whose force you dare, unrecking of its weight!   What
will you do in the eternity when there will be no cause
to fight for, no Goliath of Gath, twice your size, to sally
forth against with sling and stone?   In that paradise
that we are promised, where will be your place?   We
cannot tell.   But, if there be a just God who made your
high hearts, He will answer the question whose solution
is not for us.

The next three miles were almost level and she drove
on steadily; she had seen her pursuer's nag in the Black
Horse yard, a hairy-heeled bay with a white nose who
looked as if he had already travelled some distance.
Rob Roy had been little out of late and the cart was
empty; indeed, it was light enough to be a precarious
seat for a woman of her age.   By the time she had done
half her journey it had become dark enough to make
caution necessary, for few country travellers carried
lights in those days, and she was on the highroad which
took an eastward sweep to the coast between Perth and
Aberdeen.   She stopped once more to listen and give
Rob Roy his wind; for the last half mile they had come
up a gradual ascent whose length made up for its gentle
slope.   He did not seem distressed and the gale had
helped him, for it was almost strong enough behind him
to blow the cart forward without his efforts.

On again, this time a little faster; the solid blackness
of the fields slid by and she passed a clump of trees, creak-
ing and swaying over a patch of light which she knew to
be a mill-pond.   Three miles more, and she might climb
down from her place to rest her stiffened limbs, before
the Laird should be due and she should go to the door of

the Crown to wait for his coming. She almost wondered whether it were her imagination which had seen the cadger run back at Barclay's instigation, whether she had dreamed of the horse's feet pursuing her near the Basin of Kaims. She let Rob Roy walk.

Her hair was blowing over her face and she pushed back her soaking plaid to twist it behind her ears. In a momentary lull, a clatter of hoofs broke upon her and voices answered each other, shouting. Either her enemy was behind with some companion of his own kidney, or there were others abroad to-night with whom time was precious; she could hear the wheels grind on a newly-mended piece of road she had crossed. A cottage, passed in blind darkness, suddenly showed a lamp across the way, and, as the driver behind her crossed the glaring stream which it laid over his path, she saw the hairy-heeled bay's white nose swing into the strong light to be swallowed again by the dark. She took up her whip.

Hitherto, she had saved her horse, but now that there were only three miles to be covered she would not spare for pace. How the white-nosed beast had crept so close she could not imagine, until it occurred to her that the evil short cut taken by herself on a memorable occasion, years ago, must have served his driver too. She laid the whip remorselessly on Rob Roy.

Fortunately for her aching bones, the road improved with its proximity to the town, or she could scarce have kept her seat. As it was, she could not see the stones and irregularities in her way, and it might well be that some sudden jerk would hurl her headlong into the gaping dark. But she dared not slacken speed; she must elude her pursuer before reaching the first outlying houses, for, were her haven in Blackport discovered, she knew not what foul play he might set afoot. She resolved that she would not leave Rob Roy until he was in Gilbert's hands, could she but get the cart into the tumble-down premises of the friend whom she trusted, and for

whose little backyard behind River Street she determined to make. Blackport was a low place, and her
friend, who kept a small provision-shop, was a widow
living alone. Suppose she should be discovered! Suppose, after all, she should fail! What Barclay had said
to the cadger whose wheels she could now hear racing
behind she did not know, but his action in securing the
post-horses and in sending such a character after her
showed that he was prepared to go to most lengths to
frustrate Speid. She had known of men who lamed
horses when it suited them; the thought of what might
happen made her set her teeth. She remembered that
there was a long knife inside the cart, used by her grandson for cleaning and cutting up fish; if she could reach
her destination it should not leave her hand; and, while
Rob Roy had a rest and a mouthful in the hour or two
she might have to wait for Gilbert, her friend should run
to the Crown and tell Jimmy where she was to be found.
With a pang she renounced the joy of meeting the Laird;
her place would be behind the locked door with her horse.

Past hedge and field they went, by gates and stone-
heaps. Her head·was whirling and she was growing
exhausted. She could no more hear the wheels behind
for the roaring of the wind and the rattle of her own cart.
She had never driven behind Rob Roy on any errand
but a slow one, and it was long years since she had been
supreme on the road; but old practice told her that it
would take a better than the hairy-heeled bay to have
lived with them for the first two miles. A crooked tree
that stood over the first mile-stone out of Blackport was
far behind them and the gable end of the turnpike cottage cut the sky not twenty yards ahead.

She had forgotten the toll, and, for one moment, her
stout heart failed. But for one moment only; for the
gate stood open. She could faintly distinguish the white
bars thrust back. A lantern was moving slowly toward
them; probably some vehicle had just gone by, and the

toll-keeper was about to close them. With a frantic effort, she leaned forward and brought the whip down with all her strength on Rob Roy's straining back. Their rush carried them between the posts, just before the lantern-bearer, from whom the wind's noise had concealed their approach, had time to slam the gate, shouting, behind them.

In a couple of minutes her pursuer drove up, to find the swearing toll-keeper threatening him and all his kind from behind the closed bars. In half an hour Rob Roy stood in a rough shed, while the owner of it was hurrying through the wet streets to the Crown with a message to Jimmy. Inside its locked door, leaning her aching back against the wall, sat the Queen of the Cadgers, fierce, worn, vigilant; with a long knife across her knee.

And Gilbert, his eyes on the wind-tormented sky, lay fuming in the shelter of the disabled coach in the heart of Monrummon Moor.

CHAPTER XXX

MORPHIE KIRK

WHEN the morning of the seventh of April broke over Speid and his companions, they lashed the damaged pole together with a coil of rope and harnessed the wheelers. Progress was possible, though at a very slow pace, and they started again, the guard and outside passengers walking; from the coach's interior, which cradled the slumbers of the Glasgow merchant, there came no sound.

It was past eight when they crossed the South Lour where the river curls round Blackport before plunging into the Basin of Kaims on its seaward course; it was almost nine when Gilbert saw Jimmy Stirk's anxious face at the door of the Crown.

"Eh, Laird, ! but a'm feared ye're ower late !" was the boy's exclamation, as they clasped hands.

"Come ! Come in here," said Gilbert, dragging him into a room near the doorway.

There, in a voice lowered by reason of the slattern who was on her knees with soap and pail, Jimmy gave him the history of the last three days, from his grandmother's receipt of his letter to her hurried message of last night.

"She's waitin' ye now in River Street," he concluded.

Without further ado they went out of the house together.

What would be the upshot of the next two hours Speid did not know and did not dare to think. Cecilia's freedom would pass with their passing. Captain Somerville had said in his letter that he was writing to tell her he had summoned him, and his heart stood still as he reflected that, in the face of this, she had hastened her marriage by three days. He was puzzled, dismayed, for he could not guess the full depth of Barclay's guilt, and the boy beside him knew no more from his grandmother's message than that the lawyer had cleared Blackport of all available horses. To appear before a woman who had forgotten him on her wedding morning, only to see her give her willing hand to another man—was that what he had come across Europe to do? His proud heart sickened.

Seeing that the night had passed unmolested, Granny Stirk had fallen at daylight into an exhausted sleep; 'it needed Jimmy's thunder upon the door to awake her to the fact that Gilbert stood without. She turned the key quickly.

"Whanland! Whanland!" was all that she could say as he entered. Her face was haggard with watching and exertion.

"Oh, Granny!" he cried. "You have almost killed yourself for me!"

"Aye, but a'm no deid yet!" exclaimed the old woman. "Eh, Laird! but it's fine to see ye. A'm sweer to let ye gang, but ye canna loss a minute."

Jimmy was harnessing Rob Roy.

"But, Granny, what does this mean? She has hurried her wedding, though Captain Somerville told her I would come. What can I do, knowing that?"

"Do? Ye'll just hae to rin. Laird, she doesna ken onything. Yon tod—yon damned, leein' Barclay—he got a haud o' the letter. The Captain tell't me that himsel'. Ye'll need to drive."

"Good God!" cried Speid.

The sight of her worn face and the knowledge of what she had done for him smote Gilbert hard. Though time pressed, he would not consent to start till he had taken her to the Crown and left her in the landlady's care, with an order for fire, food, and dry clothing. Then he tore

out of the door and down the street to the spot where
Jimmy awaited him with the cart. The boy's brown,
hard face cheered him, for it seemed the very incarnation
of the country he loved.

The world which lay round them as they drove out of
Blackport was a new one, fresh, chastened by the scourg-
ing of the storm. The sky was high, blue and pale, and
there was a scent of spring; underfoot, the wet ground
glistened and the young finger of morning light touched
trees and buildings as they rose from an under-world of
mist.

When we look on the dying glory of the evening, and
again, on the spectacle of coming day, do we not regard
these sights, so alike in colour and in mystery, with an
indefinable difference of feeling? The reason is that
sunset reminds us of Time and sunrise of Eternity.

Though sunrise was long past, the remembrance of it
was still abroad, and a sense of conflict ended breathed
over the ground strewn with broken boughs, wreckage
of the night. Gilbert, as he sat by his companion and
felt his heart outrunning their progress, could find no
share in this suggestion. All cried to him of peace when
there was no peace; effort was before him, possibly
failure.

He knew that, though Cecilia was to be married from
Fullarton, the actual wedding would take place at Morphie, according to her own desire. Somerville had told
him so. It was now half-past nine and Jimmy was pressing Rob Roy to his utmost, for Fullarton was the further
of the two places, some seven miles north of Kaims, and
the horse would have to put his best work into the collar
were Speid to arrive in time to see the bride before she
started for the kirk.

The high hope and determination in which Gilbert had
left Spain had changed to a foreboding that, after all,
he might find fate too strong; but, though this fear lay,
like a shadow, over him, he would not turn from his wild

errand. Till the ring was on Cecilia's finger and she had
agreed in the face of minister and congregation to take
Crauford Fordyce for her husband, he meant to persevere.
He smiled gloomily at himself, sitting travel-stained and
muddy, on the front of a springless cart, with what was
more to him than his life depending on the speed of a
cadger's horse.

Among the crowd of relations, acquaintances, and
companions alongside of which a man begins life, Time
and Trouble, like a pair of witch-doctors, are busy with
their rites and dancers and magic sticks selecting his
friends; and often the identity of the little handful they
drag from the throng is a surprise. For Gilbert they had
secured a wooden-legged naval captain, a sullen young
cadger, and a retired fishwife with gold earrings. As
he watched the ground fly past the wheels, he recognised
that the dreadful functionaries had gone far to justify
their existence by the choice they had made.

There were dark marks under pad and breeching, for
the sun was growing strong, and, though Jimmy held his
horse together and used such persuasive address as he
had never been known to waste upon a human being, he
was now beginning to have recourse to the whip. Speid
realised that their pace was gradually flagging. By the
time they had done half the journey and could see, from
a swelling rise, down over the Morphie woods, it was
borne in on him that Rob Roy's step was growing
short. He made brave efforts to answer to the lash,
but they did not last, and the sweat had begun to
run round his drooping ears. The two friends looked at
each other.

"Ma' grannie had a sair drive last nicht," said Jimmy.

"Pull up for a moment and face him to the wind,"
cried Speid, jumping down.

With handfuls of rush torn from a ditch they rubbed
him down, neck, loins, and legs, and turned his head to
what breeze was moving. His eyes stared, and, though

he was close to the green fringe of grass which bordered the roadside, he made no attempt to pick at it.

The hands of Gilbert's watch had put ten o'clock behind them as he looked over the far stretch to Morphie and Fullarton. Jimmy, whose light eyes rested in dogged concern on the horse's heaving sides, put his shoulder under the shaft to ease off the weight of the cart. Away beyond, on the further edge of the wood, was the kirk; even now, the doors were probably being opened and seats dusted for the coming marriage.

Speid stood summing up his chances, his eyes on the spreading landscape; he was attempting an impossibility in trying to reach Fullarton.

"There is no use in pushing on to Fullarton," he said, laying his hand on Rob Roy's mane, "we shall only break his heart, poor little brute. I am going to leave you here and get across country to the kirk on my own feet. Here is some money—go to the nearest farm and rest him; feed him when he'll eat, and come on to Whanland when you can. Whatever may happen this morning, I shall be there in the afternoon."

The boy nodded, measuring the miles silently that lay between them and the distant kirk. It would be a race, he considered, but it would take a deal to beat the Laird of Whanland.

"Brides is aye late," he remarked briefly.

"Who told you that?" asked Gilbert, as he pulled off his overcoat and threw it into the cart.

"Ma' Grannie."

Speid vaulted over the low wall beside them and began to descend the slope. Half-way down it he heard Jimmy's voice crying luck to him and saw his cap lifted in the air.

The rain of the previous day and night had made the ground heavy, and he soon found that the remaining time would just serve him and no more. He ran on at a steady pace, taking a straight line to the edge of the

woods; most of the fields were divided by stone dykes
and those obstacles gave him no trouble. Sometimes
he slipped in wet places; once or twice he was hailed by
a labourer who stopped in his work to watch the
gentleman original enough to race over the open
landscape for no apparent reason. But he took no
heed, plodding on.

When he came to where the corner of the woods protruded, a dark triangle, into the pasture land, he struck
across it. The rain had made the pines aromatic, and the
strong, clean smell refreshed him as he went over the
elastic bed of pine-needles strewn underfoot. The
undignified white bobtails of rabbits disappeared, right
and left, among the stems at his approach, and once a
roe-deer fled in leaps into the labyrinth of trunks.

Before emerging again into the open he paused to rest
and look at his watch; walking and running, he had
come well and more quickly than he had supposed; he
thanked heaven for the sound body which he had never
allowed idleness to make inactive. It wanted twenty-
five minutes of eleven, and he had covered a couple of
miles in the quarter of an hour since he had left Jimmy.
He judged himself a little under two more from Morphie
kirk. The boy's unexpected knowledge of the habits of
brides had amused him, even in his hurry, and he
devoutly hoped it might prove true.

Standing under the firs and pines, he realised the
demand he was about to make of this particular bride.
He wondered if there were a woman in the world bold
enough to do what he was going to ask Cecilia to do for
him. He was going to stand up before her friends,
before the bridegroom and his relations, the guests and
the onlookers, and ask her to leave the man to whom she
had promised herself for a lover she had not seen for
nearly two years; one who had not so much as an honest name to give her. Would she do it? He reflected,
with a sigh, that Jimmy's knowledge would scarce tell

him that. But, at the same time, loving her as he loved her, and knowing her as he knew her, he hoped.

He was off again, leaping out over a ditch circling the skirts of the wood; he meant to follow the outline of the trees till he should come to a track which he knew would lead him down to where the kirk stood under a sloping bank. Many a time he had looked, from the further side of the Lour, at the homely building with its stone belfry. It had no beauty but that of plainness and would not have attracted anyone whose motives in regarding it were quite simple. But, for him, it had been enchanted, as common places are enchanted but a few times in our lives; and now he was to face the turning-point of his existence in its shadow.

This run across country was the last stage of a journey begun in Spain nearly a month since. It had come down to such a fine measurement of time as would have made him wonder, had he been capable of any sensation but the breathless desire to go forward. His hair was damp upon his forehead and his clothes splashed with mud as he struck into the foot-track leading from the higher ground to the kirk. The way went through a thicket of brier and whin, and, from its further side, came the voices and the rough East-coast accent of men and women; he supposed that a certain crowd had gathered to see the bride arrive and he knew that he was in time.

It was less than ten minutes to eleven when the assembled spectators saw a tall man emerge from the scrub and take up his position by the kirk door. Many recognised him and wondered, but no Whanland people were present, and no one accosted him. He leaned a few minutes against the wall; then, when he had recovered breath, he walked round the building and looked in at a window. Inside, the few guests were seated, among them Barclay, his frilled shirt making a violent spot of white in the gloom of the kirk. Not far from him, his back to the light, was Crauford Fordyce, stiff and im-

maculate in his satin stock and claret colour, unconscious
of the man who stood, not ten yards from him, at the
other side of the wall. It was evident from their bearing
that, by this hour, the minds of the allies were at rest.
Gilbert returned to the door and stood quietly by the
threshold; there was an irony in the situation which
appealed to him.

While he had raced across the country, Cecilia, in her
room at Fullarton, was putting on her wedding-gown.
Agneta, who looked upon her future sister-in-law as a
kind of illustrated hand-book to life, had come to help
her to fasten her veil. One of the house-maids, a scarlet-
headed wench who loved Cecilia dearly and whose face
was swollen with tears shed for her departure, stood by
with a tray full of pins.

"You had better not wait, really, Jessie," said the
bride in front of the glass, "I am so afraid the rest of the
servants will start without you. Miss Fordyce will help
me I am sure. Give me my wreath and go quickly."

The servant took up her hand and kissed it loudly;
then set the wreath askew on her hair and went out, a
blubbering whirl of emotion.

"She has been a kind, good girl to me," said Cecilia.

"Your hand is all wet!" exclaimed Agneta, to whom
such a scene was astonishing

Mary and Agneta inhabited a room together and many
midnight conversations had flowed from their bed-
curtains in the last few nights. Agneta had gone completely over to the enemy, but her sister, who, though
gentler in character, was less able to free herself from the
traditions in which she had been brought up, hung back,
terrified, from an opinion formed alone. Outwardly, she
was abrupt, and Cecilia and she had made small progress
in their acquaintance.

Robert Fullarton and his brother-in-law were ready
and waiting downstairs and two carriages stood outside
on the gravel sweep. Sir Thomas and his daughters

were to go in one of these, and Robert, who was to give
Cecilia away, would accompany her in the other.

Agneta and Mary had started when Cecilia stood alone
in front of her image in the glass; she held up her veil
and looked into the reflected face.   It was the last time
she would see Cecilia Raeburn, and, with a kind of
curiosity, she regarded the outer shell of the woman,
who, it seemed to her, had no identity left.   The Cecilia
who had grown up at Morphie was dead—as dead as that
companion with whom she had shared the old house.
Between the parted friends there was this momentous
difference: while one was at rest, the other had still to
carry that picture in the mirror as bravely as she could
through the world, till the long day's work should roll
by and the two should meet.   She thought of that dark
morning at Morphie and of her aunt's dying face against
Fullarton's shoulder, and told herself that, were the
moment to return, she would not do differently.   She
was glad to remember that, had Gilbert Speid come
back, he would have cast no shadow between them; the
knowledge seemed to consecrate the gleam of happiness
she had known with him so briefly.   But it was hard
that, when the path by which they might have reached
each other had been smoothed at so terrible a cost, the
way had been empty.   She was thinking of the time
when two pairs of eyes had met in a looking-glass and
she had plastered his cut cheek in the candlelight.
After to-day she must put such remembrances from her.
She dropped her veil and turned away, for Fullarton's
voice was calling to her to come down.

While she sat beside him in the carriage, looking out,
her hands were pressed together in her lap.   The rain-
washed world was so beautiful, and, between the woods
touched with spring, the North Lour ran full.   The
lights lying on field and hill seemed to smile.   As they
passed Morphie House she kept her face turned from it;
she could not trifle with her strength.   She was thank-

ful that they would not be near the coast where she could hear the sea-sound.

As the carriage turned from the highroad into a smaller one leading up to the kirk, Captain Somerville's hooded phaeton approached from Kaims and dropped behind, following. The sailor, who sat in the front seat by the driver, was alone, and Cecilia's eyes met his as they drew near. She leaned forward, smiling; it did her good to see him. Mrs. Somerville had declined to appear; she was not well enough to go out, she said, and it seemed, to look at her face, as though this reason were a good one. She had scarcely slept and her eyes were red with angry weeping. Since the preceding morning, when the Inspector had discovered what part she had played, the two had not spoken, and she felt herself unable to face Barclay in his presence. After the wedding the men must inevitably meet; she could not imagine what her husband might do or say, or what would happen when the lawyer should discover that she had betrayed him. She retired to the sanctuary of her bedroom and sent a message downstairs at the last moment, desiring the Captain to make her excuses to Miss Raeburn and tell her that she had too bad a cold to be able to leave the house.

The sailor's heart was heavy as he went and the glimpse of Cecilia which he had caught made it no lighter. He had tried to save her and failed. All yesterday, since his dreadful discovery, he had debated whether or no he ought to go to Fullarton, see her, and tell her that he had tried to bring Gilbert home; that he would, in all probability, arrive a few hours before her marriage. He turned the question over and over in his mind. The conclusion he came to was that, things having gone so far, he had better hold his peace. She *could* not draw back now, and, being forced to go on, the knowledge that her lover would have been in time, had she not hastened her marriage, might haunt her all her life. If

Speid arrived at the hour he was expected he would hear from Jimmy Stirk of the wedding. Should he be determined to act, he would do so without his—Somerville's —intervention; and, should he see fit to accept what now seemed the inevitable, he would, no doubt, have the sense to leave Whanland quietly. He would go there himself, on his return from Morphie Kirk, in the hope of finding him and inducing him to start before anyone should see him, and before Cecilia should learn how near to her he had been. It might well be that she would never know it, for she was to leave Fullarton, with her husband, at two o'clock, for Perth. They were to go south immediately.

The sailor was not sure whether he was relieved or disappointed to find that, apparently, Speid had made no sign. Cecilia was there to play her part; no doubt, like many another, she would come to play it contentedly. With all his heart he pitied Gilbert. Meanwhile, as the carriages neared their destination, he could see the evergreen arch which some Morphie labourers had put up over the entrance at which the bride would alight.

The kirk could not be seen from the gate of the enclosure in which it stood, for the path took a turn round some thick bushes. A low dyke of unpointed stone girdled it and kept at bay the broom and whins clothing the hillock. When his phaëton stopped, Somerville got out, and was in time to greet the bride as Fullarton handed her out of the carriage; he did not fail to notice the tremor of the fingers he touched. He went on and slipped into a group of bystanders surrounding the door without observing the figure which stood near the kirk wall, a little apart.

A movement went through the group as Fullarton appeared by the tall bushes leading Cecilia. While they advanced a man walked forward and stood in the way; a man with splashed clothes and high boots, brown with the soil; the wet hair was dark upon his forehead and his eyes looked straight before him to where the bride came, brave and pale, under her green wreath. She saw him and stopped. Her hand slipped from Fullarton's arm.

Unheeding Robert's exclamation, he sprang toward her, his eyes burning.

"Cecilia," he said, almost under his breath, "am I too late?"

The slight commotion caused by this unexpected incident had brought Barclay to the doorway; Crauford's face could be seen behind his shoulder.

"Great Heavens! Here's Speid!" exclaimed the lawyer, seizing his friend.

Fordyce moved irresolutely, longing to rush forward, but aware that custom decreed he should await his bride's entrance in the kirk; he scarcely realised the import of what had happened outside its walls while he stood, unconscious, between them. Barclay ran out to the little group round which the onlookers were collecting, and he followed, unable to sacrifice his annoyance to his sense of what was expected. Not for a moment did he believe that decency could be outraged by anything more than an interruption. In the background stood Mary and Agneta, aghast under their pink-rosetted bonnets.

"May I ask what you have come here for, sir?" he inquired, approaching Gilbert.

But Speid's back was turned, for he was looking at Cecilia.

"Come!" cried Fullarton, sternly, "come, Cecilia! I cannot permit this. Stand aside, Mr. Speid, if you please."

"Cecilia, what are you going to do?" urged Gilbert, standing before her, as though he would bar her progress to the kirk door. "I have come back for you."

She looked round and saw the steady eyes of Captain Somerville fixed upon her. He had come close and was at her side, his stout figure drawn up, his wooden leg planted firmly on the gravel; there was in his countenance a mighty loyalty.

"Gilbert," she exclaimed, with a sob in her voice, "thank God you have come." Then she faced the bridegroom. "I cannot go on with this, Mr. Fordyce," she said.

"But it is too late!" cried Robert. "There shall be no more of this trifling. You are engaged to my nephew and you must fulfil your engagement. I am here to see that you do."

"I will not," she replied. "Forgive me, sir—forgive me, I beg of you! I know that I have no right to ask you to stand by me!"

"I shall not do so, certainly," exclaimed Robert, angrily.

She glanced round, desperate. Captain Somerville was holding out his arm.

"My phaëton is outside, Miss Raeburn," he said, "and you will do me the favour to come home with me. Speid," he added, "am I doing right?"

But Gilbert could scarcely answer. A great glory had dawned in his face.

EPILOGUE

HERE, so far as the author's choice is concerned, this history closes. The man and woman, forced apart by powers greater than themselves, have come to their own again and stand at the portal of a new life, at the door of a structure built from the wreck of bygone things. Those who have watched them may augur for themselves what the future is like to be for them, and shut the book, assured that the record of these two, for whom life held so much more than they could see with their eyes and touch with their hands, will not fall below its mark.

But, to that vast and ingenuous multitude which has taste for the dotted "i" and the crossed "t," there remains yet a word to be added.

Cecilia stayed under Captain Somerville's roof while the disturbing events round her quieted themselves, and while Gilbert, who received a challenge from Fordyce, settled the score. Even she scarcely felt anxious, as she awaited the result of their meeting, for Speid chose the sword as a weapon and had assured her he would deal as tenderly with Crauford as though he were a new-born babe. This he proceeded to do, so long as it amused him, after which he scratched him deftly on the inside of the wrist, and the seconds, who could scarce restrain their smiles, agreed that honour was satisfied.

And so the jasmine-trees were planted at Whanland, the ideal horse bought; the necklace with the emerald drop found the resting-place Gilbert had desired for it. Granny Stirk, accompanied by Jimmy, went to the second wedding which was attempted in Morphie Kirk, and which, this time, was celebrated without interruption;

317

she drove there in a carriage, and the bridegroom, who was standing by the pulpit as she arrived, left his place and conducted her on his arm to a seat near the Miss Robertsons.

Crauford married Lady Maria Milwright, who therefore thought herself exalted among women, and was, in reality, much too good for him. Barclay constantly frequented his roof, making Lady Maria very happy by his expressed admiration for her husband, he might have boasted of the intimacy to the end of his life had he not covertly courted Agneta and been taken in the act by Lady Fordyce. Family dignity expelled the offender, and the only person who was sorry for him was kind Lady Maria, who rose at an unconscionable hour to preside over his breakfast before he departed, forever, amid shame and luggage.

Agneta eloped with an English clergyman and ended her days as a bishop's wife, too much occupied with her position to have a thought for that palpitating world of romance and desperation upon which she had once cast such covetous eyes.

On the death of Captain Somerville, a few years later, the lawyer took to himself his widow, who had contrived, by much lying and some luck, to conceal from him her part in the betrayal of his schemes. She looked as much out of the window and dispensed as much hospitality under her new name, and never failed to disparage Mrs. Speid of Whanland whenever that much-admired lady appeared either in the street or the conversation. These were the only places in which she met her, for her husband had long ceased to be connected, either by business or acquaintance, with the family.

THE END

Lightning Source UK Ltd.
Milton Keynes UK
UKHW021303210222
399002UK00007B/1596